First World War
and Army of Occupation
War Diary
France, Belgium and Germany

20 DIVISION
Divisional Troops
Royal Army Medical Corps
60 Field Ambulance
23 July 1915 - 1 May 1919

WO95/2109/1

The Naval & Military Press Ltd
www.nmarchive.com
Published in association with The National Archives

Published by

The Naval & Military Press Ltd

Unit 10 Ridgewood Industrial Park,

Uckfield, East Sussex,

TN22 5QE England

Tel: +44 (0) 1825 749494

www.naval-military-press.com

www.nmarchive.com

This diary has been reprinted in facsimile from the original. Any imperfections are inevitably reproduced and the quality may fall short of modern type and cartographic standards.

© Crown Copyright
Images reproduced by permission of The National Archives, London, England, 2015.

Contents

Document type	Place/Title	Date From	Date To
Miscellaneous	2109/1		
Heading	20th Division 60th Field Ambulance Jly 1915-1919 Apl		
Miscellaneous	60th Field Ambulance		
Miscellaneous	List of Casualties 60th Field Ambulance		
Miscellaneous	Wounded R.A.M.C.		
Miscellaneous	Prisoners of War		
Miscellaneous	Casualties 60th F A		
Heading	20th Division 60th F Amb Part Of Vol I July 15		
Heading	War Diary 60th Field Ambulance 23rd July 1915 To 31st July 1915		
War Diary	Cormette	23/07/1915	27/07/1915
War Diary	Campagne Wardrecques	27/07/1915	28/07/1915
War Diary	Borre	29/07/1915	29/07/1915
War Diary	Cormette	27/07/1915	27/07/1915
War Diary	Campagne Wardrecques	28/07/1915	28/07/1915
War Diary	Borre	29/07/1915	30/07/1915
War Diary	Outer Steene	31/07/1915	31/07/1915
Heading	War Diary 60th Field Ambulance 1915 1st To 27th August 27th To 31st August		
War Diary	Outer Steene	31/07/1915	10/08/1915
War Diary	Bac St Maur	11/08/1915	16/08/1915
War Diary	Outer Steene	17/08/1915	28/08/1915
War Diary	Estaire	29/08/1915	31/08/1915
Heading	War Diary 60th Field Ambulance 1st Oct 1915 to 31st Oct 1915		
War Diary	Estaire	01/10/1915	31/10/1915
Heading	20th Division 60th F.A Vol 4 Nov 15		
Heading	War Diary of 60th Field Ambulance For November-1915		
War Diary	Estaire	01/11/1915	30/11/1915
Heading	20th Div F 60th F.A. Dec. 1915 Vol 5		
Heading	War Diary 60th Field Ambulance 1st December To 31st December 1915		
War Diary	Estaire	01/12/1915	31/12/1915
Heading	60th F.A. 20th Div Vol 6 Jan 1916		
Heading	War Diary 60th Field Ambulance Lt Col A. C. Osburn R.A.M.C. Commanding For January 1916		
War Diary	Estaire	01/01/1916	21/01/1916
War Diary	Morbecque	21/01/1916	22/01/1916
War Diary	St Marie Cappel	22/01/1916	30/01/1916
Heading	60 F.A 20th Div Vol 7 Feb 1916		
Heading	War Diary of 60th Field Ambulance For February 1916		
War Diary	St Marie Cappel	01/02/1916	04/02/1916
War Diary	Herzeele	05/02/1916	13/02/1916
War Diary	Poperinghe	13/02/1916	29/02/1916
Heading	60th F. Ambulance March 1916		
Heading	War Diary of 60th Field Ambulance For March 1916		
War Diary	Poperinghe	01/03/1916	31/03/1916
Miscellaneous			
Heading	No 60 Field Ambulance April 1916		

War Diary	Poperinghe	01/04/1916	17/04/1916
War Diary	Herzeele	18/04/1916	26/04/1916
War Diary	Watou	27/04/1916	30/04/1916
Heading	War Diary 60th Field Ambulance For May 1916 Vol 10		
War Diary	Watou	01/05/1916	06/05/1916
War Diary	Calais	07/05/1916	13/05/1916
War Diary	Zutkerque	14/05/1916	14/05/1916
War Diary	Volkerinckhove	15/05/1916	15/05/1916
War Diary	Herzeele	16/05/1916	20/05/1916
War Diary	Peselhoek	21/05/1916	31/05/1916
Heading	War Diary of 60th Field Ambulance For July 1916		
War Diary	Peselhoek (Near Poperinghe)	01/07/1916	02/07/1916
War Diary	Peselhoek	02/07/1916	17/07/1916
War Diary	Herzeele	18/07/1916	20/07/1916
War Diary	Bailleul	21/07/1916	25/07/1916
War Diary	Fervent	26/07/1916	26/07/1916
War Diary	Lucheux	26/07/1916	26/07/1916
War Diary	Authie	27/07/1916	28/07/1916
War Diary	Authie Hill	29/07/1916	31/07/1916
Heading	War Diary For August 1916 of 60th Field Ambulance		
War Diary	Authie Hill	01/08/1916	02/08/1916
War Diary	I.10.C.6.6 Authie	04/07/1916	06/07/1916
War Diary	Authie Hill	07/08/1916	15/08/1916
War Diary	Authie (Hill) I.10.c.6.6	16/08/1916	18/08/1916
War Diary	Beauval G.21.a. 10.3 Sheet 59d	18/08/1916	18/08/1916
War Diary	Beauval G.21.a.10.3	19/08/1916	22/08/1916
War Diary	Bronfay Farm	22/08/1916	28/08/1916
War Diary	Divl. Bearer Post	29/08/1916	29/08/1916
War Diary	Divisional Bearer Post (Bronfay Farm)	30/08/1916	30/08/1916
War Diary	Divl Bearer Posts	30/08/1916	31/08/1916
Miscellaneous			
Heading	War Diary of 60th Field Ambulance September 1916		
War Diary		01/09/1916	01/09/1916
War Diary	Bronfay Farm	01/09/1916	06/09/1916
War Diary	Bois De Taille	07/09/1916	08/09/1916
War Diary	Corbie	09/09/1916	11/09/1916
War Diary	Bois De Taille	12/09/1916	14/09/1916
War Diary	Arbre Fourche F.27.C.3.3	14/09/1916	15/09/1916
War Diary	Carnoy	16/09/1916	16/09/1916
War Diary	Guillemont	17/09/1916	21/09/1916
War Diary	Sand Pits	22/09/1916	22/09/1916
War Diary	Morlancourt	23/09/1916	25/09/1916
War Diary	Happy Valley	26/09/1916	26/09/1916
War Diary	Bricqueterie	27/09/1916	30/09/1916
Heading	War Diary of 60th Field Ambulance For October 1916		
War Diary	Bricqueterie	01/10/1916	08/10/1916
War Diary	Meaulte	09/10/1916	09/10/1916
War Diary	Ville-Sur-Ancre	09/10/1916	12/10/1916
War Diary	E.25.d 20 Ville-Sur-Ancre	13/10/1916	17/10/1916
War Diary	Ville-Sur-Ancre	18/10/1916	18/10/1916
War Diary	Franvillers	19/10/1916	20/10/1916
War Diary	Allonville	21/10/1916	21/10/1916
War Diary	Picquigny	22/10/1916	31/10/1916
Miscellaneous			
Heading	War Diary of 60th Field Ambulance For Nov 1916		
War Diary	Picquigny	01/11/1916	02/11/1916

War Diary	Foudrinoy	04/11/1916	08/11/1916
War Diary	Picquigny	09/11/1916	15/11/1916
War Diary	Ville-Sur-Ancre	16/11/1916	30/11/1916
Heading	20th Div War Diary of 60th Field Ambulance For December 1916		
War Diary	Ville-Sur-Ancre	01/12/1916	12/12/1916
War Diary	Dive Copse	13/12/1916	23/12/1916
War Diary	Corbie (Chateau)	23/12/1916	31/12/1916
Heading	War Diary of The 60th Field Ambulance January 1917 Vol 18		
War Diary	Corbie (Chateau)	01/01/1917	01/01/1917
War Diary	Meaulte	02/01/1917	03/01/1917
War Diary	Trones Wood	03/01/1917	26/01/1917
War Diary	Franvillers	26/01/1917	31/01/1917
Heading	20th Div 60th Field Ambulance Feb. 1917		
Heading	War Diary of 60th Field Ambulance For February 1917 Vol 19		
War Diary	Franvillers (Amiens Map)	01/02/1917	04/02/1917
War Diary	Bonnay	04/02/1917	06/02/1917
War Diary	Trones Wood	07/02/1917	28/02/1917
Miscellaneous			
Heading	20th Div 60th Field Ambulance March 1917		
Heading	War Diary of 60th Field Ambulance For March 1917		
War Diary	Trones Wood	01/03/1917	31/03/1917
Heading	20th Div. No. 60 F. A April 1917		
Heading	War Diary of 60th Field Ambulance For April 1917		
War Diary	Trones Wood	01/04/1917	03/04/1917
War Diary	Lechelles	04/04/1917	09/04/1917
War Diary	Mois Lains	10/04/1917	24/04/1917
War Diary	V.30.D.	25/04/1917	25/04/1917
War Diary	V.18.c.2.8 (Sheet 57 c)	26/04/1917	28/04/1917
War Diary	V.18.c.2.8	29/04/1917	30/04/1917
Heading	20th Div. No 60 F. A May 1917		
Heading	War Diary of 60th Field Ambulance For May 1917 Vol 22		
War Diary	V.18.c.2.8	01/05/1917	13/05/1917
War Diary	V.18.c.2.8 (Sheet 57c)	14/05/1917	14/05/1917
War Diary	V.24.a.6.3	15/05/1917	22/05/1917
War Diary	H.16.D.9.5 Sheet 57c 1/40.000	23/05/1917	27/05/1917
War Diary	H.16.D.9.5 Sheet 57c 1/40.000 & C.20.D.3.6	28/05/1917	31/05/1917
War Diary	H.16.D.9.5 Sheet 57c 1/40.000	31/05/1917	31/05/1917
Heading	No 60 F. A June 1917		
Heading	War Diary of 60th Field Ambulance For June 1917 Vol 23		
War Diary	H.16.D.9.5 Sheet 57c 1/40.000	01/06/1917	03/06/1917
War Diary	H.16.D.9.5	04/06/1917	20/06/1917
War Diary	H.16.D.9.6 Sheet 57c 1/40.000	23/06/1917	24/06/1917
War Diary	H.16.d.9.6	25/06/1917	25/06/1917
War Diary	H.16.D.9.5	26/06/1917	26/06/1917
War Diary	Sheet 57c 1/40.000 Gomiecourt	27/06/1917	27/06/1917
War Diary	Gomiecourt	28/06/1917	28/06/1917
War Diary	Domesmont Sheet II Lens 1/100.000	29/06/1917	30/06/1917
Heading	No. 60 F. A July 1917		
Heading	B.E.F. Summary of Medical War Diaries For 60th F.A., 20th Divn. 14th Corps, 5th Army From 21.7.17	21/07/1917	21/07/1917
War Diary	Headquarters	21/07/1917	21/07/1917

War Diary	Moves And Transfer	21/07/1917	21/07/1917
War Diary	Moves Detachment	24/07/1917	24/07/1917
War Diary	Moves	30/07/1917	30/07/1917
War Diary	Operations	31/07/1917	31/07/1917
War Diary	Medical Arrangements	31/07/1917	31/07/1917
War Diary	Casualties Evacuation	31/07/1917	31/07/1917
War Diary	Operations Enemy	31/07/1917	31/07/1917
War Diary	Headquarters	21/07/1917	21/07/1917
War Diary	Moves And Transfer	21/07/1917	21/07/1917
War Diary	Moves Detachment	24/07/1917	24/07/1917
War Diary	Moves	30/07/1917	30/07/1917
War Diary	Operations	31/07/1917	31/07/1917
War Diary	Medical Arrangements	31/07/1917	31/07/1917
War Diary	Casualties Evacuation	31/07/1917	31/07/1917
War Diary	Operations Enemy	31/07/1917	31/07/1917
Heading	War Diary of 60th Field Ambulance For July 1917 Vol 24		
War Diary	Domesmont Lens Sheet No 11 1/100.000	01/07/1917	20/07/1917
War Diary	Proven Belgium & Part France Sheet 27 1/40,000	19/07/1917	29/07/1917
War Diary	Sheet 28 NW 1/20,000 F.10.D.4.0.Sheet 27 1/40.000	30/07/1917	31/07/1917
War Diary	A.16.B.8.8 Sheet 28 N.W. 1/20000	31/07/1917	31/07/1917
Heading	No. 60. F.A Aug 1917		
Heading	B.E.F. Summary of Medical War Diaries For 60th F.A. 20th Divn. 14th Corps, 5th Army. From 21.7.17	21/07/1917	21/07/1917
War Diary	Moves	01/08/1917	01/08/1917
War Diary	Moves Detachment	05/08/1917	05/08/1917
War Diary	Operations Enemy	05/08/1917	05/08/1917
War Diary	Casualties	05/08/1917	05/08/1917
War Diary	Operations Enemy	06/08/1917	06/08/1917
War Diary	Moves	11/08/1917	11/08/1917
War Diary	Medical Arrangements	11/08/1917	11/08/1917
War Diary	Operations Enemy	12/08/1917	13/08/1917
War Diary	Operations Casualties	16/08/1917	16/08/1917
War Diary	Moves	19/08/1917	19/08/1917
War Diary	Decorations	30/08/1917	30/08/1917
War Diary	Moves	01/08/1917	01/08/1917
War Diary	Moves Detachment	05/08/1917	05/08/1917
War Diary	Operations Enemy	05/08/1917	05/08/1917
War Diary	Casualties	05/08/1917	05/08/1917
War Diary	Operations Enemy	06/08/1917	06/08/1917
War Diary	Moves	11/08/1917	11/08/1917
War Diary	Medical Arrangements	11/08/1917	11/08/1917
War Diary	Operations Enemy	12/08/1917	13/08/1917
War Diary	Operations Casualties	16/08/1917	16/08/1917
War Diary	Moves	19/08/1917	19/08/1917
War Diary	Decorations	30/08/1917	30/08/1917
Heading	War Diary of 60th Field Ambulance For August 1917		
War Diary	A.17.A.2.6 Sheet 28 1/40.000	01/08/1917	03/08/1917
War Diary	A.17.A.2.6	04/08/1917	06/08/1917
War Diary	A.17.A.2.6 Sheet 28 1/40.000	07/08/1917	11/08/1917
War Diary	B.15.C.5.3 Sheet 28 1/40.000	11/08/1917	11/08/1917
War Diary	S.E. 9 Elverdinghe	12/08/1917	13/08/1917
War Diary	B.14.A.2.7 C.15.A.5.3	14/08/1917	16/08/1917
War Diary	B.14.A.2.7	17/08/1917	18/08/1917
War Diary	F.10.C.5.5 Lovie Woods Sheet 27 1/40000	19/08/1917	24/08/1917
War Diary	F10.c.5.5 Priory camp-Lovie Wood.	25/08/1917	31/08/1917

Miscellaneous				
Heading	No 60 F.A. Sept. 1917			
War Diary	Operations Enemy		24/09/1917	24/09/1917
War Diary	Moves		28/09/1917	28/09/1917
War Diary	Appendices		28/09/1917	28/09/1917
War Diary	Moves Detachment		08/09/1917	08/09/1917
War Diary	Moves		10/09/1917	10/09/1917
War Diary	Operations Enemy		16/09/1917	16/09/1917
War Diary	Operations Medical Arrangements Evacuation		20/09/1917	20/09/1917
War Diary	Operations Enemy Casualties		22/09/1917	22/09/1917
War Diary	Operations Enemy		23/09/1917	23/09/1917
War Diary	Moves Detachment		08/09/1917	08/09/1917
War Diary	Moves		10/09/1917	10/09/1917
War Diary	Operations Enemy		16/09/1917	16/09/1917
War Diary	Operations Medical Arrangements Evacuation		20/09/1917	20/09/1917
War Diary	Operations Enemy Casualties		22/09/1917	22/09/1917
War Diary	Operations Enemy		23/09/1917	23/09/1917
War Diary	Operations Enemy		24/09/1917	24/09/1917
War Diary	Moves		28/09/1917	28/09/1917
War Diary	Appendices		28/09/1917	28/09/1917
Heading	War Diary of 60th Field Ambulance For September 1917			
War Diary	Priory Camp Sheet 27 1/40.000		01/09/1917	04/09/1917
War Diary	Priory Camp		04/09/1917	19/09/1917
War Diary	Fusilier-ADS		20/09/1917	20/09/1917
War Diary	Pelissier Farm Fusilier A.D.S		20/09/1917	22/09/1917
War Diary	Pelissier Farm		23/09/1917	23/09/1917
War Diary	Pelissier Farm B.21.A.3.0 Sheet 28 1/40.000		24/09/1917	30/09/1917
Miscellaneous	Evacuation Arrangements During Active Operations-20th Division			
Miscellaneous	The following Will Be The Checking Sergts, At The Various		17/09/1917	17/09/1917
Miscellaneous	Report On The Arrangements For The Evacuation Of Wounded During Active Operations 20-21st September 1917 East of Langemarck		05/09/1917	05/09/1917
Heading	No 60 F.A. Oct. 1917			
Heading	B.E.F. Summary of Medical War Diaries of 60th F.A., 20th Divn. 14th Corps, 5th Army. To 3rd Corps, 3rd Army On 2/10/17		02/10/1917	02/10/1917
War Diary	Headquarters		02/10/1917	02/10/1917
War Diary	Moves And Transfer		02/10/1917	02/10/1917
Heading	B.E.F. Summary of Medical War Diaries of 60th F.A. 20th Divn. 14th Corps, 5th Army To 3rd Corps. 3rd Army On 2/10/17			
War Diary	Headquarters		02/10/1917	02/10/1917
War Diary	Moves And Transfer		02/10/1917	02/10/1917
Heading	War Diary of 60th Field Ambulance October 1917 Vol 27			
War Diary	Beaulencourt		01/10/1917	05/10/1917
War Diary	Fins		06/10/1917	31/10/1917
Heading	No 60. F.A. Nov. 1917			
Heading	War Diary of 60th Field Ambulance R.A.M. Corps For November 1917 Vol 28			
War Diary	Fins V.12.c.8.8 57c S.E. 1/20.000		01/11/1917	19/11/1917
Miscellaneous	Report On Work At A.D.S. At Gouzeaucourt And of The Bearer Divisions. 20-25th Nov 1917			

Miscellaneous	Instructions Re-Operations Instructions For O.Cs. Brigade Parties of Div. Stretcher Compy.		
Miscellaneous	A Form. Messages And Signals		
Miscellaneous	Gouzeaucourt Q36 d. 4.9	30/11/1917	30/11/1917
Miscellaneous			
Heading	No 60 F.A. Dec. 1917		
Heading	War Diary of 60th Field Ambulance For December 1917 Vol 29		
War Diary	Fins	01/12/1917	03/12/1917
War Diary	Ribemont	04/12/1917	06/12/1917
War Diary	Boubers	07/12/1917	12/12/1917
War Diary	Wardrecques	13/12/1917	20/12/1917
War Diary	Bailleul	21/12/1917	31/12/1917
Heading	No. 60. F.A. Jan. 1918		
Heading	War Diary of 60th Field Ambulance For Jan-1918 Vol 30		
War Diary	8 Rue De College Bailleul (Baillell College)	01/01/1918	05/01/1918
War Diary	St Joseph's College Bailleul (8 Rue De Benoit Cortyl)	06/01/1918	23/01/1918
War Diary	Bailleul	27/01/1918	31/01/1918
Heading	War Diary 60th Field Ambulance February 1918 Vol 31		
War Diary	St Joseph's College Bailleul (8 Rue De Benoit Cortyl)	01/02/1918	09/02/1918
War Diary	Waratah Camp	11/02/1918	14/02/1918
War Diary	St Joseph's College Bailleul (8 Rue De Cortyle Beuort)	15/02/1918	15/02/1918
War Diary	Caestre	16/02/1918	18/02/1918
War Diary	Eeckhout Casteel	19/02/1918	20/02/1918
War Diary	Omencourt	21/02/1918	28/02/1918
Heading	War Diary 60th Field Ambulance March 1918 Vol 32		
War Diary	Omencourt	01/03/1918	20/03/1918
War Diary	Ugny	20/03/1918	22/03/1918
War Diary	Matigny	22/03/1918	22/03/1918
War Diary	Languevoisin	22/03/1918	24/03/1918
War Diary	Rethonvillers	24/03/1918	25/03/1918
War Diary	Champien	25/03/1918	25/03/1918
War Diary	Roye	25/03/1918	25/03/1918
War Diary	Laucourt by Roye	26/03/1918	26/03/1918
War Diary	Roye Montdidier Road	26/03/1918	26/03/1918
War Diary	Roye-Montdidier Road Faverolles	26/03/1918	26/03/1918
War Diary	Fontaine Sous Montdidier	26/03/1918	26/03/1918
War Diary	Aubvillers	27/03/1918	27/03/1918
War Diary	Berteaucourt	28/03/1918	28/03/1918
War Diary	Boves	28/03/1918	28/03/1918
War Diary	Sains En Amenois	28/03/1918	28/03/1918
War Diary	Seux	29/03/1918	29/03/1918
War Diary	Warlus	30/03/1918	31/03/1918
Miscellaneous	Appendix To War Diary For March 1918 60th Field Ambulance		
Miscellaneous	O.C. 60th Field Ambulance		
Heading	War Diary of 60th Field Ambulance For April 1918 Vol 33		
War Diary	Abbeville	01/04/1918	01/04/1918
War Diary	Sorel	04/04/1918	06/04/1918
War Diary	Hallivillers	06/04/1918	06/04/1918
War Diary	Ramburelles	10/04/1918	10/04/1918
War Diary	Incheville	11/04/1918	17/04/1918
War Diary	Bethonsart	18/04/1918	30/04/1918
Heading	War Diary May 1918 60th Field AMB Vol 34		

War Diary	Bethonsart	01/05/1918	04/05/1918
War Diary	Chateau De La Haie Summit Near Villers-Du Bois	05/05/1918	11/05/1918
War Diary	Chateau De La Haie Summit (W 11 B.E.4 Sht 36 B)	12/05/1918	20/05/1918
War Diary	Chateau De La Haie Summit	21/05/1918	31/05/1918
Heading	60th Field Amb. War Diary June 1918 Vol 35		
War Diary	Chateau De La Haie Summit	01/06/1918	30/06/1918
Heading	60th Field Amb. War Diary July 1918 Vol 36		
War Diary	Chateau De La Haie (Summit)	01/07/1918	18/07/1918
War Diary	Chateau De La Haie	19/07/1918	31/07/1918
Heading	War Diary August 1918 60th Field Ambulance Vol 37		
War Diary	Chateau De La Haie	01/08/1918	27/08/1918
War Diary	Chateau De La Haie Summit	28/08/1918	31/08/1918
Heading	War Diary September 1918 60th Field Ambulance Vol 38		
War Diary	Chateau De La Haie Summit	01/09/1918	10/09/1918
War Diary	Chateau De La Haie	11/09/1918	22/09/1918
War Diary	Chateau De La Haie Summit	23/09/1918	30/09/1918
Heading	War Diary of O.C 60th Field Ambulance 1st October 1918- 31st October 1918 Vol 39		
War Diary	Chateau De La Haie Summit	01/10/1918	20/10/1918
War Diary	Comblingneul	21/10/1918	30/10/1918
War Diary	Cambrai	31/10/1918	31/10/1918
Heading	60th F.A. Nov 1918		
War Diary	Cambrai	01/11/1918	03/11/1918
War Diary	Avesnes Les Aubert	04/11/1918	27/11/1918
War Diary	Cambrai	28/11/1918	30/11/1918
Heading	War Diary of 60th Field Ambulance 1st December 1918- 31st December 1918		
War Diary	Lealvillers	01/12/1918	17/12/1918
War Diary	Toutencourt	19/12/1918	31/12/1918
Heading	War Diary 60th Field Amb. January 1919 Vol 42		
War Diary	Toutencourt	01/01/1919	31/01/1919
Heading	60th F.A. War Diary February 1919 No 60th Field Ambulance Vol 43		
War Diary	Toutencourt	01/02/1919	28/02/1919
War Diary	60th Field Ambulance War Diary March 1919 Vol 44		
War Diary	Terra Mesnil	01/03/1919	30/03/1919
Heading	60th F.A. War Diary April 1919 Vol 45		
War Diary	Terra Mesnil	01/04/1919	01/05/1919

2109/1

20TH DIVISION

60TH FIELD AMBULANCE
JLY 1915 - ~~DEC 1915~~
1919 APL

60th Field Ambulance

Early History

Shortly before the end of September 1914 about 3000 men were detached from the great Training Centre R.A.M.C. at Aldershot and proceeded to Tweezledown. On arrival here - a splitting up process commenced resulting in the formation of a number of Field Ambulances numbered from 29 upwards.

Birth
(End of Sept. 1914)

Thus the 60th F.A. was born. Commanded for a few days by an officer of the 29th F.A., the first officer definitely posted to this F.A. was Capt (then Lt.) DAVIDSON J. who took over temporary Command. He was joined shortly afterwards by Lt. GREVILLE C.P. & Training commenced.

Training

Training continued at Tweezledown until June 1915 when the unit was moved to Rolleston (Salisbury Plain)

Officers

At the beginning of 1915 - the Establishment of Officers had been made up by the addition of Lieuts TOZER, KENNEDY, KIRTON, BENNETT, LAWSON, MELVILLE, TAWSE. Major LAUDER joined the unit just in time to take it from Tweezledown to Rolleston. Establishment was thus complete with the exception of a Q.M. - and this officer joined at Rolleston (Lt & QM BURN) where the unit also received its transport.

Attachment to Brigade & Division

At the latter place the Field Ambulance was at length attached to its Division and came into contact for the first time with the Brigade (60th) to which it was to be affiliated.

Brigade & Divisional Training

Training proceeds on a larger scale and the men were introduced to manœuvres by day and to the joys of night operations.

Inspection by H.M. The King	By the end of June the Division was considered to have completed its training and was inspected by H.M. The King on Salisbury Plain.
Orders for Service Overseas	On the 19th July 1915 at 9 A.M. the F.A. moved out on the great adventure. 7 A.M on the 20th saw them at Southampton and at 8 P.M a start was made. Le HAVRE was reached after an uneventful passage
France	On the morning of the 21st July the unit disembarked and was marched to a Rest Camp where it entrained for LUMBRES near ST. OMER which was reached about noon on the 23rd. After a longish march billets were reached at CORNETTE. Here training was continued for the space of another fortnight. By Brigade march the unit next proceeded to OULTERSTEENE (near BAILLEUL) and after another week or so - the F.A. was temporarily split up for instructional purposes
Instructional attachment	"A" Sect was sent to the 26th F.A. at BAC-ST-MAUR - while "B" Sect was attached to the 25th F.A. at SAILLY-sur la LYS
Baptism of Fire	The Bearers of "A" Sect were detached from the Tent Subdivision (which remained at the Main Dressing Station BAC-ST-MAUR - and had their baptism of fire at FLEURBAIX - whilst 'B' Sect had the same experience & was similarly subdivided at SAILLY, the bearers going into the BOIS GRENIER Sector "C" Sect proceeded to PRADELLES and opened a Divisional Rest Station there under Lt KIRTON 3 weeks later it rejoined HQ. The remainder of the unit having meanwhile reassembled at OULTERSTEENE

and proceeded on to ESTAIRES (Sept 15th 1915).

LAVENTIE SECTOR + DRS at ESTAIRES
The LAVENTIE front was quiet and the bearers had a relatively easy time. The Div'l Rest Station was shortly after this changed - transferred to ESTAIRES and an Advanced Dressing Station (A.D.S) opened at LAVENTIE with a few bearers in the line.

Change of O.C.
Just before the unit left OUTERSTEENE for ESTAIRES - Major A.C. OSBURN took over Command of the unit vice Major LAUDER & Capt N. CANTLIE joined as Adjutant - (Shortly before Sept 15. 1915.).

BATTLE of LOOS
Shortly after this the F.A took a share in the battle of LOOS - in that the bearers were sent to reinforce 61st F.A. which was looking after 60th Bde - who were involved in the battle.

A long period was spent altogether in this portion of the line - the medical arrangements conforming to occasional sidestepping on the part of the Division and Advanced Dressing Stations were established at different times at SAILLY & FLEURBAIX.

The front remained a quiet one and casualties were light.

YPRES SECTOR
About Jan 16th 1916 the Ambulance commenced its first move to the YPRES SECTOR - spending a few days at MARIE CAPELLE before moving on to POPERINGHE - where a large Ecole was taken over as a Brigade Main Dressing Station (M.D.S) and a D.RS for Officers - the bearers being in the line with the affiliated Brigade when the Division relieved the 14th Division in the line about 12/2/16.

The Divisional front was on the North of the Salient in front of LA BELLE ALLIANCE and LA BRIQUE near ST JEAN.

ST JEAN front.
The A.D.S was established at ESSEX FARM on the Canal Bank. (ST JULIEN 28.N.W.2) C 25. a.

There was no change for two months and the sector was none too pleasant with rather heavy casualties all the time.

XIV Corps. The Division was now in the XIVth Corps grouped with the Guards & the 6th Div under the Earl of Cavan.

In April 1916 the Division was relieved by the 6th Division and went back to the WATKBU – WORMHOUDT Area to rest.

REST AREA During this time the 59th Bde and the F.A were sent back to CALAIS for 10 days.

After a period of rest as above described the Division was once more sent into the Salient where it remained until the beginning of July 1916. The H.Q F.A. were stationed at PESELHOEK N of POPERINGHE with the A.D.S. at the Asylum in YPRES and the usual Advanced

ST JEAN SECTOR Posts in the line at POTEZE & ST JEAN.

At the beginning of July the F.A was relieved and marched out – camping on the outskirts of BAILLEUL for about a week – where orders were once more received for the Division to go into the line & for a short time took over the

PLOEGSTREET PLOEGSTREET Sector. This Sector was quieter than the ST JEAN Sector and casualties were not heavy.

Once more taken out of the line the F.A. now entrained with the rest of the Division for AUTHIE just N of the

SOMME 1916 Somme Area and the D.R.S was taken over in the wood at AUTHIE while a detachment was sent to HEBUTERNE to run an A.D.S and be responsible for the evacuation of wounded of the Brigade which was in the line. The F.A. remained in this area for the first month of the Somme fighting which – after the relative failure of the offensive about BEAUMONT HAMEL, was quiet.

About Aug 6th 1916 the unit was relieved and entrained for MÉRICOURT – from where it marched to M'EAULTE. Tents were pitched here for a few days before

GUILLEMONT.

the next move - which was to the "Loop" near FRICOURT. Almost immediately after arrival the Division went into the line in relief of the 24th Div (Aug 20th 1916) taking over the line this side of GUILLEMONT. Posts were established by the F.A in BERNAFAY WOOD, the BRIQUETERIE & WATERLOT FARM. The Division was heavily counterattacked about this time and suffered many casualties.

The 61st F.A was at this time i/c of the M.D.S at DIVES' COPSE and was reinforced by 2 out of the three Tent Subdivisions of this F.A. - The remainder of the Ambulance was i/c of the evacuation of wounded from the line - itself reinforced by the Bearer Divisions of 61st & 62nd F.A.'s

On the 3rd September 1916 the Division took part in the battle for GUILLEMONT which place was captured by the 59th Brigade.

The morning was heavy and a little misty. For the battle the Ambulance was disposed as follows: H.Q. & Bearer Camp were at BRONFAY FARM, while 2 A.D.S's were being run - namely at BRIQUETERIE, and in BERNAFAY WOOD respectively - with the usual posts further forward, and squads attached to the regimental medical officers at their regimental aid posts. The short intense bombardment opened punctually at 12 noon & the men went over in perfect style. Casualties began to get heavy by about 2 P.M. - as the result of more concentrated enemy retaliation. A Brigade of the 16th (Irish) Division - suffered heavily in the afternoon on its way up to reinforce us.

The same evening a small post for walking wounded was established at The CULVERTS near BERNAFAY WOOD and cleared 140 patients during the night by means of the horse ambulance waggons which were now able to get up. Some 500 casualties passed

GUILLEMONT

through the F.A. H.Q at BRONFAY FARM - in addition to large numbers evacuated direct from the A.D.S.'s at BRIQUETERIE & BERNAFAY; the carry to this latter A.D.S was something like 3000 yds over the worst possible ground and was of a most arduous nature. The A.D.S at the BRIQUETERIE was better situated in this respect - nevertheless by the morning of the 4th the services of all available reserve bearers were necessary & these were accordingly ordered up, being heavily shelled in the process of getting there.

During the night of 3rd September Capt D.A.D. KENNEDY took out a number of squads of bearers & succeeded in bringing in a number of wounded from the shellpocked area around GUILLEMONT

About 2 days after the capture of GUILLEMONT the F.A. & 59th Bde moved back to CORBIE - on being relieved - but this was the shortest of reliefs and two more days saw them back again in the line

8th Sept. 1916

The last (3rd) Tent Subdivision was now detached from the F.A - which then consisted of HQ & Bearers only. The Tent Subdivision was sent to further reinforce the XIV Corps M.D.S which had meanwhile moved up from DIVES' COPSE to BRONFAY FARM; the bearers were still in the line in front of GINCHY in the MORVAL - LE BOEUF Sector. The conditions were very bad, casualties heavy and evacuation very arduous. After about a week in the line the Division was relieved and the F.A proceeded with the Brigade to MORLAN- -COURT; the relief was however a short one and the division once more went into the line in front of DELVILLE WOOD. The H.Q. F.A came up to a site close to BERNAFAY WOOD

RELIEF

The Bearers were detached to help in evacuating the line: conditions were if possible worse than before & casualties continued fairly heavy.

At the beginning of October the Division was once more relieved and went back again to the CORBIE Area – 59th Brigade & F.A. (H.Q) at VILLE-sur-Ancre.

Inspection by Lord CAVAN

Here the Brigade Group was inspected and complimented by the Corps Commander.

About the 20th October the Division moved back to the PICQUIGNY AREA to refit – H.Q. F.A. at PICQUIGNY. – and remained here for some three weeks among pleasant surroundings until ordered (about the middle of Nov) back to the CORBIE Area – with F.A H.Q. once more at VILLE-sur-Ancre.

About this time the whole Tent Division of the F.A. was again detached and sent to join the XIV Corps M.D.S at CARNOY – where it remained until the Division went into the line again about Dec 11th 1916.

LE BOEUF – MORVAL SECTOR

The 61st F.A were now given the manning of the line and consequently the whole Bearer Division of the F.A was detached to work under them – the Tent Division moving back to XIV Corps Rest Station.

The Division remained in this area until just on Christmas day 1916 – The LE-BOEUF-MORVAL SECTOR – the howling wilderness in front of GINCHY. The weather was bad & wet – mud appalling & casualties from sickness as high as battle casualties. By Xmas day the Division was once more back in the CORBIE Area – and a good deal better pleased than those who had gone into the line.

The F.A. consisted of H.Q. & Bearers only – the whole Tent Division remaining at the Corps Rest Station for the present. At the beginning of Jan 1917 there was a move into the line again – but this

8

SAILLY-SAILLISEL
Jan 1917.

time there was a slight side stepping and the Division relieved the Guards in the SAILLY-SAILLISEL Sector.

The F.A. was now reconstituted by the return of the Tent Division and a Dressing Station was built and opened just beyond TRONES WOOD - the bearers still working under 61st F.A.

TRONES WOOD DRESSING STATION does not fit into the usual scheme of medical arrangements in vogue at the time. It was a large Collecting dressing Station tapping the A.D.S's & was of the nature of a Divisional M.D.S - for from it cases were evacuated to Corps M.D.S. or Corps Rest Station. During this period the weather conditions were very bad & consequently the trenches as bad as they could be. Battle Casualties were moderate but the Division suffered very heavy losses from Trench foot - necessitating special arrangements and preventive measures. With the onset of very severe frost during the second half of January conditions improved and the health of the Division improved concurrently. About the end of the month the Division was once more relieved in the line & proceeded to the HEILLY AREA

HEILLY
Jan/Feb 1917

H.Q. F.A. were at FRANVILLERS. After a few days H.Q were shifted to BONNAY. During this time the frost was intense - the weather glorious - and everybody vastly preferred the Sun & Cold - to mud & rain

TRONES WOOD Dressing Station

About 7th Feb 1917 orders were once more received for the line & the F.A. once more took over TRONES WOOD DRESSING STATION. - the bearers being again detached to work under 61st F.A.

The F.A. now remained for some considerable time in this location not being ordered up until well after the beginning of the German

9.

German Retreat Spring 1917. retreat. While the enemy were retreating through Le TRANSLOY, Le MESNIL, ROCQUIGNY etc the F.A. continued at TRONES WOOD formerly a link in the ever lengthening line of evacuation which in spite of all difficulties 61st F.A. carried through brilliantly.

LECHELLE. At the beginning of April the H.Q F.A. were at last shifted up to LECHELLE close to YTRES

Capture of METZ en COUTURE On the 4th April 1917 - the day on which METZ en COUTURE was taken in a snow storm - the F.A. took over the running of the line of the affiliated Brigade again. The casualties during this operation were rather heavy and some 500 were passed through the Dressing Station which had been established at YTRES Station - half way between YTRES & ETRICOURT.

It now became absolutely imperative to move forward the Corps Station Corps M.DS & C.R.S - as the distance was almost beyond the powers of the cars and drivers, consequently early in April 1917 the whole F.A was detached from the Division for work under Corps at MOISLAINS - which place being quickly found unsuitable was given up and further constructional work taken in hand to establish the Corps M.D.S just outside FINS on the FINS-NURLU ROAD. The position was at that time a trifle exposed and more than one shell just skimmed over the tents & landed in the road (the Divisional Commander having a narrow escape there) - but this state of things did not continue for long & except for occasional reminders - was quiet - and no casualties ever occurred there.

Corps M.D.S FINS-NURLU ROAD.

While here the Bearers were detached to assist 62nd F.A who were running part of the line. The

HAVRINCOURT WOOD SECTOR

61st F.A. had been evacuating the line but on the Division been ordered to temporarily put all 3 Brigades in the line — the consequent extension of front was entrusted to 62nd F.A. The Area was quiet — the weather fine & sunny & the enemy so busy getting behind the Hindenburg line that the men had the easiest & most comfortable time they had experienced for many a long day. Nothing of importance occurred & casualties were extremely slight.

MONUMENT

NOREUIL-LAGNICOURT SECTOR.

Towards the end of May orders were received to relieve the Australians (5) in the NOREUIL-LAGNICOURT Sector N.E. of BAPAUME.

The evacuation of wounded was in this Sector shared with 61st F.A. Both Field Ambulances had their H.Q. in a field between FAVREUIL & BEUGNATRE. (H17)

This F.A. was responsible for the Northern half — but all the wounded of the Division passed through the A.D.S of this F.A. situated — dug in along the VAULX-VRAUCOURT—NOREUIL Road (C20). This A.D.S, which eventually consisted of 5 elephant dugouts, was considered as a M.D.S. but was totally unsuited as such. There was constant shelling along the valley between VAULX & NOREUIL and round about. Casualties had been very heavy while the Australians were in and it was thus a pleasant surprise that the intensity of shelling diminished in geometrical progression daily — about the time we took over; even then the Sector remained a very unpleasant one — which was never free from promiscuous attentions.

The weather during this time was perfect — warm & sunny — but the area being none too sanitary — there was soon a perfect plague of flies

LOSSES. As far as could be ascertained the losses of the Division were about 1380 in wounded alone — by the time the position were consolidated (19/8/17).

After the actual battle was temporarily over the back areas came in for a good deal of shelling and there were a good many casualties.

On the 19th August the Division was once more relieved by the 38th Div. — and

PROVEN AREA went back again to the PROVEN AREA. The H.Q. (F.A) were again near LOVIE CHTEAU. After a short period of rest — on the 12th Sept 1917 — the Division was ordered into the line again — (D.H.Q moved to the new Camp at WELSH FARM — near ELVERDINGHE) — and the evacuation of the line was retrusted to the F.A.

LINE. H.Q. were established at PELISSIER FARM. near ELVERDINGHE

Preparations were now made for the big battle all along the 5th & 2nd Army fronts which commenced on the 20th Sept 1917.

Medical Dispositions were as follows

BATTLE of 20th Sept. H.Q. 60th FA at PELISSIER FARM. A.DS at
1917. FUSILIER on Canal Bank (SUSSEX FARM A.D.S had been given up). The former forward A.D.S at GALWITZ FARM on the PILKEM RIDGE had not only been very heavily shelled during the period which had elapsed since the battle of the 16th August — but had also to some extent outlived its functions — Consequently it was largely left out of the scheme — being considered as a standbye — and a forward A.D.S. was established at CEMENT HOUSE — an excellent reinforced concrete "pill box" of large dimensions near the STEEN BEEK and not more than a few hundred yards from AU BON GITE — the old enemy strong point

Though constantly submitted to most murderous shelling this pillbox withstood everything & many casualties were evacuated through it.

EAGLE TRENCH
On the evening of the 20th Sept. a second attack was made on EAGLE TRENCH which was cleared. The wounded from both battles came in steadily all through the day & night and were cleared without hitch.

During all this time there had been very determined enemy air raids repeated not only nightly - but taking place in broad daylight. The Boches came over in great droves of 10-20 machines - and dropping bombs broadcast caused many casualties in the back areas especially: there

27-9-17.
were heavy losses in horses & mules all around ELVERDINGHE. Though it is not to be supposed the damage was confined to that area.

RELIEF.
The Division was relieved in the line by the 4th Division on 29.9.17. & moved back again to the PROVEN AREA. This was however only a preliminary to a move Southwards and between the 2nd & 4th Oct the Divisions entrained for BAPAUME.

Shortly after starting out from HOPOUTRE SIDING, POPERINGHE - the F.A. and some other units of the 59th Bde were held up for several hours by a bad bombing raid. One bomb was aimed at the train - but, dropping just behind it killed a French Soldier from a big-gun train which was standing on a siding and was presumably the actual object of attack. Detraining at BAPAUME the F.A spent a few days at BEAULEN-COURT (just N. of le TRANSLOY) proceeding on at the end of this time to take over the F.A. Site at FINS. about the 10th Oct 1917.

15.

VILLERS-PLUICH - GONNELIEU Sector.

The Division now took over the VILLERS-PLUICH - GONNELIEU Sector and there was a general feeling of astonishment and relief at finding a sector of the line which was so quiet & (pro.tem) uneventful. Shortly after the beginning of Novr. however preparations began for the projected burst through the Hindenberg Line and this Division had to prepare and make all necessary arrangements for the 6th, 12th, & 29th Divs. While medical arrangements had to be similarly made for these divisions and enormous quantities of Medical Stores, blankets, stretchers, dressings etc drawn for distribution to these divisions. It was an exciting fortnight watching the secret arrival of numberless guns, some 200 tons & the troops of the four additional Divisions.

Preparations for

Medical Dispositions before the attack were roughly as follows:— The evacuation of the line was being carried out by No. 9 F.A. H.Q. at FINS & A.D.S. at GOUZEAUCOURT; the more forward posts were northwards towards VILLERS PLUICH and eastwards along the GOUZEAUCOURT-CAMBRAI ROAD. — All offshoots from the above were naturally absorbed in the scheme of medical arrangements for the Divisions on our left (N) & right (S). — then the additional A.D.S. at VILLERS GUISLAN which had been run by 61st F.A. naturally became the Chief A.D.S. of the 12th Division on our right. The 6th Div on our left had great difficulty in finding a suitable A.D.S and it was not difficult to prophecy that many casualties would come down through our posts as indeed proved to be the case.

Just before the battle the F.A. was reinforced by all available bearers from 61 & 62nd F.A's.

On the left an advanced Post or Dressing Station was pushed up beyond VILLERS-PLUICH to SURREY RAVINE and on the right a similar advanced post, battle

1st Battle of CAMBRAI
20th Nov 1917

(F.A) Post - or Dressing Station was established in PARTRIDGE ROAD - just off the main GOUZEAUCOURT - CAMBRAI Road close behind the then - front line.

A Walking Wounded Post - (& Dressing Station) was also organized in GOUZEAUCOURT - not far from the original A.D.S. there.

Just before Zero hour the H.Q. (FA) was transferred to GOUZEAUCOURT.

Wounded began to come in after the usual interval of about 2 hours.

After the complete success of the attack was established other posts were quickly pushed forward - one being at LA VACQUERIE & one in the Hindenburg Support line on the LA VACQUERIE - MAS-NIÈRES Road. Another further North towards MARCOING. Later, when the position settled down to the well known Salient - but by no means long after the Capture of MASNIÈRES an A.D.S. was established in the BREWERY at LES RUES VERTES just S. of MASNIÈRES

A.D.S Brewery Les Rues Vertes

It was not long before the lightly metalled VACQUERIE - MASNIÈRES road became quite useless and an alternative route had to be found via MASNIÈRES - MARCOING - to VILLERS-PLUICH to GOUZEAUCOURT - And this remained the chief route of evacuation during the whole of the first phase of the battle & after - until just before the Counter-attack on the 30th Nov.

With the Movement of HQ FA to GOUZEAU-COURT - a bearer Camp had been established in Farm Ravine (16 Ravine).

Enemy Shelling which had been completely paralysed during the earlier stages of the battle gradually increased in intensity during the ensuing days particularly along the MASNIÈRES - MARCOING Road - which was rather recklessly used in broad daylight - in spite of being overlooked by RUMILLY - still in enemy hands

CASUALTIES

As regards Casualties:— On the 20th & 21st Nov. about 1750 cases were passed through the Dressing Station at BOUZEAU-COURT — comprising — as had been anticipated men — not only of our own division but large numbers from the 6th, 29th & 12th Divs — and even from the 51 Div — at the extreme North. During the 22nd another 850 were passed through (or about 2400 in 3 days) — now including a good many Prisoners of War.

During the ensuing days casualties settled down to a relatively light flow of adventitious victims of enemy shell fire.

As above mentioned however, shell fire gradually increased in intensity and by the afternoon of the 28th Nov became so heavy that it became necessary to evacuate the A.D.S at Les RUES VARTES and establish one a little further back in the QUARRIES (Crucifix X roads

25th Nov.

an additional Post being also established a little nearer MARCOING on the MASNIERES — MARCOING ROAD.

It was from this post that cases were evacuated by car — though the a/m road was under heavy machine gun & shell fire.

Pte COOK (MT/RASC) driving one of the cars during this night had the misfortune to get into a shell hole and with exemplary courage spent the whole night on this road repairing the damage* — and next morning Sgt Paterson M.T. arrived in another car & in broad daylight hauled the damaged car away.

*under heavy shell & machine gun fire.

It was but a day or so before this that two Medical Officers who were stationed at the BREWERY-ADS were off duty for a time and encountered a Sergt Major — who, they noticed, was carrying a rifle & bayonet. He disappeared shortly afterwards up a cul-de-sac & was caught

18

red handed - firing at our men. He was eventually captured and his fate though conjectured is not known

2nd Battle of CAMBRAI
Nov 30th 1917

On November 30th 1917 - at about 5AM the enemy commenced putting over a large number of gas shells. Shelling increased in intensity and was of course the precursor of the great Enemy counterattack in this sector.

Capt. Edmond R.A.M.C

Capt. Edmond of this F.A was conspicuous in the early state of the attack of his gallantry in remaining at his post (the A.D.S at the QUARRIES Crucifix X Roads - outside Les Rues Vertes) dressing the wounded until the enemy were within a few hundred yards. He then withdrew his bearers - but finding a man seriously wounded on the road, he ran back towards the enemy to get a stretcher and blanket for the wounded man, while under heavy machine gun & rifle fire from the advancing enemy infantry, and from aeroplanes. With the help of Pte BARKER R.A.M.C he carried the wounded man 6000 yards to a loading post, remained there until the man was got away safely and, having dressed a number of other severely wounded men on his way there and also at the loading post.

He succeeded in joining Capt KIRTON at the Bearer Camp Partridge Row or XVI Ravine.

Hearing that there many casualties in the neighbourhood of this gallant officer proceeded there through a very heavily shelled area & attended many of the severely wounded men. It appears that at the time where the shelling in the neighbourhood was very severe & all other troops were confined to their dugouts - he went from his own to the Hospital dugout - to attend

19

to a wounded man & was struck by a fragment of a shell in the heart and died instantly.

Meanwhile the enemy had captured GOUZEAUCOURT - and the H.Q of the 7A & Staff were just got away in time as will be described shortly.

Evacuation from the left Sector of the line was then entirely diverted and had to be carried out via BEAUCAMP Charing Cross, TRESCAULT, METZ en COUTURE to FINS - being further interfered with by an enormous Mine crater at Charing Cross - which made the road impassible & completely isolated Several cars. These cars had consequently to ply backwards & forwards as far as the crater and hand over cases there to other cars.

GOUZEAUCOURT A.D.S

The first warning of anything untoward was a sudden barrage on the outskirts of the village - between it and VILLERS GUISLAIN. As this was followed shortly afterwards by bursts of machine gun fire from the direction of VILLERS GUISLAIN it became evident that a big German attack was in progress and that, apparently VILLERS GUISLAIN had been captured. There were 30-40 lying cases in the Dressing Station at the time & cases were still coming in. Luckily an Ambulance DECAUVILLE Train was waiting and this was quickly loaded up & sent away; walking cases were dispatched by car as they arrived. At least 4 Officers were at the time bathing, shaving etc and were totally ignorant of what had occurred. Shell fire had recommenced and shells were arriving indiscriminately in the village. A 5.9" hit the Dressing Station - demolishing the wall of the room in which cases were being dressed. By this time it was about 9 A.M. and things looked fairly serious when the enemy were seen advancing at the double over

20.

the ridge between GOUZEAUCOURT and VILLERS-GUISLAN. — Some 7,800 yds away. Fortunately instead of advancing direct on Gouzeaucourt they wheeled off in the direction of HEUDECOURT with the evident intention of getting across the FINS-GOUZEAUCOURT road further back. No further wounded were now arriving and the remainder of the F.A. were collected and the A.D.S vacated. There was heavy H.V. and machine gun fire on the road — and a Corporal (Cpl HADLEY) was hit and died later of his wounds.

Half way between FINS & GOUZEAUCOURT a provisional A.D.S was chosen and on arriving back at the old F.A. (HQ) at FINS a strong detachment of bearers was organised and under Capt R.V.C ASH & Capt STALLARD (of 61st FA) went forward again and occupied this site.

It was found that the personnel had got away from Gouzeaucourt almost complete; 3 men were missing who were indeed in the hands of the enemy but eventually succeeded in escaping.

Large numbers of wounded some 3-400 of ours & neighbouring Divisions were dealt with at this improvised Dressing Station (W3 — where the METZ-HEUDECOURT road — crossed the FINS-GOUZEAUCOURT Rd) until the Guards Division took over and relieved this F.A.

The Cars continued however for some time to bear the brunt of the burden of evacuations.

By the evening Gouzeaucourt had been recaptured — and though still under heavy shell and machine gun fire Capt ASH, RAMC & Lt MARBURY M.O.R.C (U.S.A). went up again to the A.D.S there and succeeded in removing the bulk of the stores which had been left. The A.D.S was finally evacuated at dawn on 1st December and was afterwards used by the Guards - as a regimental Aid post.

Capt. McARTHUR, DAVIDSON, WILLS all former members of this F.A. were reported missing after the battle.

RELIEF The Division was relieved about the 3rd December by the 61st Division and sent to the Rest Area W. of Albert with F.A (HQ) at RIBEMONT-sur-ANCRE but moved on almost immediately afterwards to the HACQUEUERS AREA F.A HQ (BOUBERT). - to refit.

The losses of the Division had of course been very heavy and it was greatly disorganised.

After about a week the Division was moved on to the BLARINGHEM AREA (between ST OMER & AIRE) - HQ FA at WARDRECQUES - to complete the work of refitting and reorganising.

The greater part of this FA was shortly afterwards moved to BAILLEUL to form a Divisional Rest Station in a large religious école in the Rue de Collège - afterwards moved to Rue BENOIT CORTYL

There was not much more rest for the Division - which was ordered to **POLYGON SECTOR** take over in the POLYGON SECTOR about Jan 6th 1918 (D.H.Q. at WESTOUTRE)
HQ of this FA & D.R.S remained at BAILLEUL.

The evacuation of the line was in the hands of 62nd FA (HQ at WOODCOTE HOUSE).

In addition to the D.R.S at BAILLEUL - this FA. was also made responsible for staffing & running a Dysentry Centre of some 60-80 beds at HAEGEDOORNE just outside (NE) of BAILLEUL (Major C.A. Boyd i/c) and thirdly orders were received to take over a D.R.S. at WARRATAH CAMP on the RENNINGHELST-POPERINGHE Road

22

with a view to giving up the École at BAILLEUL – and coincident with a side step on the part of the Division by which an additional Sector of the line was taken over from the N. Zealand Div. – North of the MENIN ROAD.

This necessitated the A/ur readjustment of medical organisation in the areas behind the line

The Sector was a bad one – casualties pretty heavy and the conditions were execrable – the great bulk of the troops in support living in large underground tunnels; the health of the division suffered accordingly from the results of overcrowding, food & water contamination etc.

The Division held this Sector of the line until the middle of February when another move was made back to the BLARINGHEM Area

BLARINGHEM AREA
2nd Time

H.Q (TA) was at first at CAESTRE and shifted later to ECKHOUT CASTEL near WALLON-CAPPEL.

On the 20th February the unit marched to STEENBECQUE and entrained for NESLE. (D.H.Q. ERCHEU) – H.Q. TA OMENCOURT – the Division being in G.H.Q. reserve

(Lt Col OSBURN proceeded on leave from ECKHOUT CASTEL & while at home was boarded and transferred to the home establishment temporarily and struck off the strength of the unit)

ERCHEU AREA
G.H.Q. Reserve.

The stay in the ERCHEU Area was extremely pleasant and the weather lovely.

A very successful Race Meeting was held.

The TA ran a small D.R.S at OMENCOURT

It was by this time common knowledge that a great enemy offensive was in preparation – Even the date being confidently predicted

The Division was in Reserve behind the 61st, 30th, & 36th Divisions which were holding the Line before ST QUENTIN. The Areas had been previously reconnoitred and battle positions chosen for the Brigades (& affiliated F.A's) in accordance with one or more alternative schemes depending on the strength and degree of involvement in the expected enemy attack.

The F.A's (including the 60th) were definitely affiliated to the Brigades and it was expected that each would be responsible for the evacuations from its own brigade.

21st March 1918 By early morning of the 21st March 1918 the guns were thundering out a hurricane bombardment & we knew our information had been correct. On the receipt of the order to man battle stations - the Brigades moved forward & occupied the previously chosen positions in support of the Divisions involved. (DHQ to HAM) This F.A. moved to UGNY - with Reserve A.D.S.'s at LANCHY & FORRESTE. Here work was carried on for some time in conjunction with a 61st Div! F(A) - as there was no other choice of suitable places.

22/3. Although information was received at about 6 A.M. from Brigade - giving the disposition of the battalions - this was apparently out of date by the time of receipt - the battalions having been otherwise disposed.

From now onwards until some time on the 24th - dispositions had in the absence of further orders from Brigade - to be made as well as possible from information to hand and personal investigation of the state of affairs at different posts.

24

The A.D.S's at L'ANCHY & FORRESTE had eventually to be vacated - and orders were given to retire on MATIGNY.

MATIGNY was by now being heavily shelled as well as receiving the attention of enemy aeroplanes

A strong party was selected to staff the A.D.S at MATIGNY and the remainder of the unit was sent back under Capt BODIE to LANGEVOISIN - across the SOMME CANAL - for greater safety of transport & equipment

MATIGNY.

While at D.H.Q 61st Div information was received that the enemy had broken through and 61st D.H.Q were withdrawing from MATIGNY.

A temporary Aid Post was nevertheless established at MATIGNY Cross roads under Major BOYD (C.A.) RAMC and numbers of wounded chiefly of 61st Div were attended to. These were evacuated by every available means - chiefly to VOYENNES (where had been an Officers' Rest Station - constructed by this F.A.)

LANGEVOISIN

Major ASH (A.V.C) proceeded to organise LANGEVOISIN as an A.D.S. Sending his only other Officer to assist Major BOYD.

As many as 2,300 cases were passed through this post before it had to be evacuated and this was done during the night (22/23) at the last possible moment - when the enemy were entering MATIGNY and just before the bridges at VOYENNES were destroyed.

The next morning (23rd) a certain amount of information as to disposition was obtainable from Brigade H.Q now at ROUY-LE-PETIT - (just N.E. of NESLE).

A.D.S.S. MESNIL-ST NICAISE

QUIQUERRY Aid Post

Major C.A. BOYD with a strong party proceeded to MESNIL-ST-NICAISE and formed an A.D.S there - Capt BRODIE proceeding to QUIQUERRY Cross roads on the VOYENNES-LANGEVOISIN Road and

25.

Some 200 wounded were passed through this post.

A.D.S at MESNIL-ST-NICAISE

On the afternoon of the 23rd Major Boyd made an attempt to establish an A.D.S at BETHENCOURT on the Canal bank to reduce the length of the carry. Shelling was however so heavy that it could not be reached

A second attempt was made between 10 & 11 p.m. that night: having reached Bethencourt in safety Major Boyd was advised to abandon the project as the Enemy were expected over the Canal in force with daylight and there was none too good a chance of holding them. It was meanwhile arranged that the wounded should be carried back from the Canal bank to a certain sunken portion of the road between BETHENCOURT and MESNIL-ST-NICAISE - the only possible place to establish even an R.A.P. in case of further retirement. This was accordingly done & the rest of the night passed relatively quietly. On the morning of the

24/3/18

24th March the Enemy came over very fast and large numbers of walking wounded came to the A.D.S but were sent straight on to NESLE. Shelling became intense and it was decided to temporarily vacate the A.D.S and shelter had to be taken where possible - e.g. under a traction engine. Some stretcher cases were collected in a cowshed As there was no abatement of the shelling the whole party vacated the A.D.S, carrying the stretcher cases to a place at the side of the road by means of repeated journeys through the barrage - and forming a dump there. On motor lorry luckily came along steering an erratic course between the shellholes; all cases were crowded into it and got away. Major Boyd now sent the whole party off along the road to NESLE remaining himself to get the result of a message sent to HQ by motorcyclist. The party under Sgt Cheal waited for Major Boyd at the railway just outside NESLE. Many cases were picked up and were carried around the outskirts of NESLE - until the NESLE-ROYE ROAD was struck - where an opportune lorry once more relieved the stretcher bearers of their burdens - and shortly afterwards this party fell in with the rest of the F.A. who were making their way along this road to RETHONVILLERS

H.Q. FA etc
24.3.18

During the greater part of this day VOYENNES continued to function as also did QUIQUERRY Aid Post and cases continued to be evacuated to LANGEVOISIN.
Later VOYENNES became impossible & cases were diverted to QUIQUERRY. During the late afternoon LANGEVOISIN was subjected to heavy shelling as well as machine gun fire from aeroplanes.
Wounded now ceased to come in largely due to diversion of the streams via NESLE on the N & MOYENCOURT - on the South and it was decided to move the HQ FA to RETHONVILLERS.
Some 800 wounded were passed through the Dressing Station at LANGEVOISIN.
When vacating the latter at about

RETHONVILLERS A.D.S	6 P.M. the Unit was once more subjected to the attentions of enemy aeroplanes. The A.D.S at NESLE [Quiqueny crossed out] was vacated the same evening about 9.30 p.m. by orders of Brigade H.Q. The whole Unit then reassembled at RETHONVILLERS before midnight of the 24th - but was immediately sent on by Major Ash (A/OC.) with orders to retire to CHAMPIEN. Major Ash himself established an A.D.S at RETHONVILLERS
25/3/18	Work continued here during the day - but by the evening enemy were within a few hundred yards (500) & the A.D.S had consequently evacuated - & Major Ash rejoined the Unit at CHAMPIEN. In the evening information was received from Brigade that the enemy were advancing on both flanks which would entail a further retirement on our part in our attempts to straighten our line. After Consultation with D.H.Q it was agreed that it was imperative to withdraw and it was decided to march through ROYE & attempt to establish at LAUCOURT on the MONT-DIDIER Road
26.3.18.	LAUCOURT was reached by 3.30 A.M on the 26th. By this time the situation about ROYE was exceedingly critical and information was received from the O.C. of a French Infantry battalion that the enemy were then about to enter ROYE and that a line of defence was being formed between LAUCOURT & ROYE. No further information was forthcoming & as it was rumoured that D.H.Q was to be at FAVEROLLES it was decided to continue the

53 C.C.S — withdrawal along the MONTDIDIER ROAD. Hearing that 53 C.C.S was unable to evacuate its wounded - 3 attached M.A.C. cars - 4 walking wounded lorries & all the unit cars were temporarily diverted for this purpose of evacuating these cases to LABOISSIERE & HARBICOURT.

Large numbers of wounded and stragglers were now picked up along the road.

26-3-18 — 28/3/18 Arriving at FAVEROLLES - touch was regained with division & by marches via FONTAINE-SOUS MONTDIDIER, AUB-VILLERS, BRACHES - rejoined the Division on the 28th at BRETEAUCOURT near DOMART.

As the result of a conference at D.H.Q. at that time still just outside DOMART it was decided that all the Divisional Transport & 2 out of the three F.A.'s were to be got out of the way without delay retiring in the direction of ABBEVILLE.

ABBEVILLE. Accordingly the Unit marched under the orders of Lt Col. STOCK 62nd F.A. by stages to ABBEVILLE - where it refitted -. (arrived 31.3.18)

On the 4th April the Unit moved (with 62nd F.A to SOREL - near ABBEVILLE - where the F. Ambulances split and on 6/4/18 this Unit rejoined the Brigade at HALLIVILLERS - and opened a small hospl there.

After a short stay there - the F.A. marched on the 10th April (with the Bde to RAMBURELLES & so on to INCHEVILLE - (in the TREPORT-ABBEVILLE area).

Broken and disorganised as the Division was reorganisation, reequip-ment and reinforcements were an

GAMACHES AREA	imperative necessity. The latter were quickly forthcoming and before long the Division was actually overstrength: reequipment had also been proceeding apace and the stay near the sea was cut short by orders to entrain once more 17/4/18 for the AUBIGNY-SAVY Area
LENS SECTOR	(in Reserve) behind the LENS SECTOR of the line.

H.Q. (F.A) at BRTHONSART. Training was of course the order of the day & was carried out to the full.

The Division was thought ready to go into the line again in the LENS SECTOR by the beginning of May and on 3.5.18 the F.A moved from BRTHONSART and took over the Divisional Rest Station at CHATEAU de la HAIE.

O.C. Lt Col A.C. Hammond Searle	Lt Col A.C. HAMMOND-SEARLE took over Command of the unit on the 5th May from Major R.V.C. ASH who had been A/O.C. since the middle of February and had commanded the unit all through the retreat

The time at Chateau de la Haie was relatively uneventful - the LENS Sector remaining quiet after almost the entire front had become involved in active operations

The Accommodation of the DRS was considerably increased until it was capable of holding nearly 250 cases and for some considerable time just short of 200 cases were constantly in hospital.

There was still considerable anxiety as to the possibilities of a new enemy thrust and preparations were made accordingly.

Enemy bombing was very aggressive and hostile aircraft were overhead almost nightly. Especially at the end of May & during the month of June. There were one or two particularly determined raids lasting several hours which caused heavy casualties in the neighbourhood, notably in the immediate vicinity of Chateau de la Haie & in Gouy-Servins. July & August were uneventful and then began the turn of the tide and the receipt of news of Allied successes and advances in practically all theatres of war.

Towards the end of August a part of the evacuation of the line was taken over by His F.A. and an A.D.S was established at LA CHAUDIÈRE - with the usual posts in advance of this.

LA CHAUDIÈRE A.D.S.

LA CHAUDIÈRE was close to the ruins of VIMY, and came in for a good deal of daily shelling - even when other parts of the sector were quiet.

It had also the disadvantage of being approachable only by two roads which were under direct enemy observation. However, the dugout was a very deep and exceedingly well constructed one and no casualties were sustained.

Inspection by "The" Corps Commander

Towards the end of August the F.A and the A.D.S were inspected by the Corps Commander (Sir Aylmer Hunter Weston) 30.8.18.

By this time the Allied advance was in full swing and preparations were being made for possible participation in the advance - which was becoming general.

During September came all the wonderful news from the East and with the continued advance on our front LENS began to be left behind, instead of being a salient and it began to be obvious that the enemy would have to retire. Except for occasional gas bombardments which caused moderate casualties these months May to

September 1918 were not responsible for many losses to the Division from wounds. Though some 8-900 men were lost to the Division as the result of the Influenza Epidemic.

At the end of September the enemy were clearly getting on the move - backwards and we hoped to take part in the general advance - but during the first week in October the Division

Relief by 12th Div. was relieved by the 12th Division and proceeded once more to the Reserve Area (AUBIGNY-SAVY). H.Q. F.A. at

CAMBIGNEUL CAMBIGNEUL, where a small hosp¹ was opened.

On the 30th October the unit marched to SAVY and entrained for VELU from where the unit was rebussed for

CAMBRAI CAMBRAI arriving there about 5 AM on 31.10.18

On the 3rd Nov. the unit marched with the Bde to CAUROY & on the 4th on to AVESNES les AUBERT - some

AVESNES-les AUBERT 13 kilometres E of CAMBRAI & taking over the Hospital Site at the MAIRIE there.

The F.A. was now detached from the Division for work under XVII Corps direct and established a Corps Influenza Hosp¹ at the a/m site. Large numbers of cases were received from the Division which was now in the BAVAY Area and in the neighbourhood of MONS.

Shortly after the Declaration of the Armistice on 11th November - orders were received to empty the hosp¹ at AVESNES - preparatory to moving back.

In the mean time a Corps Sick Entraining Station was established where the sick from all divisions of the Corps were fed & kept before being sent on by train to CAMBRAI.

By the end of November the Division was in process of being relieved in the forward area and on the 27th Nov the F.A. marched to CAMBRAI - where the Division reassembled before being rebussed on the 30th November for the PAS Area.

LEALVILLERS The F.A. was billeted at LEALVILLERS & opened a small hospital there - but a new site was necessary and an abandoned camp near TOUTENCOURT was chosen & put into repair and on the 19th December the unit moved in - to the present site.

A great deal of work was done and the Camp eventually completed by the end of January 1919 - by which time Demobilisation was the only subject of interest to all ranks, a view not necessarily shared by unfortunate O.C.'s.

List of Casualties. 60th Field Ambulance.

Killed.—

Capt. J. A. EDMOND

Missing believed Killed.—

CAPT. DAVIDSON.

Wounded and Prisoner of War

CAPT. C. R. WILLS.

Missing

LIEUT. J. F. HORNSEY.

Killed by Lightning

PTE GASKILL

Killed

L/C GARRETT	PTE. T. ELLIOTT
PTE BURNS	" HAYWARD
" BLOWER	" HENDERSON
" COULSON	" LEWIS

Died of Wounds.

L/SGT. BOLTON	CPL HEDLEY
PTE AMOS	PTE. ETOUGH

Wounded. R.D. 16.6.

30325	SGT. J. H. BARKER, MM.		PTE BAYES
	CPL. H.C. ALLAN		" BOON
	CPL. BROOKS	32803	" BRIDGMAN J.D.
	L/C CATTANACH	31040	" BAGLEY R.R.
	L/C DAVIES		" BENNETT
35224	L/C V.A.J DOWER		" BLACKLEY
461182	L/C A.H. MINTRAM		

Wounded R.A.M.C. (Cont'd)

30823	PTE. J. BUCKLE		PTE	GLACCUM
	" BRITTAIN	461530	"	A HAYTER
	" BREWER		"	E HARPER
	" BRAINE		"	HARRISON
	" BEALE	53894	"	T. KELLY M.M.
	" BORRINGTON	101754	"	W.E. LONGMAN
	" J. BRIGHT		"	W. LOVELL
	" BARLOW		"	LILLEY
	" H CLARK		"	G. LLOYD
	" E. COULSON	37564	"	T. PAINE
	" CARTER	457330	"	N.E. WYATT
30851	" H.A. CRISFORD		"	WILLIS
	" COOK		"	E. WEST
75621	" COLLINS. W. M.M.			
34750	" J. DELANEY			
31103	" H.H. DODKIN			
43374	" J. DIGGLE			
	" DOBEY			
	" J. ELLIOTT			
	" EDMUNDS			
	" J. EMBERTON			
69216	" N. FOX			
30209	" J. FORREST			
	" FISH			
	" GRIFFIN			

A.S.C. (M/T) Wounded.

No M2/105171	PTE. J.W. HOPKINS	
105175	" A HOPKINS	
106224	" H FOSTER	
034450	" F. TREMLOW.	

A.S.C. (H/T) Wounded.

T2/016207	Dr. F.W. SHAW

Prisoners of War.

	CPL. TALBOT. W.R.	No 78448	PTE. J.P. JONES
	PTE. ATKINSON A.	88950	- O. MERRELLS
32804	" G. BRIDGMAN. M.M.	79172	- W. McCORD
	" W. BRIGHT.		- A. NEEDHAM
40492	" W.G. CLARKE.		- I. NEWMAN
30840	" G.A. GREEN	88960	- W.J.M. SMITH
	" F. HARBRIDGE		- SLEAP
	" HIORNS	34400	- H.G. WILKS.
	" HUTCHINSON		
5116	" J. HENDERSON		

Casualties Co. "H."

D/
7595

20th Division

66th F. Amb.
Part of vol I
July 15

July 1915

Army Form C. 2118

WAR DIARY
or
INTELLIGENCE SUMMARY
(Erase heading not required.)

WAR DIARY

60ᵗʰ FIELD AMBULANCE

23ʳᵈ July 1915 to 31ˢᵗ July 1915

Major F. P. Sanders R.A.M.C.

WAR DIARY or INTELLIGENCE SUMMARY

Army Form C. 2118

Place	Date	Hour	Summary of Events and Information	Remarks and references to Appendices
CORMETTE	23/7/15	4.30	Unit entrained at LOMBRES at 12.30 and marched to BULLS at CORMETTE - arrived here 4pm. A vacant building near Church selected for collection of sick of BRIGADE. On our first arrival was by R.R.S Unit for Signal Coy. Refilling point PETCQUES.	
"	24/7/15		Attend Routine & freed - ordered into - of to Lieutenant - attend on totally sick scale	
"	25/7/15		Sent 2 A. Wagons to collect sick to BRIGADE Hqrs — ?	
"	26/7/15		Sent in weekly return of sick & return of strength. Attend ordinary surgical. There to be sent to Refilling Point - no cases M.F.D. (delivered shortly). Battalion evacuated today (G.P.M.S. Shaw A.K.K.R.)	
"	27/7/15		Left CORMETTE at 10 a.m. & were in billets by 6 pm - Camping - WARDRECQUES at 11pm. Intakes in Barn report fair - officers in CHATEAU 4 cases fr. Empty use of J.Amb. Sent by D.A.D.M.S. - Lt Enden A.S.C. reverted to Infantry.	
CAMPAGNE WARDRECQ VES	28/7/15		Left C.W. at 6.30 a.m. half trying march down road - arrived BORRE at 3.30. 9 Sick Motor sent to pick up foot sore cases + stragglers. Attend 130 cases face not to duty. 5 cases admitted to J.Amb. 2 Canadians to 10, 2 to & 20 St Omer - 16 duty.	
"	"		Capt BARRE at farm - Capt Billet Orte on M.Y.O.R - marched to OUTERSTEENE arriving	
BORRE	29/7/15		There 11 a.m. - & at Battalion Recv by "C" Section. Billets insufficient — 1 section bivouacked.	

WAR DIARY or INTELLIGENCE SUMMARY

Army Form C. 2118

Place	Date	Hour	Summary of Events and Information	Remarks and references to Appendices
CORNETTE	27/7/15		Left CORNETTE at 10.a.m. and marched billeting from to 6th Echelon ZUDAUSQUES en route. Arrived CHAMAGNES-WADRECQUES at 4 p.m. and were billetted in a Barn & officers field Officers in a Château. D.A.D.V.S. sent 4 cars for Exped. over 9 BOJ Nnds. One Sick NCO & 2 O.R. (24 Section) left at Station. Officers for S. Pharagus. 5 Others.	
WADRECQUES	28th/7		Left C.W. at 8.30 a.d. After trying march had to do arrived at BORRE at 2.30. 9 Sick Nobrs. Ambulances was to pick up first-line cases. About 15 cases fell out. Little trouble with Transport. 5 cases were admitted to Hopper 2 to per 10 & 2 to 1125 M Others. 0 1 to duty.	
BORRE	29/7		Left BORRE after shorty Royal Hy at 8 am. Marched to OUTERSTEENE arriving about Noon. Established a Receiving Station by E. Schm. Billets inconvenient - Section bivouacking	
BOARE	30/7			
OUTER STEENE	31/7		Reporting Lagroid - HQM's inspection horses. 2 Ambulanshes. No true fevers	

Signed

WAR DIARY
or
INTELLIGENCE SUMMARY

Army Form C. 2118

Place	Date	Hour	Summary of Events and Information	Remarks and references to Appendices
Aug. 1915			WAR DIARY Vol I 60th FIELD AMBULANCE — 1915 — 1st to 27th August — Major F. P. Sanden 27th to 31st August — Major A. C. Osburn A. C. Osburn Major R.A.M.C. COMMANDING 60th Field Ambulance	

WAR DIARY
or
INTELLIGENCE SUMMARY

(Erase heading not required.)

Army Form C. 2118

Place	Date	Hour	Summary of Events and Information	Remarks and references to Appendices
OUTERST EENE	31/7/15		A.D.M.S. inspected horses — Horses put under protective mange —	
"	1/8/15		Examined M.O. of Service with Sani Officer (Lt Col Dew) — Have a Sanitary Conference with M.O.s of units to arrange sanitation in camping lines in this area — Sergts McPherson & Gnr Poulting inspection unit. 1 Officer admitted for Syphilis. Transferred to No 7 C.C.S. thro MERVILLE	
"	2/8/15		Sanitary Section joined unit today — 1 Sergt & 4 men. Interviewed C.O.s of D.C.O. thro MERVILLE — Inspection w Supplies with D.D. General L.Mgt of Artillery	
"	4/8/15		Arranged with local farmers to remove J. Manure from lines here	
"	6/8/15		B.M. Gnd Inspection Hospital & other about arrangements for latrines etc for a permanent camps here Suggested deep pits or trench system. Col Sherran visited I hid site at Pratt.	
"	9/6/15		Recd orders to attach 'B' Sect. to 259.Amd near Sailly 1,644 & 'A' Section to 267.Amd near Bac St Maur thru BRIDGE — for Instructional purposes. 'C' Section left to Hospitoe Lynz.	
"	10/8/15		AMB Sect marched via SAILLY leaving 'B' Sect with 259.Amd & H. Sect proceeded to 267.Amd —	
BAC ST MAUR	11/8/15		Lt Bennett went to 8 E Div Baths for instruction for 3 days — J. Mule-Surgeon in hump shelter & at front Aid Posts	

WAR DIARY
or
INTELLIGENCE SUMMARY
(Erase heading not required.)

Army Form C. 2118

Instructions regarding War Diaries and Intelligence Summaries are contained in F. S. Regs., Part II. and the Staff Manual respectively. Title Pages will be prepared in manuscript.

Place	Date	Hour	Summary of Events and Information	Remarks and references to Appendices
BAC ST MAUR	15/8/15		"C" Section moved Hospital for Girls School to a place near farm of Mon La Fosse. Men & Officers billeted in farm.	
"	16/8/15		Pte Argyll Plum & Pvt H "a" Section Fires & Sentries duties to Chief & Room. Sent to Portable X Ray Supp. Pr 22q RE jn diagram I cwn.	
WATERSIDE NE	17/8/15		Sept 26 I. Pet at Spa. returned to Outstation 6:20 & trenches nr McLelin	
"	18/8/15		1 car 2 st. heads downward to wards to any for 6:15 pm at Pontbelle.	
"	21/8/15		E'fect. Others A.T.s at PARADE G 45 CHATEAU U - B' Section Fk and T Staysighton & Bennett Bde unit to join an amo. to Mr R. Bde ordered & ordered to J.C. Stayyight P. & Pheccile " " " " T Twomoto	
"	22/8/15		2 cars J. Huster for PRADELLE - visited DADZ5 and down for Trouble.	
	22/15 8		Pte care P.G.S. Wood leave - leg infection	
	23/8 8		Capt Carlie joined unit triplace Lt Bennett - Pecor	
	24/8		Recd instr re charge of units staying on to bring others on his arrival	

WAR DIARY or INTELLIGENCE SUMMARY

Army Form C. 2118

Place	Date	Hour	Summary of Events and Information	Remarks and references to Appendices
OUTER STEENE	25/8		Visited PRADELLES D.B.S. & Fied Sergt Cuthbertson in charge of about afr. Tato - brief	
do	26/8		He was severely reprimanded. Visited ESTAIRES & inspected billets & attempt to hire the College which I think is going to take over for J.A. Hub No 128. Col Sherman inspects I think & suggests [1] Been held for particulars (2) Motor Lorry - for transport of College Ho C.C.Ste	
do	27/8		Visited ESTAIRES & Selected billets for J.Amb. Officers, refer other arrange. I day to take over J. Amb.	
OUTER STEENE	28/8		Took over charge of Patients - and Command of No 60 Field Ambulance from Major J.P. LAUDER. R.A.M.C. A.C. Osborn Major R.M.C	

Visited ESTAIRES. and arranges to take over Agricultural College buildings in of from No 128 Indian Field Ambulance allotted rooms for Residential Patients - and saw College authorities above conditions of our occupation. Gas & water supply &c.

WAR DIARY
or
INTELLIGENCE SUMMARY
(Erase heading not required.)

Army Form C. 2118

Place	Date	Hour	Summary of Events and Information	Remarks and references to Appendices
OUTER-STEENE	28/8/15		Visited Div. Rest. Station PRADELLES - Saw Colonel Skinner D.D.M.S. III Corps Reported personally to A.D.M.S. XX Division. Sent all Patients to ESTAIRES	
ESTAIRES	29/8/15	7.45 AM	Left billets and marched to ESTAIRES - arriving 9.45 P.M. - Transport horses and Tents pitched. Sgt Hillet and Corps visited Ambulances - Cook house - Latrines - etc. D.D.M.S. III Corps visited Ambulances - Cook-house - Latrines etc. Indents for extra Blankets and general cleaning up Bolègue - and general cleaning up Cleaning and disinfecting D.A.D.M.S. Re Sgt Hughes A.S.C. Conway and event the matter. Saw Details of College - and event for 83rd Light Infantry and French Interpreter - Remove for Officers duplicating - dermuduring urgent call for College continued stationary and M.F.O re Cleanliness and Sanitation	
		2 P.M.	Cleaning to of College continued. Visited the Men of A.B. Sections Left brushes, cans of their clothing and Baths, was of Economy - Equipment to. unpaid Promoted to Acting Lance Sergeant James Corporal " " Corporal Pte Conroy (Mahon) " " " Pte Sloss (?) The following promotions were made	
" "	31/8/15		Further cleaning to of College - note made of dilapidation in buildings re 16lb pounds of glass broken - generally in very bad repair - Report A. C. Osburn Major RAMC	

Army Form C. 2118

WAR DIARY or **INTELLIGENCE SUMMARY**
(Erase heading not required.)

War Diary
60th Field Ambulance

Vol III

1st Oct 1915 to 31st Oct 1915

Major A. C. Osburn
R.A.M.C.

Oct. 1915

WAR DIARY
or
INTELLIGENCE SUMMARY

(Erase heading not required.)

Army Form C. 2118

Place	Date	Hour	Summary of Events and Information	Remarks and references to Appendices
ESTAIRES	1/10		Visited new line of Aid Posts in trenches – and front line trenches as far as "BACQUEROT STREET" - Communication trenches waterlogged. Inspected Ad. Dressing Station. He & given 9 "C" Section sent in to A.D.S (from trenches). Saw R.S. in charge of Brandy & Champagne. spare supply returned to B Coy. Brandy & Champagne took to No. 7 C.C. Station. 35 sundry detail and D.R.S. reports.	
"	2/10		D.D.M.S + A.D.M.S. inspected ambulance. Having left his detachment (5 men) for duty at MERVILLE (No. 2 C.C.S.) Lt TAYLOR returns here duly. 110 Jcs (or during?) Gendarmerie claim to be relieving ? broke ourselves — we let 9 by our carrying at the R.E. to fail to keep 20/? truck labels etc — sent to S.A.O.S Q.M. to take then 3 Oxygen cylinders of funnel to 59th Brigade. Lt TAYLOR returns to MERVILLE by direction of A.D.M.S.	

WAR DIARY or INTELLIGENCE SUMMARY

Army Form C. 2118

Place	Date	Hour	Summary of Events and Information	Remarks and references to Appendices
ESTAIRE	3.10/15		Inspected trenches in front line - as regards removal of wounded from trenches under Propst - from line trench water topped - but wide enough - between Pakeman and Bedford Road, problem is fairly free; WANGERIE front trench is peri of MASSELOT fully water - quite impassable at present	
—	4/10/15		Between O.C. F.A.W. lines re billing on vehicles - repair & damage motor cycle & return of 3 men of M.T. laden - application to A.Q.M.G. Saw A.D.M.S. - re Bugler & A.P.M. re Officer's servant - infantry they will accompany their quartermasters. Then account settled, question re P.E. Brooklyn mending run — Gun account settled. Barker killed. Transport moves into new post - also lack of personnel - 2 Tents damaged to be sent back to Ordnance - number are 26 now used as Mortuary. 1 small tent used as Mortuary. Arrange for stabling for Transport in new pens A.D.M.S unable about Baths working of Patient cloths to arrived from D.R.S and to 6 Divisional Baths	N.Y.D. A.D.T Book (a) & A.D.M.G
—	5/10/15		Patient from D.R.S aretup to 6 Divisional Baths the day before then Surgleft	

WAR DIARY or INTELLIGENCE SUMMARY

Army Form C. 2118

Place	Date	Hour	Summary of Events and Information	Remarks and references to Appendices
FITANÉ	5/10		Visited A.D.S. "A" pst - issued our 2 tube cylinder & 2 funnels - for oxygen	
		6pm	Inspected night duty party, 2 experts 1 corporal and 16 men - Sgt Major not a single N.C.O. or man including Sgt Major noted this – Knew the fire alarm through the Keyhole – the Fire I had constantly been read out in parade. The Sgt Major in consultation with the Sgt Major (who never does so) ordered these 10 men? the men stated they knew nothing of 3 weeks ago - and ? the men stated they knew nothing of it, many said that they had been told it on a bugle. Saw read about a pulley to lift a stretcher & P.Lt.R. nots to. arranged with Kitu re– bolts, waits &	
			D.D.M.S visited A.D.S. Officer Brigade major to evacuation. Jud orders visited A.D.S. - also Brigade Major again now intro [front trenches] Brigade runs out still indefinite - Brigade may again move into (front trenches) Brigade plan now to cylinders - Brigade gets 3 cylinders he has now 4 cylinders 8 advanced post A/post 3 at MDS (6 at A/DS and 1 at A/Catro 3 at A/DS 3 at MDS) + funnel will keep M.O.s on arrival whether he will keep M.O.s on arrival also the correspondence with O.	
	6/10		2 men whole R. Lt Togo truly also he correspondence with O. Saw R.O. ref R. Lt Togo truly also he correspondence with O. also to buoke Sgt Major about yesterday occurrences - he admits that he has not 2 weeks ago 2 weeks to give all ranks information on to give all ranks a disgraceful performance on Sunday Slave done it as above he admits it was a disgraceful performance if all concerned	

Army Form C. 21

WAR DIARY
or
INTELLIGENCE SUMMARY
(Erase heading not required.)

Place	Date	Hour	Summary of Events and Information	Remarks and references to Appendices
ESTAIRES	7/10		Went to A.D.M.S. about Laundry Equipment & other [illegible] Case — and D.R.S. Anchors & other Division Life sent to A.P.M. on R.T.O. Expects R.T.C. men late to [illegible] — employ own — expect duty in regard to operations 24/26 Bat. Sent in report on position of Payments Regarding trip &c. A.D.M.S. visits D.R.S. — one [illegible] of allowance will be visits A.D.S. Report sent in on Pumps. Perrines Duo Tobacco 575 S.R.S. 50. total 385.	
ESTAIRES	8/10		Sent in Report on fat Caps. Saw Liaison Officer A.D.M.S. — reference allotments & occupation & otherwise shown her III visitors & Arrange to claim cups from Front of NIEPPE — & trucks from LAVENTIE. Sent instructions re disposition not carried out — to L A.D.S.M.S. no officer apparent available — [illegible] — also men assisted by Sgt Moran about — See Instructions drew up new O re Pumps Facing to our Rght. visits A.D.S. Rept. — Heavy Firing to our Rght. A.D.M.S. visits D.R.S. — a C.F. (Captain) upon unknown informs me they he has order to change the Chaplain attached here — also sees grains and Principal College note sent to A.D.M.S. re officer do [illegible] so kerosene [illegible] change. Further Scout instructions 2 [illegible], 12 men detailed for R.T.O. to Admiral book to reach here by 9 p.m. taking [illegible] shelter Re, & oxygen cylinder to	

Place	Date	Hour	Summary of Events and Information	Remarks and references to Appendices
ESTAIRES	9/10		Make A.D.S. in parts at Advanced Post.	
			Visited advanced post and communication trenches — busy bus carrying Lieut Townsend. Set numerous enquiries underfoot for the wounded continuing. Surprising number of german bullets flying about & of the lie wounded about 4 wipes been seen during visit by the last look — the most striking feature in a bad one, but simply better teamed available. It townsends fondour in a bad one, but simply better teamed available — ordens are now stopped — A.D.M.S. came into send enquiries later. Not wounded officer each to receive	
	10/10		Recalls 20 men r/Sgt Murridge from A.M.S. — on their way back Wty Camsu a disturbance in the road outside Lt A.D.M.S office — He was reported to me — by Captain Coates — about 12 noon — at 3 am Set enough men on examining — anything known nothing? He commences — Set enough men in situ under to otto evaluation. Note that is has summary and been formed 12 aniving columns returns from A.M.S. about 12. by O.C. 2 Both Chaplains changed. Rev C.E JAMES & Rev H.A.TURNER reports their arrival. The end and Rev P. STEWART + R.W COATES their duration to No 6ct F.A. Provisional	
	11/10		3 men from 14 days CB disturbances rules when having dressed Head quarters — A.D.M.S. mentioned their Good moral discipline &c 1 Official accidents "wounds" only inflicted — ruces sent to 62nd Field 2 core accidents B.R.Q. notified Ambulance on future. 6 624 mobile trigale All sick care in future	

WAR DIARY or INTELLIGENCE SUMMARY

Army Form C. 2118

Place	Date	Hour	Summary of Events and Information	Remarks and references to Appendices
ETAPLES	12/10		Orders for re-occupying park. 24 beds at 24, 6 A+C park – Lt Kinton in charge with one cyclist – property of Lieut Duncan Halliwill, Cruden, par cotton whiteholder – to act as storekeeper. 1 Motor Cyclist to ADS – Capt Cantlie in charge ADS. 8 bearers & B teleph to ADS for full duty. 1 Cyclist to D.H.Q. (59th). 4 Cars and 3 Horse ambulances to ADS. Reported Sick for day. Arrangement made for bearing men – Cars on continue per Squire – L Kinton gave up divisions in Lozingham. 1 Coy ever temporarily on bandary of Lozingham & theatre & motor removed. Change arose 5 Room, 3 Rooms & station – walls "A" fort – 1 Store ambulances all open but three. Very heavy firing started about 11.30 am to open – Sgt Auster is in charge D.C. fort. Division Red Station change L Auster many slated building near dug out – trouble many slated building near dug out Sgt men - wounding - & nightly duty Room also changed.	
—	13/10		8 Hamels about returning men to duty – 9 Other Corps & Foreigner R.A.M.C.s beyond status they are on spared on our – 9 & reporting room Stray units. They anyhow well to R.T.O. Bealls all extra personnel at 7.30 am except Capt Cantlie & to leave to medical; Dentist & sopathis accommodate on Truck	

Army Form C. 2118

WAR DIARY
or
INTELLIGENCE SUMMARY
(Erase heading not required.)

Instructions regarding War Diaries and Intelligence Summaries are contained in F. S. Regs., Part II. and the Staff Manual respectively. Title Pages will be prepared in manuscript.

Place	Date	Hour	Summary of Events and Information	Remarks and references to Appendices
ESTAIRES	14/10		A.D.M.S. visited M.D.S. D.D.M.S. —.— M.D.S. Suggests new equipment for D.R.S. Capt Coulter returned from A.D.S. also 12 men recylist 3 deaths - two wounds - many guns - faulty equipt by D+O Gibbs. — To be withdrawn Don Ration Inspection. Tube Helmet instruction. — DDMS also suggests new table for D R S 8/. Check otk on the pck kit. — also 96 C.R.2 — also	was as equip
	15/10		visited A.D.S. — Obtained word from O.C. 96th C.R.2. — also Cmdt at Brick from LAVENTIE — Polu from La VIEPPS ward Sais LAVENTIE is inundating at his own	Amitilln
	16/10		V/ Crothers Transport for duty at A.R.S. — as a charge — at his own regiment — he has been on look list to 5 days.	
	17/10		Took over two men been for D.R.S. — number between 70 & 80 men two men misaplying boar 9 knew trenches other defences DAJMS marks ambulance —	
	18/10		New ADMS who turned to me 2 Officers in rely — also decused service - to Dentist - DDMS agrees that under present circumstances Lucky mobile Lt WALL orders L relieve Lt ANDERSEN — in charge 10th K.R.R vehicles trucks detachment at La Pugnoy — Major RYAN 10.C.C Crichton's at A.D.S. 200 done Lt KIRTON inoculating	

WAR DIARY or INTELLIGENCE SUMMARY

Army Form C. 2118

Place	Date	Hour	Summary of Events and Information	Remarks and references to Appendices
ETAIRE	19/10		Lt LAWSON - left at 1 pm on 7 days leave - have to report on meeting 26.8.02 to relieve Lt LAWSON & Lt WALL. Lt ROBERTS arrived at 6.30pm saw O.C. of 10th K.R.R. who asks if Lt McINTYRE might be kept on D.R.S. on account of urgent need of Coy officer. Pitched tent in yard for night duty party - arranged Quarters for 60 men in billets - saw Leave Officers - also DDMS 11th Corps Saw MO 10 KRB at white house - some firing of machine guns about M 12 c 17.18	
	20/10		Visited Dr Balls with DADMS & O.C. 6 c 29 Always driving Regmt (Major Scott) for D.Rs. Lt McIntyre still less DC 96 7Co called; he to keep his 18mm down - asks him to leave his M.O. here for consultation	
	21/10		Case of D.T. soldiers - letter to dentist re crocodiles Saw Leave Officer about Cas - & arrangement for payment. Sgt Knopp to Tpers for Rgts - to those time for those been continued Rowing 3 all schools begun - Tommy's have been continued	

Army Form C. 2118

WAR DIARY
or
INTELLIGENCE SUMMARY
(Erase heading not required.)

Place	Date	Hour	Summary of Events and Information	Remarks and references to Appendices
LITTAIRE	22/10	11 AM	D.D.M.S. Lt SKINNER Unattached M.D. Station. (DADMS called about 10.a.m) DDMS criticised Lt DAVIDSON's Treatment & expense, — he inquired why O.C. did not visit 7 Ambulance in other divisions. — My good Shortage of Officers was pointed out to him 3 have been away for a month in detachment — 2 are relieving Reg M.O.'s Is leaving only 2, 1 D.C. & 9 Medl as Field at LAVENTIE — Trickey & Bullen Severe respect Ambulances; Transport lines — officer Supervision — have but Red Station all regime Supervision — office work also	
	23/10		loads kept on Officer going — DADMS. — he agrees as to Discussed points raised yesterday with DADMS. — Shortage of Officers — Fresh Difficulties arose (or all DADMS. holds Others re Dugouts &c — always	(2 Evacuees)
	24/10		Pending 7 Horse & Motor Transport delayed, no trains (Service column) arrived yet.	Ambulance Boy

WAR DIARY or INTELLIGENCE SUMMARY

Army Form C.2118

Place	Date	Hour	Summary of Events and Information	Remarks and references to Appendices
ESTAIRS	25/10		WATER TESTING apparatus tried — returned Tech. 3 Officers instructed. Supreme Smoke Goods for use in W. Cans. Loan arrangement allows to send A.D.M.S.	
—	26/10		FRONT LINE trenches — Lt KIRTON & Lt WALL — arrangement for 10th K.R.R. mess — and for Emergency arrangement for coroners if 10th K.R.R. made an attack on the "Ducks Bill" German if 10th K.R.R. (a bell communicates and news-instrument)	
—	27/10		A.D.M.S. visited Ambulance — complaints about Water Cart — investigated — Missing box of Lemons, Q.M. agrees at fault — re Collite & debility. C.O.J. 10th K.R.R. advised not Colibri & debility. Colonel Douglas Pennant. Lt. TOZER Lt. KENNEDY & 18 N.C.Os. men returns from 24/10ct Lt. TOZER gazetted CAPTAIN from 24/Oct — to Bsc or Maur. La Pugnoy.	
—	28/10		Forms fielden re Abdominal & chest wounds Lt LAWSON returns from Eau Lt. ROBERTS sent to No 62. Lt WALL Lt ANDERSON return to the 10th K.R.R.s Regt. from Eau	

1875 Wt. W593/826 1,000,000 4/15 J.B.C. & A. A.D.S.S./Forms/C.2118.

Army Form C. 2118

WAR DIARY
or
INTELLIGENCE SUMMARY
(Erase heading not required.)

Instructions regarding War Diaries and Intelligence Summaries are contained in F. S. Regs., Part II. and the Staff Manual respectively. Title Pages will be prepared in manuscript.

Place	Date	Hour	Summary of Events and Information	Remarks and references to Appendices
ESTAIRE	29/10		Capt DAVIDSON on leave — until 5th Nov. Lt KENNEDY to 11th R.B. to relieve Lt STEPHENSON. Colonel Inspects Present Occupants. G.O.C. 20th Brigade & A.D.M.S. visits Ambulances & G.O.C. 59th Brigade. 59th Brigade G.O.C. inspection during the morning.	
—	30/10		A.D.M.S. visits Ambulance & Dr. Post Station. D.D.M.S. — Ambulance now uses own Gas, stoves, fuel &c. announced now own Gas, bought at present, in Laundry arranged Cupboards also stoves used. — Stoves cannot be bought at present, in Gas taken into use. Manufacture & to operate the town. Major Scott specialed. — to Verma	
—	31/10			

A. C. Osburn
31/10/15.

Major R. A. M. C.
COMMANDING
60th Field Ambulance

66 K. Ja.
tds 4

121/7678

Amd

20th November

Nov 15.

Nov 1915.

WAR DIARY
or
INTELLIGENCE SUMMARY

Army Form C. 2118

War Diary
of
60th Field Ambulance
for
November — 1915

Major. A.C. Osburn. R.A.M.C.
Commanding.

WAR DIARY
INTELLIGENCE SUMMARY

Army Form C. 2118

Place	Date	Hour	Summary of Events and Information	Remarks and references to Appendices
ESTAIRES	1 Nov		Units position on Map Sheet 36a 1/40000 Main Dressing Station + D.R.S. Advd. Dressing station (Sheet 36) Ref. Doncy from Duckmann Farm. A.D.M.S. visited ambulance. QMarks and all to send for Coke - opened from Duckmann-Boyd. Bucking & lines been nearly completed - roofing begun. Weather very favorable for building & laying roads - very heavy rain — mud up to axles of wagons.	L 29. 6. 5.5 G 34. C 8. 2
-.-	2 Nov		Saw A.D.M.S. re Dental Corps - also about leave k. Saw O.gC. Divisional Rolls re change in laundry arrangements	
-.-	3 Nov		5 Stores purchased at MERVILLE. weather very cold wet. Continues making dining room for Personnel - Both lorries and polls - 3 cases ? trench foot	
-.-	4 Nov		Newletter waistcoats issued to personnel. 1 case ? lumphago	
-.-	5 Nov		Billeting Outposts completed sent in	
-.-	6 Nov		Stead of return obtained —	

Army Form C. 2118

WAR DIARY
or
INTELLIGENCE SUMMARY
(Erase heading not required.)

Instructions regarding War Diaries and Intelligence Summaries are contained in F. S. Regs., Part II. and the Staff Manual respectively. Title Pages will be prepared in manuscript.

Place	Date	Hour	Summary of Events and Information	Remarks and references to Appendices
FS THRE	7/11/5		Lt Wall to A.D.S in charge. Lt TAYLOR to 11th KRR for temporary charge.	
-	8/11		Claris Officers seen re patients and Revt also claims it & Revt	
-	9/11		Sgt Major Spence to leave 63 days	
-	13/11		Cases of Revd kept beginning to assist — all patients or doubtful wounded. Kerax or Afternoon on now to be sent to Bac St Maur. Capt DAVIDSON to 10th R.B. in medical charge. 26th Field Ambulance. Corporal PIBLE to Capt TOTER - Sgt. Complaints by the Convoy our Ambulance of Officers obvious to prevent them being lost or misplaced in evacuation of casualties 4 months.	
-	15/11		Even Ambulance of wild Cabs now charge of A.D.S from Lt Wall. Lt. KENNE by will Cabs now charge of 11th S.F.O.	
-	17/11		Lt. Veall to Nues charge of 11th S.F.O.	
-	18/11		O.T. on leave for 7 days.	

WAR DIARY or INTELLIGENCE SUMMARY

Army Form C. 2118

Place	Date	Hour	Summary of Events and Information	Remarks and references to Appendices
ESTAIRES	18/11/15		A.D.M.S. visited Ambulance & visited proposed new A.D.S. at SAILLY. O.M. to inspect proposed new A.D.S. at SAILLY. Billets & horse lines below inspected.	
	19/11		Continued work in Horse lines, making roads to D.R.S. A.D.M.S. paid us visit. O.O. 70-16 recd. new kit for A.D.M.S. O.O. 10-16 Recd. instructions received of A.D.M.S. Lt. Keiton & Sgt. Armitage (with all equipment as before) 18 men / 1 NCO to A- post 18 " / 1 NCO to C- post Lt. TAYLOR to visit Lt. Kennedy at A.D.S. & bearer subsection NCOs at A.D.S. movements completed & reports to G.O.C. 59th Bde & 8th 1 motor car Travel post — A.D.S. sing bearer ambulance Closing up — Horse lines — this morning except 10"R.B. & Tetels call all Guides.	
	20/11		[sketch]	
	2/12		Visited Advanced Posts "A" & "C" — nothing doing Détachement withdrawn.	

WAR DIARY
or
INTELLIGENCE SUMMARY

Army Form C. 2118

Place	Date	Hour	Summary of Events and Information	Remarks and references to Appendices
ESTAIRES	22/11 Nov.		O.O. No 15 rec'd. Visited SAILLY + LAVENTIE. Cooking ranges at home have been completed.	
—	23/11		Lt TAYLOR & 6 Beavers to SAILLY QM accompanied them. Found report on condition of building. Drew P.O.S. at LAVENTIE with Sgt Major. Lt WAIL transferred to D.A.C. Lt 76 hunter transferred to 6th F.A. O.O. No 15 continues no. 2	
—	24th		Round visits Ambulance — & Colonel Skinner at 11 am — and Q Marti Round visits A.D.S. LAVENTIE at 11 am. Lt KENNEDY procured A.S.C. Guards Division transport. SAILLY being cleaned up.	
—	29th		Capt E. TOZER. to medical charge of 10th R.B. Lt KENNEDY Transport officer — Unit is unchanged — at present portion of Brown Survey School at Brun Culver.	Sheet 36 1/40000 L. 29. B. 5. 5. L. 34. c. 8. 2 G.22 b/s u Sheet 36 [?]

WAR DIARY
or
INTELLIGENCE SUMMARY
(Erase heading not required.)

Army Form C. 2118

Place	Date	Hour	Summary of Events and Information	Remarks and references to Appendices
ESTAIRES	30/11/15		Completed organisating 9 Horse Lines, roadway Round, sheet 36 town bury cleared. New A.D.S. at SAILLY G.22.6.5.4 also new walks & filled up with rubble – stores main evacy station Paths & roadways completed at main evacy station (D.R.S. & Ambulance) Total sick & wounded in hospital – 86 Osburn Major RAMC Officers 5 Commanding 60th Field Ambulance Other Ranks 81	

60 te Fa.
Vol: 5

2en D[?]

Flibo 11

Dec 1915

War Diary
60 Field Ambulance
1st December to 31st December 1915

A.C. Osburn

Major R.A.M.C.
COMMANDING
60th Field Ambulance

WAR DIARY or INTELLIGENCE SUMMARY

Army Form C. 2118

Place	Date	Hour	Summary of Events and Information	Remarks and references to Appendices
ESTAIRE	Dec 1. 1915		Positioning unit Main Dressing Station Adv² — "— 1/40000 map sheet 36ᵃ " " 36	L 29. B. 4.4. G 22. 8. S.S.
	1.12.15		Board of 5 med Officers held on 61 cases Scabies (?) sent in by febrile 10ᵗʰ R.B. (Capt Tozer). all found free of scabies	
	2.12.15.		1 case of Mange discovered amongst Horses — Isolation of all and the canteen taken of Sgt & Cable. Meatrical disinfected — waggon pole flames of Horse wagon pole & A.D.S. ad (Forms) New aid post & accommodation visited, Area to be occupied very exposed to shell fire, civilian occupants H25.d.77 sheet 36 40000 snow of two places, and country poor — all very insanitary Trivial infections + antigen: cases of new A.D.M.S works all Boils, Calcul — Cases sent to large Barn afresh Impetigo & scabies. Sgt Hanley & 6 men sent on to re-inforce P.S. A.D.S.	62ⁿᵈ B.Fld.
	3.12.15.		preparing to	

WAR DIARY or INTELLIGENCE SUMMARY

Army Form C. 2118

Place	Date	Hour	Summary of Events and Information	Remarks and references to Appendices
ESTAIRES	4/12/15		A.D.S. at SAILLY G.22.b.5.5. handed over to 62nd F. Amb. and new A.D.S. taken over from 62nd at H.25.d.7.7. paid a visit to trenches with Capt Buchanan – Trench is in a bad condition about 18 inches of water – Sand bags rotting, dug outs caved in, communication trench unusable (wounded) except V.C. avenue & Cordonnerie Trench. Transport now parked in Gendarmerie Horse lines unknown by further draining it. "Scabies" treatment begun at A.D.S. 7 cases – our working into putting both parries in order/ carting dung, digging drains, making paths, re Shortage of Blankets. Q Merlin investigating – about 10-11.45 am visited Advanced A.D.S. & F.A. post with D.D.M.S. III Corps near H.33.6.7.7. on & over H.33.a.c.d. Col Skinner. Heavy shelling all over – splendid going all over on alt rides Guns hit – no batteries within 500 yards or so A.D.M.S. called in afternoon.	
	5/12			
	6/12			

WAR DIARY or INTELLIGENCE SUMMARY

Army Form C. 2118

Place	Date	Hour	Summary of Events and Information	Remarks and references to Appendices
ESTAIRES	7/12		Moved my A.D.S. between 3.30 & 5.30 p.m. will Capt Davidson and Lt Gowan - again very heavy shelling 180 shells falling within 150 yards. CROIX-LE-CORNET - torn on road - about 15 men near hit. Splinters making it impossible for my ambulance Wolfram to P.U. pass this Crossroads - the road is about 400 yds off A.D.S.	
	8/12		Capt Lauthe & 4 men left for England. 7 days leave. Lt Kieran relieves Lt Wall (on leave) in medical charge of D.D. Column. Splinter proof shelter begun at A.D.S.	
	9/12		Area around A.D.S. continues to be shelled daily: 11 cases up to to-day re air raid. 3,000 sandbags & Timber to A.D.S.	
	12/12		received from C.R.E. - 90 yards double with canvas brought obtained from C.R.E. - 90 yards double with canvas brought up. Works continued at A.D.S. filling sandbags &c.	
	15/12		Again very heavy shelling. Lt Johnson & Lt Lawson & myself nearly hit by H.E. shell. Passed all round EATON HALL. Visited trenches will Ambulance taken in day	
	16/12		Capt. Tozer + 4 men to England on leave	

WAR DIARY
or
INTELLIGENCE SUMMARY
(Erase heading not required.)

Army Form C. 2118

Place	Date	Hour	Summary of Events and Information	Remarks and references to Appendices
	17/12/15		Visited Trench with Capt Morrison & Capt Anderson - some improvement in general condition of trench - much sniping going on especially near Celler Farm. 22 cases of contagious drained at A.D.S. Capt Curtis return from leave. Condition of road is seriously affecting use of Motor cycles & cycles. Courland repair needed to Cycles. About 6 men daily anxious from wound - many Bombs & Bayt today. R.M. TURNER 10 R.B.	
ESTAIRES	20/12/15			
ESTAIRES	22/12/15		Very large requisition for Anti-fire solution rec'd from Reg'ts & at 10.30pm. All our stock exhausted. Urgent indents at the Status Form. 24 cases now under treatment. Heavy shelling continues - a few wounds during in 5 pounds Personnel Transferred to Guard berrain. Reserve of 900 lbs of Sulphate ordered to be kept.	

WAR DIARY or INTELLIGENCE SUMMARY

Army Form C. 2118

Place	Date	Hour	Summary of Events and Information	Remarks and references to Appendices
ESTAIRES	Dec 23		A.D.M.S. visited Ambulance. 2 Officers admitted with Rheumatism. Sent Orders from 5th Brigade No 21 re: of inquiry 22/23. Continued memorandum about Officers sick on Division.	
—	24		Sgt Hanley & 1 Armitage 748 were relieved from A.D.S. Coy. Stretcher Jas Attack postponed. A.D.S. at Sailly G 22 B.S.S. & houses over A.D.S. H 23 d 77. Took over A.D.S. at Sailly G 22 B.S.S. & houses over to R.A.P.8	
—	25.12.15		A.D.M.S. visited Ambulance. 181 Coy R.E. brought in dead to R.A.P.8. P'te GROVES 1st Lemm. R'gt attached (Stomach to No 5 Laboratory) No cause ? Enemies to Patients 5.30 - 8.30 pm	
—	26.12.15		P. Mortem on P'te GROVES held. (Stomach & No 5 Laboratory) 9 acute alcoholism. death found.	
—	27.12		Lt. Johnson took over medical charge of 90 Brigade. Relieving Lt Grant who has Tonsillitis.	

1875 Wt. W593/826 1,000,000 4/15 J.B.C.&A. A.D.S.S./Forms/C. 2118.

WAR DIARY or INTELLIGENCE SUMMARY

Army Form C. 2118

(Erase heading not required.)

Place	Date	Hour	Summary of Events and Information	Remarks and references to Appendices
ESTAIRES	29/7		Lt Grant returns to 90 Bgde R.F.A., & Lt JOHNSON returns here for duty.	
	30/7		Capt Tozer reported his arrival off leave, and took over charge of A.D.S. Lt Taylor brought in from A.D.S. at LE TROU from his been sleeping. Near our proposed post. Have been shelled by shell fire since yesterday. A.D.M.S. visited Ambulance. 5 Officers & 112 Other Ranks in D.R.S. and Field Ambulance.	
ESTAIRES	31/7/15	2pm	Lecture to all Personnel & Patients re precautions shown for Helmets &c. Lt TAYLOR & 4 men to England. Guard to Patients 6-8 hm. on leave. Position: Main Dressing Station: Pont? Dressing Station sheet 36	40.000 a. sheet 36a. L. 29. B. 4.4. G. 22. B. 5.5.

A. C. Osburn
Major R. A. M. C.
COMMANDING
60th Field Ambulance

60th S.A.
20th Div.
Vol. 6.

Jan 1916

WAR DIARY
or
INTELLIGENCE SUMMARY

Army Form C. 2118

War Diary
60th Field Ambulance R.A.M.C
Lt. Col. A.C. Osburn.
commanding
for 1916
— January —

WAR DIARY / INTELLIGENCE SUMMARY

Army Form C. 2118

Place	Date	Hour	Summary of Events and Information	Remarks and references to Appendices
ESTAIRES	1st Jan 1916		POSITION ON MAP OF UNIT.	
			MAIN DRESSING STATION L.29.B.4.4. Sheet 36a/ 20000	
			Advanced " " G.22.B.5.5. Sheet 36a	
		2 p.m.	Gas Helmet Drill - all ranks Patients in Hospital Officers 7	
			Lt Taylor 14 men on leave. (including D.R.S) men 112	
	2nd		A.D.M.S. called	
			Gas helmet drill E. Section with practice of carrying patient	
			1 abdominal wound & Pte St Maur	
			Lectures re SMOKE HELMET to Personnel & Patients by O.C.	
	3rd		A.S.C M/S sent 2 Sgt.s for Temporary Commissions	
			Rode March A. Section	
	4th		Lt Kennedy returned from leave	

WAR DIARY
or
INTELLIGENCE SUMMARY

(Erase heading not required.)

Army Form C. 2118

Place	Date	Hour	Summary of Events and Information	Remarks and references to Appendices
ESTAIRES	5/1/16		D.D.M.S. visited Ambulances & saw Sick Officers. Sgt Beverley He below promoted by order G.O.C.	
	6.1.16		Secret orders re Divisional Move. Med Boards on 4 Officers — A.D.M.S. address Norm Eve Sick Officers (review)	
	7.1.16		D.M.S. 1st Army (Gen'l Pike) DD.M.S III Corp & A.D.M.S. Division ord inspection of Ambulance & D.R. Station. Surgeon Genl Pike Expressed himself as very well pleased with the condition of the Ambulance and informed me that the condition of all concerned, & D.R.S. reflected greatest credit on every one	
	7.1.16		4. R.M.O's of 59th Brigade called for instruction re enemy patients en route — treated 59th Brigade H.Q. M.O. Lahr Sqdn. 3. Secret Ord Dis R.O.M.G. No 2 refering to enemy envenime more.	

Army Form C. 2118

WAR DIARY
or
INTELLIGENCE SUMMARY
(Erase heading not required.)

Instructions regarding War Diaries and Intelligence Summaries are contained in F.S. Regs, Part II. and the Staff Manual respectively. Title Pages will be prepared in manuscript.

Place	Date	Hour	Summary of Events and Information	Remarks and references to Appendices
ESTAIRE	8/1/16		Lt Tolman promoted to Captain. Gas attack. Lt Hulton to R.A.P. to spend day. Lt Hynes Act. para at LA BELLE HOSTESS trailed. New Divisional Res opened. 32 Sulcher cecil in emergency at R.A.P. Gas attack. New Divisional Res opened. Gas attack. Lt Hulton to R.A.P. for emergency at R.A.P. Gas attack. Lt Hulton to R.A.P. at LA BELLE HOSTESS — accommodation. Arrangements made for Act. Post at LA BELLE HOSTESS (to be occupied by 1 personnel) to be sent. It is 1½ miles. Acc Horses (1 personnel) by road road. Poor 21 over the Horses by road road. From M.D.S. french 16 miles by road to. Picked up a severely wounded French soldier at SAILLY & took to HAZEBROUCK. Put up a dangerous wounded French soldier in critical condition. Put him into M.D.S. MEZIN brought. Lt. Hinton returns from SAILLY. Point to E.22.6.6.4. BERQUIN rd. next to 6 men. ↓3 days return. Gas attack delivered during night 8/9 & 10"FF.A., 59. Hd. a Reg. supporting no casualties. Gas. 2 motor ambulances Bn C, 61st PKuhelien to company at 62 inField Ambulances to some.	LA BELLE HOSTESS
	9/1/16			

WAR DIARY
or
INTELLIGENCE SUMMARY

Army Form C. 2118

Place	Date	Hour	Summary of Events and Information	Remarks and references to Appendices
ETAPLES	9/1/16		Capt TOZER 21 men left for new Aid Post La Belle Hotesse C.21.D.10.4. with necessary equipment. Capt LAWSON [struck through] and 7 men continued sham having been changed to carry on at A.D.S. at Sailly. Lt Curry in at A.D.S. 57th Brigade. Visited H.Q. 57th Brigade. Lt KENNEDY & LAWSON [struck through] relieving Lt. Z— LAWSON attends a court martial at H.Q.	
	10/1/16		R. Pitelley & — to N.D.S. Sgt Collins & 3 men to N.D.S. Lt. Taylor returns from leave.	
	11/1/16		Instructions to return to A.D.S.	
	12/1/16		Postmd office shifted to BLARINGHEM handed over at 11 am to O.C. 25 F. Amb. Stretcher Aid Post VIEUX BERQUIN rounds nr L.O.C. 6129 9 Amb returned. Temp. Aid Post Lt Kates relieved at 6 pm. B Gen HAMBRO A.A Q.M.G. II Corps inspected D.D.M.S. & ambulance — re Rifles, Officer caut feet, Lewis bomb & stove in pack store.	

Army Form C. 2118

WAR DIARY
or
INTELLIGENCE SUMMARY
(Erase heading not required.)

Instructions regarding War Diaries and Intelligence Summaries are contained in F. S. Regs., Part II. and the Staff Manual respectively. Title Pages will be prepared in manuscript.

Place	Date	Hour	Summary of Events and Information	Remarks and references to Appendices
ESTAIRE	14/1/16		Visited A.D.S. at La Belle HOTESSE, VIEUX S.	
	15/4/16		Before at Rue St Maur	
	16/4/16		Lt Kirton & Lt Taylor to charge of 10 O.R. & 20 R.P.O. — Bomb. men cancelled. at 9 p.m. — Bomb. men – 2 officers cancelled.	
	17/4/16		A.D.V.S. inspected horses. Drummond Training begun – (as to have been said), ready	
	18/4/16		Lectures – Drummond evacuated – French – Civilian evacuated – convalescent	CHARLEBROUCK
	19/4/16		Court martial held on Driver McMillan. 8 p.m. received orders to leave ESTAIRE by 9 a.m. tomorrow – 7 officers + 81 other ranks. Sick in Hospital – evacuated 23 men & officers to No 2 & No 7 C.C.S. Merville.	
	20/1/16		Packed during night – completed by 1 A.M. See surplus stores in shed near A Echelon R.E. Corporal Saville + 2 men left in charge	

WAR DIARY
or
INTELLIGENCE SUMMARY

(Erase heading not required.)

Army Form C. 2118

Place	Date	Hour	Summary of Events and Information	Remarks and references to Appendices
ETAPLES	21/4/16		Handed over to No 7 Field Ambulance 60 patients (men) and 3 sick Officers - Others evacuated night from 6 & 24 Field Ambulances - Receipt obtained for 703 cases other items - In no claims to make - Presd in charge (College) State - Gas Bell & Billeting certificates signed Ambulance - Gas Bell & Billeting certificates - Paid receipt obtained	
		9 a.m.	Marches via LA MOTTE & MORBECQUE	
MORBECQUE		2 p.m.	arriving MORBECQUE. Billetted and 62 in Field Ambulance	
	22/4/16	8. a.m.	Marches at 8 a.m. via St WALLON CAPPEL	
			Transport and Personnel arriver 1 and subdivision followed it	
			at 0.30. a - 2.8. - 6.7. - 2.8. - about 27	
			3 farms. Hospital accommodation for 15 in Girls School St MARIE CAPPEL	
ST. MARIE CAPPEL.			Hospital accommodation from LA BELLE HOTESSE farm and at St WALLON CAPPEL	
			Capt TOZER & Transport Carts during June - 1 Cow German breed	
			Supplied crew of Carts during June	
	24/4/16		Evacuated	
	26/4/16		Capt TOZER to Charge 2 11/2 KRR	
			Capt JOHNSON to Charge 7 TE Company - Bourbourg 2 R.E. Hsp	
			Lt KIRTON Relieves from Charge 2 10 KRR	
			Capt DAVIDSON to have attend lecture on "GAS" Treatment at OXELAERE	
			Lt KIRTON	

WAR DIARY or INTELLIGENCE SUMMARY

Army Form C. 2118

Place	Date	Hour	Summary of Events and Information	Remarks and references to Appendices
St MARIE CAPPEL	27/4/16		Lt. BURN evacuated sick to No 11 C.C.S. Capt LAWSON to be temporary Quartermaster. Draft of 12 men arriving.	
--	28/4/16		Recd notice of Lt's promotion to Lt Colonel (London Gazette 25/4/16) Early practice of stretcher work drill by all section.	
--	29/4/16		Lectures and experimental marching by compass map & instruction given by section. Officer inspection by G.O.C. 2nd Army — personnel, horses &, S.O.S. & wagon packs &c. now vaccine/personnel pigeons &, G.O.C. 2nd Army. Started inoculating all new vaccine/personnel — G.O.C. 59th Brigade — much pleased will	
--	30/4/16		Inspection — satisfactory —	

R.C. Osburn
Lt Col
R.A.M.C.
Commanding 60 of Ambulance

5 Feb. 1916

60 F A

60. F. A.
20th Div
Kokota
Vol. 7

Army Form C. 2118

WAR DIARY
or
INTELLIGENCE SUMMARY
(Erase heading not required.)

Retro

War Diary
of
60th Field Ambulance
for
February. 1916
Lt. Col. A. C. Osburn
RAMC
Commanding.

WAR DIARY
or
INTELLIGENCE SUMMARY

Army Form C. 2118

Place	Date	Hour	Summary of Events and Information	Remarks and references to Appendices
ST MARIE CAPPEL	January 1st		POSITION OF UNIT Headquarters + Hospital Show 27. tooo P. 19.6.8.9. (Girls school in village) O.30.a.2.8.	
	2nd		Transport + Personnel - minor - 1 car ambulance - communions on Sgts EVEN + COLLINGE sent to England for Commission Infantry. - Advance party sent to HERZEELE. Ambulance empd - collected on Road. March continued. Cent.	
	3rd		Capt LAWSON to leave to England - Billeting pasty - order given to leave tomorrow for HERZEELE	
	4th		marched at 9 a.m. via CASSEL, HARDIFORT, WORMHOUDT billet was HERZEELE Show 27. D.8.C and D.9.9.8.	
HERZEELE	5th		Hospital accommodation 20 patients 9.0.6. C in Chief SIR D. HAIG inspected billets at 4 p.m	

WAR DIARY or INTELLIGENCE SUMMARY

Army Form C. 2118

Place	Date	Hour	Summary of Events and Information	Remarks and references to Appendices
HERZEELE	6/2/16		Cleaned and improved Hospital & new billets	
	7/2/16		D.M.S. 2nd Army inspected Hospital & Personnel. Route march carried out	
	8/2/16		99 men inoculated against enteric. Capt Davidson, 3 N.C.O's and 18 men + 2 A.S.C. M.T. sent on a advance party to 44th (Fd) Ambulance in POPERINGHE to take over Main Ambulance at POPERINGHE	
	10/2/16		Capt TOZER and 20 N.C.O's men posted new area. Capt TOZER and 20 N.C.O's men called to take over A.D.S. at ESSEX FARM. to new area. Bumm Trenchfield. A.D.M.S called. Car &	
	11/2/16		A.D.M.S called.	
	12/2/16		Lt. KIRTON to Reme	
	13/2/16		Marched at 8.30 am. on HOUTKERQUE – WATOU – St JANS TER College ; took over ST STANISLAS (in Rue BIEZEN to POPERINGHE – took over ST STANISLAS (in Rue College ; took over grenade & them – also about Brittain) found 85 wounded & them – also about 40 sick . Heavy fighting has been going on since 10th – on Brigade . his Heavy Canals	
POPERINGHE				

WAR DIARY or INTELLIGENCE SUMMARY

Army Form C. 2118

Place	Date	Hour	Summary of Events and Information	Remarks and references to Appendices
POPERINGHE	14/2/16		MAIN DRESSING STATION - Fitzclarence College G.1.B.53. (Sheet 28) Advanced dressing station taken over on YSER CANAL at ESSEX FARM C.19.C.43. (Sheet 28) 1 Officer, 1 NCO 12 men AID POSTS - SKIPTON ROAD C.13.a.53. 4 men AT - LANCASHIRE FARM C.13.d.103. 4 men - LA BELLE ALLIANCE C.20.d.3.3. 4 men (2 men out with ambulance) - BRIELEN (village) B.29.a.8.1. 1 NCO 5 men 1 Motor Ambulance - BRANDHOEK G.6.d.2.8. 1 NCO 2 men Evacuation through YPRES. Water Tower Road. 70 men wounded came in during the 24 hours - a lot number of sick - 3 deaths. D.D.M.S. 14th Corps - Col SHINE & DSMS called. Visited Advanced dressing Station from 9 am to 11 pm. C. Reynold H.D. 	
	15/2/16		A.D.M.S. called - Capt TOZER took over chair 3rd RE Capt JOHNSON returned to Ambulance - (59th Brigade went into trenches on night 12th/13th)	
	16/2/16		30 sick 22 wounded -	

WAR DIARY
or
INTELLIGENCE SUMMARY

(Erase heading not required.)

Army Form C. 2118

Place	Date	Hour	Summary of Events and Information	Remarks and references to Appendices
POPERINGHE	17/2/16		22 sick 19 wounded in Hospital	
--	18/2/16		Capt Cantlie returns from A.D.S. Relieves A.D.S. 8 p.m. to midnight. Hostile Zeppelin & aeroplane over POPERINGHE (midnight (30 bombs) + 3 a.m. & 7 a.m. POPERINGHE bombed dropping in gardens at rear 2 Fr. D. Station no falling in chalet	
--	19/2/16		BRIELEN post shelled College. Pte Schmunk wounded Fracture R.F.69 R.	
--	20/2/16		Bombs dropped near POPERINGHE. Killed. Brielen shelled and POPERINGHE shelled.	
--	22/2/16 (11.45 pm)		Bombs dropped near Chapel - door blown in - no casualties.	
--	23/2/16		Took over aid post at LA BRIQUE - at C.26. d.0.5. from 17th Field Amb 615 F.Amb LANCASHIRE FARM given up & Station again shelled	
--	24/2/16		9 trench feet admitted - Skates again room Lt. Kirton returns from leave	
--	25/2/16		Heavy snow fall. Lt Taylor returns to Ambulance - hostile aeroplane driven off by A.A. guns	

WAR DIARY or INTELLIGENCE SUMMARY

Army Form C. 2118

Place	Date	Hour	Summary of Events and Information	Remarks and references to Appendices
POPERINGHE	24/9/16		Continued cleaning repairing College buildings. Obtained bricks for floor lines by purchase 2000 to 50 frs. Hostile aeroplane over several times.	
—	25/9/16		Further fall of snow — visited new advance at LA BRIQUE	
—	26/9/16		Took over M.I. Room / NCo 13 men at PESCHOEK A22 a S.S. from 62⁰ Field Amb	
—	27/9/16		11 Officers in hospital sick (wounded)	
—	28/9/16		Pte Hopkins wounded at ESSEX FARM. Lt Johns arrived for duty	
—	29/9/16		Further cleaning repairing repairing of College &c	

A. C. Osburn
Lt Col RAMC
Commanding
60⁰ Field Ambulance

S.

March 1916

60th Y Ambulance

Army Form C. 2118

60 F Aml

WAR DIARY
or
INTELLIGENCE SUMMARY

(Erase heading not required.)

Vol 8

War Diary
of
60th Field Ambulance
for
March 1916

A.E. Ahern
Lieut. Col. R.A.M.C.
COMMANDING
60th Field Amb.

WAR DIARY
or
INTELLIGENCE SUMMARY
(Erase heading not required.)

Army Form C. 2118

Place	Date	Hour	Summary of Events and Information	Remarks and references to Appendices
POPERINGHE	1916			
	1. March		<u>Position of Unit</u> on MAP Sheet 28.	
			MAIN DRESSING STATION. G. 1. d. 6. 2.	
			ADVANCED DRESSING STATION C. 19 c 4 3	
			AID POSTS. 1. LA BELLE ALLIANCE. C. 26 d. 6. 1	
			2. LA BRIQUE C. 20 d. 6. 5	
			3. YPRES I. 7. I. 6. 2	
			DETACHMENTS AT. Ch^{au} de Trois Tours. B. 28 a. 5. 2	
			PESELHOEK A. 21. a. 5. 5	
			— also at G. 1. d. 6. 2	
			Officer Divisional Rest Station — Officer sick in Hospital 2.	
			A.D.M.S. visited Rest Station. 10. Other ranks — sick wounded 10.	
			40. Other ranks — sick wounded 2.	
	2. March		Returning forms & report to make during warm [?] personnel.	
			Hours. — Gas Alert 10 am	
			O.G. 10. R.B admits will re-arrive [?]	

Army Form C. 2118

WAR DIARY
or
INTELLIGENCE SUMMARY
(Erase heading not required.)

Instructions regarding War Diaries and Intelligence Summaries are contained in F. S. Regs., Part II. and the Staff Manual respectively. Title Pages will be prepared in manuscript.

Place	Date	Hour	Summary of Events and Information	Remarks and references to Appendices
POPERINGHE	3rd March 16		Returned from leave. 1 N.C.O. & 6 men sent on a working party to new A.D.S. on Canal Bank. Lt. Mullan reported his arrival for duty with F.A. New infantry pattern equipment issued to unit. 1 NCO & 4 men attached to Batt. for duty at noon. The D.Y. was shelled 10⁵⁵ P.B.	
	4.3.16.		Capt JOHNSON - sent on duty with M.M. Gun Brigade. Capt TAYLOR " " " " to Ambulance 81 scale. 11 wounded, include 11 Officers. Inspected Horse lines in very bad condition.	the building is potente — shelling bombing & Corwelia house
	5.3.16.		Arrangements completed for moving somewhere at leisurely sheels — When the point of the town act 3 hours to Remy personnel to Pearl Hook about 3 hours town. There has been any heavy. no 1 to has been mended	
	6.3.16.		Spence overs shed Kundal cars shell struck re. & also Kondon.	

WAR DIARY or INTELLIGENCE SUMMARY

Army Form C. 2118

Place	Date	Hour	Summary of Events and Information	Remarks and references to Appendices
POPERINGHE	7.3.16		Visited A.D.S. and Aid posts – fairly heavy shelling near Essex Farm – one car hit	
	8.2.16		Arrangement being made to strengthen roof of D.R.S. Pavilion. Removed horse lines nearer M.D.S.	
	9.3.16		Visited A.D.S. and aid posts – Ypres shell being killed – aid posts in Ypres – cut Tour Major away for a review and posts under canvas near front	
	10.3.16		3 Reinforcement arrived – pt Bays relieved under front	
	11.3.16		Lecture repeated [incomplete] to Corps & G.O.C. 14th Corps 20 officers in hospital – Saluochin will all instructors form } Gas	
			Lt Col [?] Officer 122 others G.O.C. [illegible] and officers of [illegible] arrived in Pop. [illegible] ambulance and forts in trenches at 11 p.m. sick -	
	12.3.16		built out posts in [illegible]	18. – } 151
	13.3.16		Patient in Ambulance Officer [illegible] Other	131. 2.
			[illegible] Home line Gas condition every breath – but improving Chlorine Gas [illegible] on shovel began	
	14.3.16		Q.M. Lt Walpole on special leave Arrangement for 3 Motor Ambulances complete.	

WAR DIARY
or
INTELLIGENCE SUMMARY

Army Form C. 2118

Place	Date	Hour	Summary of Events and Information	Remarks and references to Appendices
Poperinghe	16th Mar		Capt McLean relieves Capt Kirton at A.D.S. Visited A.D.S. at 11 p.m. Heavy shelling of road between VLAMERTINGHE & YPRES	
	17th Mar		Visited A.D.S. at 11 p.m. & out into YPRES bay hardly shelled at all. Convoy in of assisted others suffering without exception the symptoms of a few doubtful infectious cases sent to M.S.T. except Headache.	
	18th	--	Capt KENNEDY relieves Capt KIRTON at A.D.S. Transport brought down to R.A.C. section from building at 7 a.m. as bombs dropped	
	20th	--	3 TAUBES over main building	
	21st Mch		Capt TAYLOR relieves Lt Spaul - Rt Group R.F.A.Artillery ad post. - ammunition of four men cover left.	
	22	--	Visited A.D.S. & ad post. — mores opening Thalis ambulance — more to wire lines	
	24"	--	Sa.Sm. Sir A. BOWLBY visited Ambulance to send to up 10th K.R.Rs works. 3rd Fret station to Capt Anderson (sick) will	
	25"	--	Capt KENNEDY returns	
	26"	--	Two in Home lines - Cowal of Engung visited Home lines damage done made good by Pte Meade & Baines M.S.Corps	

Army Form C. 2118

WAR DIARY
or
INTELLIGENCE SUMMARY
(Erase heading not required.)

Instructions regarding War Diaries and Intelligence
Summaries are contained in F. S. Regs., Part II.
and the Staff Manual respectively. Title Pages
will be prepared in manuscript.

Place	Date	Hour	Summary of Events and Information	Remarks and references to Appendices
POPERINGHE	30 March		Capt MOILAN - C.O. M° % 20 = F.A. Column during Capt Wall's absence. Capt CANTLIE proceeded on leave. Town still occasionally shelled.	
	31.		Visited A.D.S. and the Poppr. Adv. post. Heavy shelling of our area & Guards area — also from St Eloi direction. Completed removal of all Horse Transport to G.H.Q. D.S. Further felt it expedient to order C.O. to annoying air attack. no sickness now amongst troops — rather two sickness amongst civil popul. is on Temporary Adv. post in YPRES. evacuated to wounded sick	
			Officers 2 — 8 other Ranks 7 — 78 Total 95	
			31/March/1916	
			A.C. Osburn Lt Colonel R.A.M.C. Commanding 65th Field Amb.	

Army Form C. 2118

WAR DIARY
or
INTELLIGENCE SUMMARY
(Erase heading not required.)

Instructions regarding War Diaries and Intelligence Summaries are contained in F. S. Regs., Part II. and the Staff Manual respectively. Title Pages will be prepared in manuscript.

Place	Date	Hour	Summary of Events and Information	Remarks and references to Appendices

1875 Wt. W 593/826 1,000,000 4/15 J.B.C. & A. A.D.S.S./Forms/C. 2118.

No. 60. Field Ambulance.

April 1916.

COMMITTEE FOR THE
MEDICAL HISTORY OF THE WAR
Date 2 - JUN. 1915

Army Form C. 2118

60 J Amb
Vol 9

WAR DIARY
or
INTELLIGENCE SUMMARY
(Erase heading not required.)

Place	Date	Hour	Summary of Events and Information	Remarks and references to Appendices
POPERINGHE	1.4.16		(Officers) Divisional Rest Station	
			POSITION ON MAP G. 1. d. 6. 2.	
			(Sht 28) —do— C. 19. c. 4. 3. (Canal Bank)	
			ADVANCED —do—	
			AID POSTS. (1) LA FILLE ALLIANCE: C. 26. d. 6. 1.	
			(2) LA BRIQUE C. 20. d. 6. 5.	
			(3) "YPRES" Town 9. 7. b. 6. 2.	
			DETACHMENTS AT Ch. d. TROIS TOURS B. 28. a. 5. 2.	
			PESELHOEK A. 21. a. 5. 5.	
April 1st 1916			D.M.S. M. Anny & Surg Gen A. Bowlby visited Australian Hospital & both expressed themselves very pleased – no criticisms	
			Summary of Evidence on Sgt CUTHBERTSON taken arrangd with O.C. 26 Field C, for more material for enemmy cars. Sent O.C. 61st D.A. re evacuation of sick also Apl ml.	
			2 men Officers admitted to Fld station E61. 12 Patients in Hospital 80 – very few casualties. Bombs. Town again shelled & bombed. Agreement signed with College dropped on my old Hve here. Authorities to make no claim.	

1875 W. W593/826 1,000,000 4/15 J.B.C. & A. A.D.S.S./Forms/C. 2118.

WAR DIARY or INTELLIGENCE SUMMARY

Army Form C. 2118

Place	Date	Hour	Summary of Events and Information	Remarks and references to Appendices
POPERINGHE	2.4.16		Conference with A.D.M.S. 3 pm. Applications to 7 F.C.M. on Sgt CUTHBERTSON arranged with Interpreter for statement to be obtained from Belgian authorities re condition of building. 13 Officers sick + wounded in rest station. Heavy shelling continued during yesterday + last night - a few casualties amongst artillery and many about 45" on Canal Bank. About 6 pm visited Major 9 D.C.L.I at ELVERDINGHE CHATEAU - very busy - Salvaged S.9 a number 9 casualties. Shelling an annual thin'. — Visited A.D.M.S. for Hazebrouck 6.15 but Brigade Capt Clayton's horse arranged with much on shelling.	
"	3.4.16			
"	4.4.16		C.M. on Sergeant Cuthbertson. A.D.M.S. visited ambulances. Sent Cypher Received. Arranged disposal of Surplus Equipment. Investigates ?km ? Wales Station.	

WAR DIARY
or
INTELLIGENCE SUMMARY

(Erase heading not required.)

Army Form C. 2118

Place	Date	Hour	Summary of Events and Information	Remarks and references to Appendices
POPERINGHE	5th		A.D.M.S. visited Hospital, and made a round of Wards, Horse Lines &c. Weather tried after Rain.	
	6th		Notification received that Surg. D. Cutherbert tried by F.G.C.M is returned to the ranks from the 3rd Inst.	
	7th		Lieut Ingram R. RAMC (T.C.) reported his arrival for duty on this date from the 48th Field Ambulance 3rd Division.	
	8th		A.D.M.S. visited Ambulances. Capt. Mullan returned from duty with 20th Divisional Amm. Column, and took over Temporary Medical Charge of 20th Divisional R.E's for one day. Suit John H.J. (RAMC. (T.C.) was struck off the strength of the unit being ordered to report to A.D.M.S. 34th Division for Duty.	

WAR DIARY or INTELLIGENCE SUMMARY

Army Form C. 2118

(Erase heading not required.)

Place	Date	Hour	Summary of Events and Information	Remarks and references to Appendices
POPERINGHE				
	9/April 1916		Orders from D.D.M.S. 14th Corps that O.C. 60th Field Ambulance Lt Col O'Brien will take over duties at D.M.S. Guards Division in addition to his other duties.	
			Field Corps H.Q. transport also going front line for the duration – also field service of A.Q.M.G.	
	10th April		Visit to No. 9. Field Ambulance – an casualty clearing station – ASC&S Correspondence – held by Lt Myard Guard down with trench fever – Car struck by shell near Puven field trench PRISON – Car O.C. 17.15 (Fld)	
		9 p.m.	R.A.S. at St Jean & accommodation at St Jean & (P.O).	
			time input – accommodation in funerals shells 6 killed (3 R.A.M.C. 3 Guards unit) No 9 Fld Amb cancels order O.C. to evacuate all but 3 medical officers & less team	
	11th April	8 p.m.	14 wounded ordered bombarg shower in cars (15 to) to be evacuated, also to Conscience now the station & team journey, school now — chateau billow probable by journey intention of Corps Headquarters – point determined	
	12th		Conference 11 a.m. ready to undertaken, 81 wounded the billets, 1st 7th Sunny Com Cap Cazes. A.F.E. billets, pointchen	

WAR DIARY or INTELLIGENCE SUMMARY

Army Form C. 2118

Place	Date	Hour	Summary of Events and Information	Remarks and references to Appendices
POPERINGHE	12.4.16	1 p.m.	Saw A.D.M.S. field driver re ambce & Gt. Nrd Brit.game inspected building in town – at LARRE FARM orders sent to be ready for next – at ambulance to an emergency. Visited A.D.S. the evidence of our troops heavy attack yesterday (12th) of our from very heavy. Saw regt. wired us Division – heavy casualties in own lines through our A.D.S. then went. Visited Sewers Division A.D. Poi on Canal Bank also B.P.D. 59th and my own (6th & 7th) A.D.S. – found quiet – 1 German prisoner ad-mitted (Louis BONDEROUX) 10th JAEGER REGT.? Advance H.Q. & CAPPELLE of KEMMEL to prepare to to. 16th Division. began packing equipment, howeling over No.	
	13.4.16		Visited marched to HERZEELE D.G. d.&.S. billets to No 17 Fres Amb.	
	14.4.16			
	15.4.16	8 a.m.	Visited plan re 248 patients to No. 7 Amd Building dump of No 20 Res Boschepe Convoy to No 7 Amd heavy shell into Railway over Ypres	
	16.4.16 17.4.16		A.D.S. EGGS FARM handed over at 10 pm. to battery showed – patients – taken into shelter taking into Cars hit heavy – OR one hit. Capt. LAWSON – no casualties.	

O.C. by Capt LAWSON

Place	Date	Hour	Summary of Events and Information	Remarks and references to Appendices
HERZEELE	18.4.16		Early route march – bathing, cooking, cleaning manoeuvre, clearing of camps & having cookery equipment, clothing & kit washed. we have had 5 & 6 weeks camp (some yearly & wet weather) & am now into same. Cadre (cont.)	
	24/4/16	Rec'd orders for Capt. Coulter to proceed for 10 days duty to D.A.D.M.S. 14th Corps. & Capt Kennedy to take charge. Divisional bathing at works near Ypres. Lahore Section continuing training.	
HERZEELE	26.4.16		Rec'd orders from CHATEAU or Dg.d.8.8 to HOSPICE at K.4.6.7.5. leaving HERZEELE and hunting on 6.62. 20 patients from Regiment over from 6.19.15. patients at 10 a.m. – about 22 men fell out of Hawking. Party moved at 2.30 p.m. – Ambulance Advance party at 9 a.m. notes on 9 gun positions on 12 bus. Mess registered as to the men falling out – no man over 45 was relieved to Regiment. 10th & 11th K.R.R. Imade inquiries 14th Corps Cavalry Divn.	

Place	Date	Hour	Summary of Events and Information	Remarks and references to Appendices
WATOU	27/4/16		Inspection of Farms, Rest Billets, Latrines & poultry cleaning of cookers, Rose Beds & poultry cleaning Horse lines & carried out by a Cappm. 10" M.E. P.B. marched about 25 men. Then on to our audiences at Tyns.	
	28/4/16		Capt Mullan to relieve Cap'n STEVENSON in charge of M.T.R.s. Notification rec'd special move of 59th Brigade on night of 30/1st may 59th Brigade H.Q. arrangements for the above night operation broken.	
	29/4/16		Capt Taylor on leave. Capt KIRTON to relieving Capt Taylor in charge of B.H.Q. (Signal Station). 59 m. Coy 59 Pioneer Coys Mr. Bellew 159 Co R.E. 96 wo C R.E Capt Davidson melay of units in WATOU & M. Volaras taken under H.Q. 59th Brigade.	

WAR DIARY or INTELLIGENCE SUMMARY

Army Form C. 2118

Place	Date	Hour	Summary of Events and Information	Remarks and references to Appendices
WATOU	30/4/16		4.45 pm "A" C Reservation & "C" Two Subdivision with O.C, top Convoy, Kitchen, 1 Sh Infirmary marches to OPERINGHE, joining up there with 59th Brigade — proceeding via VLAMERTINGHE to B.20 d.5.7. NW of BAILEN. Reconnaissance in force by 59th Brigade to Canal Bank, bridge 25 GN & VLAMERTINGHE — 12 wounded — 4 orig. cases carried by in two columns W to Detained Subdivision formed an Aid Post at H.8.3.9 in VLAMERTINGHE and sending back Column returned independently to VLAMERTINGHE all wing left. No. casualties till 6.30 a.m on 1/5/16. — G.O.C J Brigade & in person ordered (noted) H.Q of Evn pd at B.23.6.2.4. — about OC Ten wing on top near half column. — night June 30 wounded. 4.2 frees & enemy on top starlight, going numerous shell WA. 3 men second fatigue & peon & attending numerous shell WA. from 10 R.E.E.	

Maj. A C Osborn R.A.M.C.
COMMANDING
60th Field Ambulance

Army Form C. 2118

WAR DIARY
INTELLIGENCE SUMMARY
(Erase heading not required.)

May 1916

1/60 J Amb

Vol 10

WAR DIARY
60th FIELD AMBULANCE
FOR MAY 1916

COMMITTEE FOR THE
MEDICAL HISTORY OF THE WAR
Date 26 JUN. 1916

Place	Date	Hour	Summary of Events and Information	Remarks and references to Appendices
	May/16			

Army Form C. 2118

WAR DIARY
or
INTELLIGENCE SUMMARY
(Erase heading not required.)

Instructions regarding War Diaries and Intelligence Summaries are contained in F.S. Regs., Part II. and the Staff Manual respectively. Title Pages will be prepared in manuscript.

Place	Date	Hour	Summary of Events and Information	Remarks and references to Appendices
WATOU	1/May/1916		Poitering Unit	
			Main Dressing Station "HOSPICE" R.4.b.9.5.	
			Section under training R.11.a.4.2.	
			at Farm at	
			Collecting work to form — 59th Brigade	
			is very carried out	H.Q. & signal section
				59th M.G. Coy.
			patients Hospital	59th I & II Trench howitzer batty
			O.R. 24. Sick	10th & 11th R.B. — to
				10th & 11th K.R.R.C.
		also —	10th K.R.R.
		20th	11th K.R.R.
			11th & 12th Infantry sub park
			Evacuated to ammunition column
			Mobile Vetinary Section
			A/O and visited Ambulance	159th M.A.C.
			also to visit Corps Orders	96. F.3. Co. R.E.
				all serial cases of dysentery

1875 Wt. W593/826 1,000,000 4/15 J.B.C. & A. A.D.S.S./Forms/C.2118.

Army Form C. 2118

WAR DIARY
or
INTELLIGENCE SUMMARY

(Erase heading not required.)

Instructions regarding War Diaries and Intelligence Summaries are contained in F. S. Regs., Part II. and the Staff Manual respectively. Title Pages will be prepared in manuscript.

Place	Date	Hour	Summary of Events and Information	Remarks and references to Appendices
WATOU	2/5/16		Hd. Qurs. moved & pt. G.O.C. 59th Bde. conferred re Harwich Louisline. Col. Kennedy relieved of command of (L8) was Ypres Col. Kennedy by Capt. Kinton.	
	3/5/16		Capt Kennedy took over charge of Bde. Hdqrs. 59/1 & 59/2 T.M. Batts., 59 M. Gun Coy., 159 Coy A.S.C. & 96th Coy R.E. engaged in Physical exercises, Route marches, and lectures. Weather very fine and warm.	
	4/5/16.		Detailed orders to fires in Billets issued by Division these instructions are to be impressed on all ranks.	
	5/5/16.		Physical Exercises for men.	

WAR DIARY
or
INTELLIGENCE SUMMARY

(Erase heading not required.)

Army Form C. 2118

Place	Date	Hour	Summary of Events and Information	Remarks and references to Appendices
WATOU	April 6		Day spent in packing up equipment, & loading wagons preparatory to moving. 9 patients were taken over by the 62nd F. Amb. Capt. Cantlie rejoined the unit from the post of A/D.A.D.M.S. XIV Corps. Marched from WATOU at 6 p.m. via ABEELE to HOPOUTRE siding at L.17.d.6.6. (Sheet 27). Entrained together with 159 Coy Divisional Train. Unit here, sharing the train with 159 Coy Divisional Train. Entraining was done quickly and without accident. Train moved out at 11-20 p.m.	
CALAIS.	7.		Arrived at BOULOGNE STATION via HAZEBROUCK and ST OMER and CALAIS at 5.30 a.m. The unit was here detrained, and marched 3 miles to No 6 Large Rest Camp. (BEAUMARAIS CAMP.) Got the hospital, 59 patients were taken over from 61st Field Amb, about 30 of whom were "detained cases". "A" Section equipment & tents were used for setting up a Small Hospital.	

WAR DIARY
or
INTELLIGENCE SUMMARY

Army Form C. 2118

Place	Date	Hour	Summary of Events and Information	Remarks and references to Appendices
CALAIS	April 8th		Camp Rules, and Town orders for CALAIS were read out to the men. 50% of men are allowed into CALAIS in afternoons. Wet and cold weather.	
	9th		Route march for men with Packs to the beach and back. Bathing Parade for all Ranks.	
	10th		Bathing Parade in morning. Admissions to hospital are very low. Weather fine and warm.	
	11th		Camp was inspected by Col. SLAYTER. A.M.S. and Major Conway Darling. Special accommodation of cook houses was pointed out, and the flooding of Camp in wet weather, and consequent washing of grease traps and urine pits etc. The personnel inspected on parade by A.D.M.S. Officers on parade. Lt. Col. Brown, Capt. Cantley, Capt. Deliusson, Capt. Sowden, Capt. Mulleon, Capt. Mulleen.	
	12th		Bathing Parade in morning, followed by Routemarch.	

WAR DIARY or INTELLIGENCE SUMMARY

Army Form C. 2118

Place	Date	Hour	Summary of Events and Information	Remarks and references to Appendices
CALAIS	13th		Raining most of the day. At 5 p.m. sudden orders came to move at 7.30 p.m. with the Brigade. Cases in hospital were evacuated to Lahore General Hospital, to 30 General Hospital and Seaside cases to No.1 Isolation Court.	
		7.30 p.m.	Capt. Samson, with billeting party was sent in advance. The Ambulance moved off behind the Brigade, and moved via PONT D'ARDRES and NORTKERQUE to ZUTKERQUE, billeting there for the night. Sub Unit WESTFIELD was left behind at BEAUMARAIS Camp to hand over to the incoming unit.	
ZUTKERQUE	14th		Left billets at 10 a.m. and marched in rear of 59th Inf. Bde. via NORDAUSQUES – WATTEN – WOLVERDINGHE to VOLKERINGHOVE, and billeted there for the night. 35 cases fell out on the line of march, and 30 men of 59th Machine Gun Coy had their equipment carried in Ambulance wagons. Most of these cases were admitted Evening. 12 cases were admitted.	

WAR DIARY
or
INTELLIGENCE SUMMARY

(Erase heading not required.)

Army Form C. 2118

Place	Date	Hour	Summary of Events and Information	Remarks and references to Appendices
VOLKERINKHOVE	15th		Vacated billets at 10am and marched Independently to Brigade via cross roads at B.19.d.5.5. (Sheet 27) —ZEGGERS CAPPEL — ESQUELBECQUE — WORMHOUDT to HERZEELE arriving at 3 p.m. 3 Horse Ambulances marched in rear of 59th Brigade for cases falling out on the line of march, all of which were returned to some Evening to their unit. Men fatigued after marching roughly 15 miles in 4½ hours, & in hot weather, and full packs. "C" section was opened at the Chateau HERZEELE D.9.d.8.8. (Sheet 27).	
HERZEELE	16th		Lt. Col. Odlum granted leave from 16th to 23rd. Capt. N. Cantlie in Temporary Command of the field Amb. The day spent in unloading and repacking equipment to harness. Cleaning Bathing, washing. Visit form of A.26.c.7.5. (Sheet 28) to there it out as a main warm weather. Dressing Station. A.D.M.S. visited Ambulance. Congratulatory note from the Corps Commander	
"	17th			

WAR DIARY
or
INTELLIGENCE SUMMARY

Army Form C. 2118

Place	Date	Hour	Summary of Events and Information	Remarks and references to Appendices
HERZEELE	17th		On the fine performance of the Brigade march from CALAIS. Route marches, and lectures for men.	
"	18th		Training of men generally continued.	
"	19th		Capt. Lawson and 10 men went as an advanced party to POPERINGHE. 1 N.C.O. and 4 men went to the CONVENT, RUE DE BRUGES to take over from 9 F.A. 1 N.C.O. + 4 men to Farm at PESEL HOEK (A.26.c.8.4) Sheet 28, and take over billet from Guards D.A.C.	
HERZEELE	20th		Preparing up unit preparatory to move. Moved out of billets at 8 a.m. and handed over to Advance Party from 10 H.F.A. Followed the Brigade after WATOU, but marched with 10th R.B. only for WATOU via HOUTKERQUE. (Very hot day), but only 13 men fell out from the Brigade, and were from our own unit. Arrived in billets at Farm or PESELHOER and A.26.c.8.H. at 1 p.m. A lot of cleaning billets, refuse and manure was needed.	

Army Form C. 2118

WAR DIARY or INTELLIGENCE SUMMARY

Place	Date	Hour	Summary of Events and Information	Remarks and references to Appendices
POPERINGHE & PESSELHOEK	21st		The day spent in continuing to clear away refuse, fixing up Pack Store, Dispensary, Wards, and Billets. ADMS major Conway visited the Ambulance. Arranged with O.C.'s 61st and 62nd F. Ambs regarding Dental and Eye cases which to be collected at CONVENT, RUE DE BRUGES. Wards for patent very warm and fine weather.	
	22nd		Completed, and fatigues on manure carting, grease traps, latrines &c continued. Case of the Reserve Brigade Field Ambulance have the duty of conveying all cases to and from the DRS. at WORMHOUDT. O.D.M.S + D.ADMS visited the Ambulance. Invalid CONVENT, RUE DE BRUGES, which Capt. Ryton has been put in charge. Suggestions for making it into a Dressing Station & receive wounded. Capt. Taylor took over Sanitary charge of Town of POPERINGHE. Temporarily under instructions from A.D.M.S. Fleeing of Injured Warders. Continued.	
	23rd		Continued. from to nowhere 23rd	

WAR DIARY
INTELLIGENCE SUMMARY

Army Form C. 2118

Place	Date	Hour	Summary of Events and Information	Remarks and references to Appendices
RESELHOEK	24th Sept		Visited the CONVENT, RUE DE BRUGES with the Town Major of POPERINGHE and arranged to take over the lower floor of the CONVENT, giving up the Schoolroom at present occupied. Visited DADMS. visited RAMC advanced Ambulance, and under his instructions on duty with a supply of dressings posted at Town Hall POPERINGHE Telephone communication fixed up between M.D.S. and CONVENT.	
	25th		Visited 62nd Field Ambulance for information on Aid Posts + arrangements for evacuating wounded from front line. Lt Col. Osburn returned from leave, and took over command of the Ambulance. Visited the 11th Calf Cantile the Asylum YPRES and inspected the accommodation for wounded, went on thro YPRES to aid Post at POTIJZE WOOD, then returned to PRISON where 61st Field Ambulance has an advanced A.D.S. with good accommodation – noted TOWN MAJOR in Prison.	

Army Form C. 2118

WAR DIARY
or
INTELLIGENCE SUMMARY
(Erase heading not required.)

Place	Date	Hour	Summary of Events and Information	Remarks and references to Appendices
PESCHAER	26		Clearing and clearing fatigues continued. Took over collection of sick and wounded from 63rd Field Ambulance beginning from 6.am 27th inst of Left Brigade Group. The Advanced Dressing Station at Asylum was taken over by Capt. Mutullan and 10 other Ranks. Canal Bank Aid Post C.25.a.13 (Sheet 28) taken over from 63rd A.Fy. Capt. Mullan, INCO + 3 O.R. proceeded there. St Jean Aid Post C.21 d.33. H.O.R. POTIZE Aid Post I.4.a.8.2. INCO H.O.R. Everything done on quiet night	
	27		Every man proceeding east of YAMERTINGHE must wear a steel helmet. Sick and wounded few in number. ADMS and Mullan and Capt Artillery activity ADMS and DADMS visited Ambulance. Notificated that 8 cases of Epidemic Jaundice have occurred in the Area several later cases.	

WAR DIARY or INTELLIGENCE SUMMARY

Army Form C. 2118

Place	Date	Hour	Summary of Events and Information	Remarks and references to Appendices
PEESELHOEK	28th		ADMS & DADMS visited Ambulance. Briefing of Roads, building Incinerators re continued. Capt Rutter is in medical charge of Transport lines of 59th Bde. POPERINGHE was heavily shelled this evening and during the night by heavy 250 pounds few casualties reported, by Capt Rutter, only 2 men being admitted. Station area and ELVERDINGHE road suffered most.	
	29th		Car visited by ADMS & DADMS. Capt. Davidson, 5 Nursing Orderlies, and Lt J. Dusty Motor Lorries proceeded to OSYLUM at YPRES on 27th inst. and reinforced Capt. Lawson there. No 4 MAC cars evacuate cases from ASYLUM to C.C.S., so that cases are thoroughly treated, at the ASYLUM. The 10 Canadian Fuid Ambl. also evacuate this ASYLUM with 1 MO. and about 10 O.R. Accommodation for 84 Stretcher cases in tent occupied	

Army Form C. 2118

WAR DIARY
or
INTELLIGENCE SUMMARY
(Erase heading not required.)

Place	Date	Hour	Summary of Events and Information	Remarks and references to Appendices
VLESELADEN	29th		by us, and additional 90 cases in porton occupied by Canadians	
	30th		Capt Kennedy relieved Capt Mullen at CANAL BANK Aid Post, and Capt Lawson returned to M.D.S. from ASYLUM. A.D.M.S. and D.A.D.M.S. visited Ambulance.	
	31st		Position of Unit MAIN Dewey Station Advanced —"— Asylum Aid Posts. 1. CANAL BANK. C.25.d.1.3 2. S.t JEAN C.27.d.3.3 3. POTIJETZE I.4.a.8.2	Shed 28 A.26.c.8.4 H.R.d.7.5 W.J.Osborn Lieut Commanding Field Amb

1875 Wt. W593/826 1,000,000 4/15 J.B.C. & A. A.D.S.S./Forms/C. 2118.

July
20. Army Form C. 2118
60 F Amb
Vol 12

WAR DIARY
or
INTELLIGENCE SUMMARY.
(Erase heading not required.)

COMMITTEE FOR THE
MEDICAL HISTORY OF THE WAR.
Date 5-SEP '45

AF Shurn
Lieut Col
R.A.M.C.
COMMANDING
60th Field Ambulance

WAR DIARY
OF
60th FIELD AMBULANCE
FOR
JULY 1916

Place	Date	Hour	Summary of Events and Information	Remarks and references to Appendices
July 1916	5			

Army Form C. 2118.

WAR DIARY
or
INTELLIGENCE SUMMARY.
(Erase heading not required.)

Place	Date	Hour	Summary of Events and Information	Remarks and references to Appendices
PESELHOEK (near POPERINGHE)			POSITION OF Unit at midnight 30/6/16 — 1/7/16	
			M.D.S. (shew 28 hours) A.26.c.8.4.	
			A.D.S. "Asylum" — H.12.d.7.5.	
			Ad Pos⁺ (i) Canal Bank — C.25.d.4.1. ⎫ 57 B.g⁶⁵ in Reserve
	1.7.16		(ii) St Jean — C.27.d.3.3. ⎬ handed over pro
			(iii) Potijze — J.4.a.8.2. ⎭ temp to 62ⁿᵈ F²Amb.
			(iv) Convent Rd Brukes — G.2.d.4.7. East Lawrence F.A. O.R.
			wounded taken in Ambulance — beck 32 hours? 2.	
-"-	2.7.16		F.G.C.M. hearted on Pte KELLY. A.A. action VIII (para 2) 7.7.16	
			Some shelling of Poperinghe — Elverdinghe road 11 a m — noon	
			Area near M.O.S. bombes between 7 + 8.30 pm, no damage	

WAR DIARY
or
INTELLIGENCE SUMMARY

(Erase heading not required.)

Army Form C. 2118

Place	Date	Hour	Summary of Events and Information	Remarks and references to Appendices
POPERINGHE.	2.7.16		1 man transferred to 1/1st F.A. Amb.	
—	3.7.16		Lt. HARKIN returns from duty	
—	4.7.16		H. Convoy evacuated. Enemy aeroplane circled — on duty. 4 enemy aeroplanes travel over & C.62.a.9 & 7.5 Point.	
—	5.7.16		Field Post (No 4) Convent POPERINGHE 59th Brigade returns to trenches — relieves 58th Brigade & posts 1.2.&3. from 62nd Inf 7.8 Point.	C.27. d.2.3. J.7. a.9.8. Canal Bank C.25. d.4.1. H.12.d.7.5. about 2.8
—	6.7.16		A.D.S. ASYLUM. Bombing about 7–9 pm — very little damage done.	
—	7.7.16		Enemy aeroplanes active. Bombing about 7–9 pm + 1–2 am. Enemy rapid — very little damage done.	
—	9.7.16		1 Car struck by a shell at POP/126 body pierced by level 9 shell & took up middle with fragments — shrapnel from bullets — Barrel pierced also by frag & another shell exploding on igniting no casualties. 1 Car damaged by running into a live wire caused by a breaking Shell at Lt. HARK. Driver wounded — no casualties.	

Army Form C. 2118

WAR DIARY
or
INTELLIGENCE SUMMARY
(Erase heading not required.)

Place	Date	Hour	Summary of Events and Information	Remarks and references to Appendices
RESELHOEK				
	10.7.16		Col KENNEDY Anchored from Hospital — to Lijssenthoek	
			POPERINGHE shelled 11.30 a.m. — to 1 p.m.	
			1 reinforcement — M.C. — M.T. arrived	
	11.7.16		POPERINGHE shelled at 4 p.m. — 6 p.m. — wounded 4.9. in trench	
			Column around Boundary in area around — voluntarily	
	12.7.16		POPERINGHE shelled from 8 a.m. — to 4 p.m. — intermittently	
			6 p.m. to 8.30 p.m. Expressively round scrap + old M.A.S.	
			2 M.A.C. A.T.C. drivers killed — (attached company) in front	
			of POPERINGHE — regular reinforcement and Col 06. Col Nightingale	
			of 37 wounds in trench 145. 7? Amb 06. Col Nightingale	
	12.7.16		G.O.C. 50t Division inspects ambulance + the Con dumps.	
			by shelling — POPERINGHE shelled — inspects old M.O.S. in Doci Bertin.	
	13.7.16		POPERINGHE HERZEELE Couthilles	
	14.7.16		1 Car damage via VLAMERTINGHE by artillery horses & fire	
			Sgt J PATTERSON awarded Military Medal.	
	15.7.16		visited A.D.S. at Herfrum Advance parties to HERZEELE + BOLLEZEELE	
	16.7.16		visited A.D.S. at Asylum — 16 to 18 7 Amb. P.O.T.1125 to 10t 7 Amb }	
			noon transports M.O.S. of ST Jean and took at ST Jean { to 10t 7 Amb }	
	16/17		midnight transferred over + M.D.S. at ASYLUM.	

WAR DIARY
or
INTELLIGENCE SUMMARY
(Erase heading not required.)

Army Form C. 2118

Place	Date	Hour	Summary of Events and Information	Remarks and references to Appendices
POPERINGHE	17/7/16	Noon	Marched via WATOU & HERZEELE D.9.d d.8 billets over from 16th & 2nd And.	
HERZEELE.	18/7/16		Advance party walked from BOLLEZEELE Orders to pack up ready for further move.	
—"—	19/7/16		Capt KIRTON & 6.O.R. B/M & advance party to billets over Audkirk at NEUF EGLISE T.20.a.8.4. 2 R.A.M.C. details burns unit. Following Austins also taken over KANDAHAR FARM T. 10. 6. 5. 7. RED LODGE. T. 18. a. 5. 5. + 2 Wof. Med junk T. 6. d. 8.5. T. 12. a. 5.5.	
HERZEELE.	20.7.16	8am 10am 2pm	Transport under Capt Mullan & Capt Taylor - marched to Bailleul united S.16.c.2.4. & join O.C. 72nd Fd Amb & new M.D.S. at S.16.c.2.4. by motor bus to new M.D.S. at S.16.c.2.4. Personnel + 20 patients Shares billets with 72nd Fd Amb MAJOR EDWARDS comdg	S.16.c.2.4.

Army Form C. 2118

WAR DIARY
or
INTELLIGENCE SUMMARY
(Erase heading not required.)

Instructions regarding War Diaries and Intelligence Summaries are contained in F. S. Regs., Part II. and the Staff Manual respectively. Title Pages will be prepared in manuscript.

Place	Date	Hour	Summary of Events and Information	Remarks and references to Appendices
BAILLEUL	21.7.16.		Capt CANTLIE struck off strength transferred to No 12 C.C.S. Lt WRIGHT joined for duty. 72 & 73 Amb detached at 10 a.m. Visited Adv. posts. (Col FAWCETT D.S.O. Comdg 108th F.A.)	
BAILLEUL	22.7.16.		108th & 73 Amb arrived & chose billets. Took over to 108th 73 Amb.	Shed e8.
-"-	23.7.16		D.R.S. in trenches Visited aid posts.	Amb posts at T 20 A 8.4, T 10 B 5.7.5 Kans 28 open T 12 a 5.5 to 108 F Amb T 28 a 5.5 Rest aid posts
-"-	23.7.16		Lt WRIGHT commenced with 8 Amb	
-"-	24.7.16		LOCRE — WESTOUTRE to HOPOUTRE arriving 1.30. 0 m on 25.	
BAILLEUL	24.7.16 10 pm		marched via LOCRE — WESTOUTRE to HOPOUTRE entrained — proceeded via HAZEBROUCK	
	25.7.16		Hopoutre und entrain. & St Pol to FERVENT.	
FERVENT	26.7.16	9.30 AM	obtained & marched via BOUQUE MAISON to LUCHEUX Cars picked up at LUCHEUX at 5.30 P.M. Capt KINNEST reported unwell	

WAR DIARY or INTELLIGENCE SUMMARY

Army Form C. 2118

Place	Date	Hour	Summary of Events and Information	Remarks and references to Appendices
LUCHEUX	26-7-16	1.30 pm	Unit marches bia HALLOY & THIEVRES to AUTHIE. Motor lorries from workshop.	
	26/7/16	6.30 pm	Unit arrived AUTHIE. - Billets undergone - Lt. BALLANTYNE. Signal Officer 59th Bgd. evacuated - shown him his home to route.	
AUTHIE	27/7/16		Conference at A.D.M.S. H.Qr. at J.26.central. Capt KENNEDY T.O.R. took over with advance parties K.15.B.3.4. Capt Taylor 1 Q.O.R. J.16.d.10.5. Inspected proposed new M.D.S. at I.10.c.6.6. Selected a new inspection room in AUTHIE U.11.095 opening station at I.16.central. Visited Corps Operating room at I.16.central. Visited A.D.S.'s at HEBUTERNE & SAILLY DELL - a few machine gun bullets coming over village of HEBUTERNE between 5-7 pm otherwise quiet	
	28/7/16		Visited COIGNEUX. Walk A.D.M.S. to select a new M.D.S. Capt TAYLOR withdrawn from J.16.d.10.5. advance party Q.O.R. & K.15.B.3.4. this morn abouts cancelled - Capt Taylor to remain J.16.d.10.5 to 62 to 7 Anl 6. Handed over A.D.S. at J.16.d.10.5. to No 35 C.C.S. Lt HARKIN & 7. O.R. sent to I.10.c.6.6. AUTHIE Hill Corps D.R.S. (hits in Wood)	
AUTHIE	28/July		Unit moved at 4 pm to I.10.c.6.6. AUTHIE K.15.B.3.4. Capt DAVIDSON to relieve	

Army Form C. 2118.

WAR DIARY
or
INTELLIGENCE SUMMARY.
(Erase heading not required.)

Place	Date	Hour	Summary of Events and Information	Remarks and references to Appendices
AUTHIE	All		visited areas around SAILLY DELL, ROSSIGNOL FARM (T.3.c.9.7) Euphon	
			found site for M.D.S. 800 yards	
	29.7.16		N.W. would turn to be carried up hill of new M.D.S. arranged for evacuation of wounded direct from SAILLY DELL by M.A.C.	
	30.7.16		A.D.M.S. visited HEBUTERNE with me — The A.D.S. there has been shelled during previous 24 hours — 1 shell coming in trench close to dug out. Report on damage to Corps sent out — for Commission to going up when finished.	
			Came on chance from any of Camps — making enquiries re D.E.	
	31.7.16	1314 7 And. 2M. at 6 am	M.M.S Came in during morning	
			D.D.M.S. 14th Corps & M.M.S. reinforced — total 2 Officers 42 men —	
			HEBUTERNE. A.D.S. — 1 Officer 174 men	
			SAILLY DELL. — —	
			— 1 Officer —	
			— 1 Ration; 6 Cart Anti gas clement	
			500 Ration drawings; 300 Reserve Rations and up to HEBUTERNE 16 Gallows Kerosene	
			to 4 ambulances twitches dug outs gas proof.	
			Latrines; Carpenters tools	

31/7/16

A.J. O'Brien
A.L. Lt Colonel
Comdg 60th Field Ambulance

WAR DIARY
or
INTELLIGENCE SUMMARY.

Army Form C. 2118.

60 60 F.A.

War Diary
for
August 1916
of
60th Field Ambulance
O.C. Been serving at
Sept Been
A.C. Osburn
Lt Col Commanding

COMMITTEE FOR THE
MEDICAL HISTORY OF THE W.
Date -5 OCT. 1916

Place: [illegible]
Date: Aug 1916

WAR DIARY or INTELLIGENCE SUMMARY

Army Form C. 2118.

Place	Date	Hour	Summary of Events and Information	Remarks and references to Appendices
AUTHIE HILL T.10.c.6.6.			M.D.S. & D.R.S.	
	1.8.16		Position of Units midnight 31/7/16	
			M.D.S. T.10.c.6.6. (sheet 57d)	5 Officers 149 men
			A.D.S. (A) HEBUTERNE K.15.b.3.7	2 Officers 42 men (2nd sanitary section)
			(B) SAILLY DELL T.16.d.10.5	1 Officer 74 men Capt Taylor
			Patients in hospital 33 sick 1 wounded	{ 2 officers obtained 1. - & 7 O.R. send to 35 C.C.S. 6. 35 C.C.S. 5 men sent to Bath
			Continued - clearing M.D.S. & making roads	
			Lt HARMER & 5 men returned from 35th C.C.S. - 2 men being return there.	
	2.8.16		Capt KENNEDY returned from A.D.S. relieving 65	
			Lt HARKIN.	

Place	Date	Hour	Summary of Events and Information	Remarks and references to Appendices
I.10.c.6.6 AUTHUILE.	July 4th		6 men returned from ATHUILLE. Baths at I.16.a.5.8. Taken up to OKS Stretcher Hospital 89 patients (sick & wounded). Continued making roads — clearing camp for water supply &c.	I.O. Officer surveying
	5th		Visited Brigade Headquarters. Patients in DRS. 100 sick. Arrangements for twenty walk at O.And. Isolts.	
	6th		Visited Brigade HQuarters Patients in DRS 109 sick. Trench mortar at Saully Dell.	

WAR DIARY
or
INTELLIGENCE SUMMARY.
(Erase heading not required.)

Army Form C. 2118.

Place	Date	Hour	Summary of Events and Information	Remarks and references to Appendices
AUTHIE Hut	Aug 7.15		Lt DENNING reports for duty	
	Aug 8th		Reconnoitred road & in front of SAILLY as far as trolley railway run HEBUTERNE — this valley road from in front to below TRANVERSE — ruinous condition. Major R.B. BROWNE, Bg. Major 55th Regt admitted to Hosp. ill. R.B. in hospital to answer.	
	Aug 9th		Inspected by G.O.C. 20th Division — Gen'l satisfied — he has done a great deal of heavy work in commence the new roads ie & that Th place had been making anciet improved.	
Pry	11th		Visited HEBUTERNE and COURCELSEN. — dug out nearly finished. Reduced labour owing to 70.R. going into division as working parties. Lt.Col. Gladstyne Cham Sailly Dell.	

WAR DIARY
or
INTELLIGENCE SUMMARY.
(Erase heading not required.)

Army Form C. 2118.

Place	Date	Hour	Summary of Events and Information	Remarks and references to Appendices
AUTHIE HUT	Aug 12th		Capt Kirton relieves Capt Taylor at SAILLY DELL. Lt HARKIN returns from HEBUTERNE. Capt DAVIDSON returned at his own request at A.D.S. 112 took 6 wounded in DRS	
	Aug 13th		Went over site at Coigneux - started up to speedy clear up by evening. J.g.a. 10.2. new M.D.S. 50 Sch shelters &c. used up to A.D.S.	
	Aug 14th		Put up 2 huts at Coigneux. Clarke Gelson prepare Rain in Patings - Saw linen other Interpreters to Bern Hendrick by Farmer. Turned to G.P. Division order Beds & hang over 136 was 6 wounded in D.R.S.	
	Aug 15th		Saw ADMS. Second from reference wandering over A.D.S. at HEBUTERNE, COIGNEUX & SAILLY DELL. D.R.S. to be handed over to No. 4. A.D.S from M.9. to Auth. No. 9. Found took over COIGNEUX.	

WAR DIARY
or
INTELLIGENCE SUMMARY
(Erase heading not required.)

Army Form C. 2118.

Place	Date (April)	Hour	Summary of Events and Information	Remarks and references to Appendices
AUTHIE I.10.c.6.6	Aug 16th		Advance party from No 9 F. Amb. to A.D.S. HEBUTERNE. No 61 & 62 F. Amb. Sent in their kit to S.P.S. as they are moving into BEAUVAL. Cars allot by III Corps. A.D.S. HEBUTERNE to No 9 F. Amb O/C SAILLY DELL " " " " Handing over " " COIGNEUX " " "	
	17th		1 Officer T.O.R. arrived from No 4 F. Amb. and assumed duty. Visited BEAUVAL and selected site for F. Amb. 6.M. infectious ward in charge arranged for men fit for light duty to be sent on by Lorry Convoys now A.D.M.S of? Corps. 135 Pts in hospital Unit packing up to hand over all patients to No 4 F. Amb O.S. opening orders from A.D.M.S. in cob to BEAUVAL Motor nos? to march at 7am.	
BEAUVAL G.21.a.10.3 Sheet 59d	18th		Marched at 7 a.m. 100 patients brought over by Bus — 2nd F. Amb to BEAUVAL including 43 town cases to move to (29 lorry from III R.B.) Capt CHANDLER arrived for duty (returned unwounded) Opened Amal Hospital at BEAUVAL arrived at BEAUVAL 11-30 A.M. Saw A.D.M.S	

WAR DIARY
or
INTELLIGENCE SUMMARY.

Army Form C. 2118.

Place	Date	Hour	Summary of Events and Information	Remarks and references to Appendices
BEAUVAL	19.8.16	G.21.a.10.3	Horse Transport - Lieut & Lieut-Col - left at 9 a.m. marches to VILLERS BOCAGE by K.P. at 9.p.m KIRTON (fell whilst shaving). Lieut Capt. MULLAN & KENNEDY. visited BEAUVAL. L/Cpl Brown visited VILLERS BOCAGE – Drums surplus stores at BEAUVAL village.	
	20.8.16		All personnel entrained at 5.30 a.m. CANDAS STATION – In MERICOURT L'ABBÉ wh. Mob. Ambulance tyre left at 10 a.m. left Lozen arrived 1 P.M. wh. Mob. Ambulance MEAULTE – arriving 3.p.m. MERICOURT L'ABBE to MEAULTS – fed men in bivouac Personnel marched from striking inepassible – fed men – Roads very bad Billets allocated but striking inepossible Town Major. In Price N 9 born by overground all town bivouacked In o price N 9 born Every place Crowded.	
	21.8.16	F.21.6.7.3	CITADEL (shed Albert) Every place crowded. Orders 2/a marches to 1 NCO & Brown to draw Corps – Orders 2/c with dummy march – {Capt Davidson Hawkins L. Benning's Capt 2.Taylor & Liviano Clarke to C.M. Survey delin at 7.24 6. (to Transport) Clarke to 06 wh. Ten horses - equipment & club under L/Cpl Morey 06. G. N? 10 M.A.C. to be sent to mob. Ambulance at A.R. Cycle BEOMFAY FARM horses mrs Dr. our motor (6. G. No 10. M.A.C) visited BEOMFAY FARM 72 F P Amb. New orders G.O.G. 59 Bgd. - Orders to take charge. 06 Roan Divisiono conference will G.O.G F.29.d.77. & took over from 72.73. ℓ74 Field Amb Co	
	22.8.16		Marched to BEOMFAY FARM 4 p.m.	

WAR DIARY or INTELLIGENCE SUMMARY

Army Form C. 2118.

Place	Date	Hour	Summary of Events and Information	Remarks and references to Appendices
BERNAFAY FARM	22/6/16		Orders to 10th Commanding. Took over Rt & Lf Brigade personnel at BERNAY BEARER POSTS of F.29.d.7.7. Rt / Lf Brigade BEARER POSTS of BERNAFAY WOOD S.22.a.9.½ C.6. } 26th Bn 7 Bn A & Co BRIQUETERIE (BRICKYARD) A.4. b.6.4. – C.6. } 26th Bn 7 Bn A & Co Report Wood Difficulties with M.A.C. — long delays present — inquiries Report Wood difficulties Corps H.Q. the only remedy! Evacuate to CORPS H.Q. and S.O.R. Rgt. Pst well only C.6 1 stretcher Case Capt KENNEDY } Rt Rr Post 4/1 Vol " " 5 " " Capt KIRTON } (BRICKYARD) Capt FOAMS } Lt Pst & S.O.R. Right Post well only Camp at BRIQUETERIE COWE } Hd Br Post & S.O.R. now in Camp at BRIQUETERIE ROBERTS } (BERNAFAY) 15 Officers & 375 men R.A.M.C now in (Rt Quales & Trichus 6) JONES " Lt 188 Bearer Post & Bath Brigade (Rt Quales & Lock) accommodation invited boil evacuation & road very bad — Lock for 111 Brigade 2200 per hyd Spetula hon evacuation two — across Yard, Carry for 111 Brigade 2200 per hyd to wounded – evacuation (Chapel in MONTAUBAN) 1 hour killed (hound) 15 Officers & 6 Others	
	23/6/16		Casualty 161 OR & Others. MP.C arrangements no Car to 7 hours – remove Broke down again in M.P.C. arrangements between BERNAFAY & BRICKYARD Post Black in wounded	
	24/6/16			
	25/6/16		Pt Slight Wounds. Parties relieved at Post 120 men sent up – worked out Casing change prepared. Medical arrangement the 10. In S Corps Division & a copy & Lack Brigade For Division to do duty as C. Collecting Station Lt. HARKIN sent up to do duty as C. Collecting Station	

WAR DIARY
or
INTELLIGENCE SUMMARY.

Army Form C. 2118.

Place	Date	Hour	Summary of Events and Information	Remarks and references to Appendices
BROMLEY FARM	26.8.16		Visited both Brow Posts & Brigade H.Q. - Likely site for a new loading post on road W. of BERKLEY WOOD. - Inspects trench tramway from Lt. B? Post. Saw C.R.E. about laying a carpet to divert my working party & about overhead in L. Work. Casualties. O.R. 363 Officers 11 = 374 all ranks.	
	27.8/16		Fatal of 6 Officers Lt Roberts, Coue. Jones & Lft out post Adam. Kennedy (both wounded) & R.E. outpost. Men continue to be covered & delays in obtaining M.A.C. convoy wounded. - Saw Capt. Pellew & Majors Brigades (59"&61") = 266 arrivals. Casualties. 25F. O.R. & 13 Officers = . Saw C.R.E. reinforcement about reserve to loading huts.	

WAR DIARY
or
INTELLIGENCE SUMMARY.

Army Form C. 2118.

Place	Date	Hour	Summary of Events and Information	Remarks and references to Appendices
BRONFAY FARM.	28/8/16		Saw C.R.E. about Roads - Loading put shells in. Operation again postponed. Saw Capt Philpin re Sewers breakdown in 2nd M.C. evans - Beaufort 14 hours without car - 2 Officers & 236 wounded & gassed passed through post. 3 men wounded dying at Left Regt Landing Posts. Capt CRAWFORD came back to M.D.S. Capt LEAHY evacuated " KIRTON " to M.D.S. for 4 days rest " CHANDLER " to 7th D.C.L.I. to replace Capt. BURT. " JONES " " 12th R.B. " TOZER " " M.D.S. for examination. Profs. R. Ryads (S.S.4) & their examining Condre StaffCaptain sanitation. Joint difficulty with ads forty stretcher bearers Staff Captain 59th Bgde. notification of warden of supply, Bryd HQs Div Staff Captain 59th Bgde. Bristol bolts BEARER POSTS & Bryd HQs Div Staff Captain 59th Bgde. materials now loading tents. Every brick & rubble to Working workers returned via MARICOURT - road. 120 elks (china based Stn to 60th Brigade. Joined Boards passed — 120 elks (china based Stn to 60th Brigade MONTAUBAN are road improved through MONTAUBAN. Arrangements made with M.A.C. for all traffic except 4 horsed limbers through MONTAUBAN to motor cyclists & lace traffic. CULVERT. Arrangement made for permanent loading banks at Bronfay Camp — soon fell in camp owing to freq. breakage Enemy aeroplane	

WAR DIARY or INTELLIGENCE SUMMARY

Army Form C. 2118.

Place	Date	Hour	Summary of Events and Information	Remarks and references to Appendices
Stn. BEARER P.O.D.	29.9.16		Total casualties Bearer post + A.S.S. CARNOY Wounded O.R. 213. Officers 2 } 311. Sick O.R. 92. Officers 4 } Sgt. Major Stones led dismtd. 160 men, bivouc. & relief sab. 90 men left at 3 am for front line. Working parties to repair road through MONTAUBAN down to pioneer park loading post at CULVERT (No 2) at S.27.6.9.8. taking BERNAFAY WOOD road & unloading post at S.28.6.6. working parties constly. 2 or 3 & 2.9.9. heavy shellfire made it impossible to finish. Bearer post again very troublesome in M.D.C. enemy much machine gun fire. O/C Bearer Post again very perturbed — saw all C.R.E. mains, police all stretchers all probably due to heavy cavalry & roads. Enemy dispersed and charged? 8.9.8. positions & stone tower — and came into one of road trenches ? further postponement ? Report M.O.S. to inform me of again report patrol. ... 2.30 pm. enemy + Capt RAWSON Pad. Pritchard went to new 3 or 4 hour reconnoitring road in MONTAUBAN + trench leading from B.P. park in building village work to out park — Enemy began storing + in building village work hut + shelling house — Pte Gaskell struck by flying shell bowling alarm, carried in House H. over H.E. shell bowling over (4 pm) Capt Rawl knocked over — hit Evans builder bagans place. No car sent to MORVAL for passages on unfavourable — expect to post passenger at Mt A.E. Carnoy Road. T C.Pats. k.k. See Capt PEILE in LINZEE is broken in (on duty)	 Wounded 10. } 14. Killed 2. } Sick 1 accidents — Enemy shells about 10 pm to 2am.

Total casualties arrived.

Army Form C. 2118.

WAR DIARY
or INTELLIGENCE SUMMARY.
(Erase heading not required.)

Place	Date	Hour	Summary of Events and Information	Remarks and references to Appendices
DIVISIONAL BEARER POST (BRONFAY FARM)	30.8.16		(Operations again postponed on account of "Road & Weather.") Messages received during night from O/C R.E Bigads Beau: Post & from O.C No 10 M.A.C. becoming impassable to that roads from MARICOURT to BRICKYARD (2000 yards) motor traffic - arranged for H.Amb waggons to be in readiness - but on bridge was always wind Asdus asking that services of Corps R.E. might be sent forward on account. By road repair O/C Lt Bigads "Bunn post" report our working party at 500y² S.t Major Stance & O/C Lt Bigads Beau West Coll. 2 BERNAFAY WOOD at 500y² 60 men have repairing rains on BERNAFAY bridge by R.E. swept in bay & shell hole which would be completed also by our working party kept exploits proof shell completed to attended two loading pad opposite R. Pat. to town in & roads back end into to others bank stretcher also Ramp to car R. Pat. party heavily shelled - L Patschild stream of traffic opposite 8 stretcher cars. hill accommodate arrange during noon under a Tarpaulin for men location by two - hour returns from BEQUVAL with Pt. Bearers & stores. - T. K. 7 day Clothes 360 Stretcher events for urgent - now Medical comforts available to Bearer Post before from Reserve - T.Key have now Reserve 1(1) Dressings 1000 in each & shell dressings also (2) Rations 200. Iron Rations & know of (3) Stretcher 100. + Satchets where covered (4) Blankets 100. (5) Comforts tools in bir. (6) arrangement for Hot soup to be valence. + 3 Officers + 40 Bearers + (53) total but not including availably oils

WAR DIARY
or
INTELLIGENCE SUMMARY.
(Erase heading not required.)

Army Form C. 2118.

Place	Date	Hour	Summary of Events and Information	Remarks and references to Appendices
Div¹ BEARER Posts.	30.8.16		F.29.d.7 - Albert - Weather outlook bad - Operations again postponed bring S.S.O. in touch of Reun & Cake, bad roads a good deal responsible difficulties continue with M.A.C. Casualties. 6.9.a.m - 291 OR. 07 officers wounded { 416 122 OR. 2 - sick Heavy Bombardment 3 p.m. very heavy rain August floods create difficulties continue in river. have been carried away 7 am at Brigades relief carried out 5th Div MA Lifting 1 officer { 335 wounded 215 OR. wounded 1 officer 118. O.R. sick	
	31.8.16.		Casualties. 6.9.a.m today (24 hours) Our 9 Field Fd securing owing to Bad weather. Mr Bombardment Arrangements being made for Bearer posts Capt Tredegar by Rd Rd Tredegar Capt Taylor Rd Rd relief of 108 even vSt officers and & Beaver post M.A.C. car comes full Reun & Cake obtained - but it appears any imbalance last Fellow called Sloting that it did not comply to & acl of x use MARICOURT- BRICQUETERIE Road) - 1 NCO impends 60 Personnel arrange for 2 Horse Ambulance wagons units. - 2 men carrulty 6am wounded Funerals at Goodwill 5 pm	

A.E. O'Burn
A.E. O'Burn Ambas A.C. Lefime
O.C. 6th Fred O'Burn Ambu Lefime
Divisional Ross Posts
(Bearer Divisions)

Army Form C. 2118.

WAR DIARY
or
INTELLIGENCE SUMMARY.

(Erase heading not required.)

Instructions regarding War Diaries and Intelligence Summaries are contained in F. S. Regs., Part II. and the Staff Manual respectively. Title pages will be prepared in manuscript.

Place	Date	Hour	Summary of Events and Information	Remarks and references to Appendices

Army Form C. 2118

WAR DIARY
or
INTELLIGENCE SUMMARY
(Erase heading not required.)

140/1794

WAR DIARY
— OF —
60th Field Ambulance
(& Sgt. Bean reviewing)
— FOR —
SEPTEMBER — 1916

COMMITTEE FOR THE
MEDICAL HISTORY OF THE WAR
Date 30 OCT. 1915

Ashburn
Pvt. rome

WAR DIARY
or
INTELLIGENCE SUMMARY.

Army Form C. 2118.

Place	Date	Hour	Summary of Events and Information	Remarks and references to Appendices
	1916 1st September		Position of Unit midnight 31/8/16 – 1/9/16.	
			Trench number. Other ranks 150 All Ranks 60% 2 Front	1 Bow Down in Furn Blow
			" " 149 " " 6 " "	
			Machine gunners 10th Machine (includes 150ft men) " " 62 " "	
			Grenades – 91	
			Divisional Bomb Post near BEAUFAY FARM.	Sheet 57 bis F.29.d.77
			LH Brigade Bomb Posts } BERNAFAY WOOD. 3 Officers + 54 men } S.22.d.9.1.	
			RH Brigade Bomb Post } BRIQUETERIE (BRICKYARD) 2 Officers + 54 men } A.4.6.6.4.	
			Loading points at CULVERT. S.27.6.0.8.	
			INCO 17 mm	
			CASEMENT TRENCH A A.4.6.44.	
			& BRICKYARD	
			Pt. Beal 60" F.A. { wounded } t/c Exam " "	

WAR DIARY
or
INTELLIGENCE SUMMARY
(Erase heading not required.)

Army Form C. 2118

Place	Date	Hour	Summary of Events and Information	Remarks and references to Appendices
Beaufoy Farm	F.29.d.0.6.			
	1.9.	16	M.O. 7th Fusiliers wounded — Capt Massey sent in his relief — Reports sent immediately & was sent to C.M. 87th Bn — East Farm 627 yards to 7th Fusiliers to await Capt Black's arrival from 113.57.Mule.	1/c 627 yards
			Pte. William Hills } 627 yards L/c Slater wounded }	
			9 wounded 60" Coy on 3yd. Capt Pridmore wounded. Replaced by Capt Taylor from Bronfer Farm Capt Taylor relieved by Lt. Harken from WW C. Post. Capt Robert to WW C.P.	
			At Beau Mots McGyven Capt Taylor & Reid. 65 O.R. including Cookspost	
			Remotary Capt Pridmore Trulley, Massey 75 O.R.	including Cookspost
			Consulta. Officer 9. OR 465. (17 game).	

WAR DIARY or INTELLIGENCE SUMMARY

Army Form C. 2118

Place	Date	Hour	Summary of Events and Information	Remarks and references to Appendices
Bronfay Farm F.29.d.9.6	2.9.16		Capt Hoskin went to W.O.P. Pte Barnes killed (60 & 23 Amb) Capt Black returned on arrival Pte Rowe Pte Blakeborough 3 F.A. 113 & 2nd Aust. Brick row Bernafay (only road & tracks) Casualties: Officers 7 O.R. 396 Regt. Aid Posts reported: 7th KOYLI – A.5.6.8.2 20th Sco Rau – L.1.C.5.7 38th Bgde. R.F.A. – A.3.0.7.4 6th Cam. d'Rouge S.24.C.9.8. Ft Halfway put in Trones Wood at S.23.d.6.3 Heavy shelling of Montary road & Maricourt area Water supply of water – supply by R.E. not following cable 10 p.m.	

WAR DIARY or INTELLIGENCE SUMMARY

Army Form C. 2118

Place	Date	Hour	Summary of Events and Information	Remarks and references to Appendices
Bronfay Farm	F.29.2.8.6			
	3.9.	16.	Day of moves attack along whole Army front. Lost between visited posts at 6 am. Visited posts at Vignon individual between 10 a.m. & 9 p.m. Journeyed going well Connaught Avenue was offered to Rum, Sgt Tate R.F.C. absent from his post times [illeg] a prisoner. Several casualties among R.A.M.C. personnel 25 OR, 61 & 66 at 111th Field Amb. Bayopte Wood Post 14 & 116 OR foot our Connaught 6 OR Lost Middleau recovering them in evacuating wounded or freeze.	
		6 p.m.	Lost Prestam wounded — Lost Irwin sent up to take his place. " Murphy Connaught Rangers wounded. " Knipe sent up to Connaught Rangers to relieve. Capts Black & Knipe	
			Casualties Officers 19 OR 571.	Col.
			30 Roussians arrived — fell in with steel helmets & sent to Corps Pat. Bondsmen old great coat. Bowden & Clarke in charge there. —	

WAR DIARY or INTELLIGENCE SUMMARY

Army Form C. 2118

(Erase heading not required.)

Place	Date	Hour	Summary of Events and Information	Remarks and references to Appendices
Brufay Farm			F.29.d.8.6 60th Field Amb.	Otter Field Amb. by Letter
	4.9.16		Casualties R.A.M.C. Since arrival at this Post 9 Kms	5 killed & 3 drowned

Killed. Pt Gaskell 29/8/16
" Leviss 3/9/16

Wounds
Plough 24/8/16
Stobie 27/8/16
Yk. Barn 31/8/16
Beal "
Brogen "
Willett 1.9.16 (gum)
Borough "
Galloway "
Henshaw "
Gregory "
Blackburn "
Temm 4/9/16
Ayres 2/9/16
Blackwood 2/9/16

Convoy
Officers 33
O.R. 672
Buckyard   Capt Dennis, Lady Kennedy Kenton & 143 men
Benrofay   3 Officers 101st & 190 men   excluding about 150 founded wounded
Wakin (wounded)

Bowling Post Cpl Sparrow LC t P.Burch
returns   Cpl Baker t P.Clarke

WAR DIARY
INTELLIGENCE SUMMARY
(Erase heading not required.)

Army Form C. 2118

Place	Date	Hour	Summary of Events and Information	Remarks and references to Appendices
Bronfay Farm	4/9/16 (continued)		113 7.O.R and 3 officers +114 men reports for duty. Capt Uchida. — Ferguson — Moffatt } +114 men sent to "Bernafay" known for duty — Thoma Capt Mueller 070 men left on furr. 2/11/16 Total to B. Pats — Brigadier twenty childless about 5pm — was taken to 2/11/16 30 Bouzincourt casualties sent to D.A.D.S Citadel. 2 men sent to Pronown Cas 1 " 112 way. Batty #65 Position of Brigades from what we are evacuating wounds is now as follows: 59th Brigade ERNOY — MONTAUBAN Rd (Cellar) 60" —"— BERNAFAY WOOD Pot (North) 61" —"— CARNOY. (Tod House) 47ᵃ —"— BRICK ALLEY 48" —"— DUMMY TRENCH 49" —"— BRICQUETERIE	

WAR DIARY
or
INTELLIGENCE SUMMARY.

Place	Date	Hour	Summary of Events and Information	Remarks and references to Appendices
BRONFAY FARM F.29.d.8.6	5.9.16		Evacuating being carried on continuously following units are now in Camps under my command	
			113th Fd.Amb. Bearer Division - Officers 4 OR 114 rTransport mules 3 HH horses	
			112 " " " - " 4 OR 106 " " " 3 "	
			111 " " " - " 4 OR 107 " " " 3 "	
			61st " " - " 4 OR 105 " " " 3 "	
			0 " " - 1 Tow'd Oddicon - 1 OR 15 " " " 1	
			62nd " " - Beaucourt - 3 OR 108 " " " 3	
			60 " " - 1 Tow'd End 3 } OR 119 " " " 3	
			3 }	
			22 OR 674 - 18	
			M.S.Md 16 O.R. 1 Lt. Col Penner visited camp for debut & overnight	
			Casualties sick Offs 7 OR 21 Carnoy Bucquoy Beaudry pr.	
			wounded Offs 27 OR 308.	

WAR DIARY
or
INTELLIGENCE SUMMARY.
(Erase heading not required.)

Army Form C. 2118.

Place	Date	Hour	Summary of Events and Information	Remarks and references to Appendices
Bronfay Farm F.29.d.8.6	6.9.16		During day handed over to Lt.Col Bennett O.C. 113" D=Mn.b. Charge of Camp Beau & Lindsey PMB — & all cracualing arrangements including shop, plans, orders, &c.	
		Noon	66: 2nd Amb marched to R.M.7 6.8.4 - Bois de Taille.	
			Notice sq!. To b; army van to O.C. 62 w. D=Mn.b.	
			Orders sent to Loch Pus & Philip to move	
Bois de Taille	7.9.16		Men resting	
			Staff of 10 P.M.M.C. now arrived, also 3 R.F.C. of 140 Horse	
			All routes on 1½ gallon of water daily.	
			Capt Reid with Beau Stream & 1 Tent subaltern arrived.	

Army Form C. 2118.

WAR DIARY
or
INTELLIGENCE SUMMARY.
(Erase heading not required.)

Instructions regarding War Diaries and Intelligence Summaries are contained in F. S. Regs., Part II. and the Staff Manual respectively. Title pages will be prepared in manuscript.

Place	Date	Hour	Summary of Events and Information	Remarks and references to Appendices
	8.9.16		(K.17.B.5.3)	
BOIS DE TAILLE			Bttlle marched at 6pm. to CORBIE arrived 10 pm.	Marches via MORLANCOURT.
CORBIE.	9.9.16		Proposed draft of A.S.C. & R.M.C. starts cleaning Regt. Shoulder Braces	O.4.a.8.2
CORBIE 10.9.16			Training & Shoulder Braces	
	11.9.16		Marched at 8.30 a.m. to BOIS DE TAILLE found Bois in a very foul condition — reports to G.O.C. and several other inspection visits to Coy's, Commanders. Drew up Rules for Standing Orders for Camp, Brigade, & to work By.Major	
BOIS DE TAILLE	12.9.16		Cleaned up Camp continuing training Running and establishing Lewis gun training. Capt Taylor takes 2.Off+Sgmjrs G.M.D.S.	
	13.9.16		Continued work at Camp	
	14.9.16		Marched to ARBRE FOURCHE at 2.30 p.m. (Happy Valley) Bois no Captain Townsend	

Army Form C. 2118.

WAR DIARY
or
INTELLIGENCE SUMMARY.
(Erase heading not required.)

Instructions regarding War Diaries and Intelligence Summaries are contained in F. S. Regs., Part II. and the Staff Manual respectively. Title pages will be prepared in manuscript.

Place	Date	Hour	Summary of Events and Information	Remarks and references to Appendices
ARBRE FOURCHU F.27.c.3.3.	14.9.16		arrived 4 p.m. from Bois de Taille + bivouacked	
	15.9.16	6 a.m.	marched to CARNOY SOUTH CAMP arrived 9 a.m. (F.23.d.5.3) + bivouacked	
CARNOY.	16.9.16		Lt. Whitehead reports his arrival for duty	
			marched at 4 a.m. to Talus Bois A.14.6.9.5. marches from Talus Bois at 9 p.m. to A.D.S. at S.30.6.6.6. + loading Post GUINCHY (T.13.C.9.1.) Took over from Guards at 2 a.m. 360 cases during next 24 hours. Ground very heavy. A.D.S. rough + inadequate protection	Capt. Lawson Muirhead Flemming Whitely at A.D.S
17.9.16 GUILLEMONT.			Transport + A.D.S. to BRIQUETERIE LINES (A.10.6.2.8. evacuation worked well — 16 sehr men from M.D.S. for stretcher work Capt. Johnston, wounded — Lt. Whitehead took over charge of 10th R.B.	
GUILLEMONT.	18.9.16.		Capue etc. + Capt. Garrett, Hayman, Coulson killed Carbin, Wood Major Griffin, Griffiths, Brooks, alkinson (capel wounded). Evacuated collected from Coles etc. many casualties from to Division. Heavy rain. Conditions very bad + troops miserable	

WAR DIARY
or
INTELLIGENCE SUMMARY.
(Erase heading not required.)

Army Form C. 2118.

Place	Date	Hour	Summary of Events and Information	Remarks and references to Appendices
Guillemont	19.9.16		Capt Mullan & Kennedy relieved by Capt Denny & Davidson. Fords Cars are only working up to S.29.d.7.5. Pte Burn killed. Kerr, Wilson & Down wounded. Fair number of Casualties. Loaders Post moved back to T.19.a.9.4 formerly at T.19.c.4.2. Heavy rain – ground impassable, clearing out wounded. M.A. wagons with 10 horses – getting bogged, are detained now at T.19.c. Quid T.19.c.7.3	
	20.9.16		Capt Taylor relieves Capt Lennern. – Denny with reserves A.D.S. to S.29.d.8.4 – visited A.D.S.	
	21.9.16		Heavy rain continue. Lt Denny sent back sick, replaced by Capt Keelan. Cars can now only land near A.D.S. — All effort to collect M.A. Coppers Corps at T.B.c.9.1. engaging orders to be relieved by Guards division at 9 a.m. tomorrow	

WAR DIARY
or
INTELLIGENCE SUMMARY.
(Erase heading not required.)

Army Form C. 2118.

Place	Date	Hour	Summary of Events and Information	Remarks and references to Appendices
SAND PITS	22.9.16		E.18.D.2.4. marched at 12.20 Noon to MORLANCOURT — Men billeted in town. N.C.O. & Officers in meadow. K.C.3.6.6. Capt Davidson to Mess charge of 10th R.A. Lt Harken sick (jaundice) Lt Stirring evacuated. All Rest of Platoon	
MORLANCOURT	23.9.16		(K.8.6.10.6.) Lt Col. Blacklock to Corps for Relation. Men cleaning weapons etc etc. Recommendation for Gallantry sent in. 1 Officer & O.R. from 60 & 9 R.B.	
	24.9.16		Divine Service. Holbeck. — Capt Cowan returned from M.D.S. Capt Harken down in his place. Capt McArthur reported for duty from England. Strength 9 officers 8 men reported for duty. Repelling & Blankets Available — Stores &c.	

1577 Wt.W10791/1773 500,000 1/15 D. D. & L. A.D.S.S./Forms/C. 2118.

Army Form C. 2118.

WAR DIARY
or
INTELLIGENCE SUMMARY.
(Erase heading not required.)

Instructions regarding War Diaries and Intelligence Summaries are contained in F. S. Regs., Part II. and the Staff Manual respectively. Title pages will be prepared in manuscript.

Place	Date	Hour	Summary of Events and Information	Remarks and references to Appendices
MORLANCOURT	25.9.16		Message sent O.C. Bearer section re: derelict H.A. Wagon 7 runners returning relieved by Corps M. Dressing station.	
		4 p.m.	Bgde. moved to Happy Valley. F.27.c.3.3	
		6 p.m.	bivouacked in Happy Valley.	
HAPPY VALLEY	26.9.16		Issued 20 stretchers to each Regtl Brigade = 80. (38 were afterwards abandoned when Bgd. had moved off.) sent 6 Bgr. of major 8 stretcher Bearers and 6 each Regt. also stretcher Capt "Kenny" sent to relieve Capt Townsend 11:15 A.M.	
		3 p.m.	marched to BRICQUETERIE (bivouac) 5:30 p.m. Capt. MacArthur + 6 men sent to W.W.C.P. nr MALTZ HORN FARM	A.6.a.central
			visited MALTZ HORN FARM. 7 p.m. good dugout - but few wounds come there.	
BRICQUETERIE	27.9.16		6.2 & 6.1.a. Lt. Trimb. Bivouacked alongside. Sgt Ewyn Stone sent back to Bronfay Farm C.M.S. relieve Pte Lt. Walfield Massey and Pte Lt. Statham to join advanced Bric section	

Place	Date	Hour	Summary of Events and Information	Remarks and references to Appendices
BRIQUETERIE A.4.d.2.2.				
	28.9.16		Capt Kennedy relieves Capt Townsend in Med charge of WKFRR Capt Townsend to duty with 60th 2 Fd at Corps M.D.S. Capt McARTHUR reladmined as decorum from MALTZHORN FARM dugouts. – 57 Brigade HQ now Arrowhead Copse to CARNOY.	
	29.9.16		Lt Ph Waite Westfield dispatch to England in accordance with instructions from G.H.Q. Lt PAYNE at HARWICH to form the convoy relief. Lt HARKIN evacuated sick with dyspepsia (ex Cdn M.D.S.). Lt GIVEN reports on duty on arrival from convoy.	

Army Form C. 2118.

WAR DIARY
or
INTELLIGENCE SUMMARY.
(Erase heading not required.)

Place	Date	Hour	Summary of Events and Information	Remarks and references to Appendices
BRICQUETERIE	30.9.16		A.A.d 22 Beau Brisjour H.R. Morgan – salvage from shell hole near GINCHY. Lt. R. Govan took over one chain of 10th R.B. tree Lt Whelan who reported sick last night some explosive last night Sgt Major A. Spence. wounded and Lewis. Lt. and on Sgt. Major arrived from M.D.S. Capts Lawson, Kirton. Taylor Officers now present with wound are Capts Townsend at Coy H.Q and Capt Millan, (McArthur) & Lieut & Capt Townsend at Bronfay Farm	
		No 3/13N/C	W.C. Davis promoted Corporal — Granted Military Medal for his courageous conduct under war gas on 17/8. Kept at GINCHY.	

N.C. Osburn
Lt. Colonel
P.M.C.
Comdg 60: Field Ambulance

Army Form C. 2118.

WAR DIARY
or
INTELLIGENCE SUMMARY.
(Erase heading not required.)

WAR DIARY
OF
60th FIELD AMBULANCE
FOR
October 1916

COMMITTEE FOR THE
MEDICAL HISTORY OF THE WAR
Date -9 DEC. 1916

Army Form C. 2118

WAR DIARY
or
INTELLIGENCE SUMMARY.
(Erase heading not required.)

Instructions regarding War Diaries and Intelligence Summaries are contained in F. S. Regs., Part II. and the Staff Manual respectively. Title pages will be prepared in manuscript.

Place	Date	Hour	Summary of Events and Information	Remarks and references to Appendices
BRICQUETERIE	1 Oct 1916		POSITION OF UNITS A.4.d.22 BEARER Division In Bivouacks. Officer O.C. Lieut Lawson. Kirton Taylor TENT DIVISION Rect & Corp M.D.S. BRONFAY FARM F.29.d.6.6 Officer Capt Mullan McArthur Townsend - Surgt. 5F Bgr N.P. CARNOY 20 Dn H.P. FORKED TREE. Men resting - twenty.3 in charge erecting graves - filling shell holes - washing cloths the sanitary work. 6 officers 7 N.C.O.'s bivouacks near.	Albert column shut to trains.

WAR DIARY
or
INTELLIGENCE SUMMARY.
(Erase heading not required.)

Army Form C. 2118

Place	Date	Hour	Summary of Events and Information	Remarks and references to Appendices
BRIQUETERIE	2.10.16		Enemy shelling camp over – a few casualties near us. Men cleaning kit & wagons. Lt Whitehead evacuated sick on 1st wnt from C.M.D.S.	
	3.10.16		Capt Cowan sick not hospt. we are a S/Sergt (NS/Sergt Kent) Con al Aucun only 2 officers Capt Kirton & Taylor & 2 wnts.	
	4.10.16	—	Battle horse and arriving T.7. Selected a site for artillery horse pant at T.7.a 2–6. 8 men & 1 NCO sent this eft ened equipment – HQ Rn & dug in fort – some shelling NE corner Delville wood. 2 herts. A.D.S.	

WAR DIARY or INTELLIGENCE SUMMARY

Army Form C. 2118.

Place	Date	Hour	Summary of Events and Information	Remarks and references to Appendices
BRICQUETERIE	5/10/16		During night 4/5 + 5/6 59th Bgd moved into position with No 5 at S.6.d.8.1 (?). Capt Taylor + 55 other ranks (wounded) at 12 a.m. (midnight) to ADS at Bernafay Wood to work under Colonel Gill there. Bearers to proceed by relays to Bearer post at N.32.c.6.4 and evacuate wounded ? 59 Bgde. Cavalry Patrons H.A. Waggons to work from ADS to Patrons to Cocoa Trench at S.17.c.8.2. The O.O. from Brigade re report of their position received at Capt M.O.S. moved to A.13.b.3.8. A.13.b.6.3.8. + W.b. CP at S.28.c.8.4 + No.10. M.A.O. Moved in to F.9.a.9.6 near Fricourt. Not many casualties - some shelling ? Delville Wood + Bernafay - Montauban Valley (North). Artillery Bd Post changed from T.7.a.2.2 to T.7.d.6.3 to shorten carry for Bearers. Weather very bad. Heavy rain - roads + footpaths almost impassable. H.A. Waggons continue working to Delville Wood T.18.c.8.10. Bearers disposed as follows — Artll + Bearer Post 9, Brigade (4 regt) 32, Bearer post at N.32.c.6.4. 50.

Army Form C. 2118.

WAR DIARY
or
INTELLIGENCE SUMMARY.
(Erase heading not required.)

Place	Date	Hour	Summary of Events and Information	Remarks and references to Appendices
BRIQUETERIE	6.10.16		Weather extremely bad – took ourselves fortunately very few casualties.	
			Camp again shelled – obliged to vacate temporarily – were put into dug out in old german trench – but these are all caving in. Arrangements completed with O.C. 62nd Bn for Captain Taylor and 50 of my bearers to relieve Cruikshank as we to continue to collect from divisional artillery.	

WAR DIARY
or
INTELLIGENCE SUMMARY

Army Form C. 2118.

Place	Date	Hour	Summary of Events and Information	Remarks and references to Appendices
BRICQUETERIE	7.10.16		Relief completed last night. Capt McArthur & Capt Taylor & teams returned - scout them at Artillery Beam Pat when we were relieved. Coll OC. 62nd 2. H.Q. Horse. 139th H.Q. at DUMMY TRENCH S.23.C	
		7 pm	Lamp again shelled - men in Canada dugouts. Casualties nom rumour in front line.	
		11 P.M.	O.C. 62 nd requests assistance. 1 Officer & 11 other ranks + 33 bearers sent to A.D.S. Beaufry Wood.	
	8.10.16		9. OR still at Artillery Beam Pat. Thes relief to move out bryside at 11 a.m. - no 6/bs Artillery Beam on Relief by 62 n 12 hours late to OC. 62nd. Weather very bad - roads almost impassable - marched chiefly 11 am via Montauban - CARNOY - MAMETZ - FRICOURT to billet in MÉAULTE	
MÉAULTE			Note received Capt McArthur that he has been relieved and is on his way to report cond.	
	9.10.16	10.30 a.m.	Marched from MÉAULTE at 9.30 a.m. to Billets in VILLE-SUR-ANCRE - arrived Capt McArthur & Rearly and to 62.y field ambulance arrived at 4 pm	

WAR DIARY
or
INTELLIGENCE SUMMARY.
(Erase heading not required.)

Army Form C. 2118.

Place	Date	Hour	Summary of Events and Information	Remarks and references to Appendices
VILLE-SUR-ANCRE.	9.10.16		E.25.d.2.0. R.V.C. under Canvas. Ground in very bad state. Congratulatory Telegram to 20 Division from 4th Army Commander on their good work & success on the Somme front.	
	10.10.16		Lt. Adye-Curran joins for duty. Proceeded to CARNOY. C.M.D.S. Classes began for Stretcher Bearers	
	11.10.16		Lt. Edmonds joins for duty – D.D.M.S. notified as duly on arrival of new Quarter Master.	
	12.10.16		Relieved? Parade by Corps Commander inspection. Classes & lectures for Stretcher bearers continued	

Army Form C. 2118.

WAR DIARY
or
INTELLIGENCE SUMMARY.
(Erase heading not required.)

Instructions regarding War Diaries and Intelligence Summaries are contained in F.S. Regs., Part II. and the Staff Manual respectively. Title pages will be prepared in manuscript.

Place	Date	Hour	Summary of Events and Information	Remarks and references to Appendices
VILLE-SUR-ANCRE	E.25.d.2.0.			
	13.10.16		Application for extra mass to A.S.C. & Letters to D.D.R. McMurry Special leave for Corporal Langdon & Pte Callen refused by Gen Inspection by Corps Commander & Brig Commander — High praise given to all ranks for the work and for their qualities turn-out & drill. Capt Browne evacuated sick (hyperhydrosis.)	
	14.10.16		Kit Inspection - Capt KENNEDY & TAYLOR to C.M.D.S. Capt TOWNSEND return to H.K.R.R. Capt MULAN to Head Quarters. Sketches drawn from Bydo	
	15.10.16		Cleaning repairing kit. two-georgs Cleaning repairing waggons. Lib Lecture to Personnel by Lt Schwerdt.	
	16.10.16		Capt KIRTON + 2 men to leave.	
	17.10.16		S.B. Classes continued. cleaning kit, waggons	

WAR DIARY
or
INTELLIGENCE SUMMARY.

(Erase heading not required.)

Army Form C. 2118.

Place	Date	Hour	Summary of Events and Information	Remarks and references to Appendices
	18.10.16			
VILLE SUR ANCRE			Orders to march at 11 a.m. (horse) marches via TREUX-BUIRE billets in FRANVILLERS. C. 29. 9.3.3. sheet 62 (D). ref 6. 21 C.C.S. at CORBIE.	
FRANVILLERS	19.10.16		Heavy Rain. S.B. clearing pack equipment.	
FRANVILLERS	20.10.16		Marched 8 a.m. via LA HOUSSOYE – PONT NOYELLES – QUERIEU to ALLONVILLE order ne 2 6 roofs. A.D. Boots from midnight 20/21st Division now attached to 8th Corps.	
ALLONVILLE	21.10.16		Capt Mullen + 2 OR to learn. Marched at 9.30 a.m from billets in Allonville via POULAINVILLE – LONGPRÉ – ARGŒUVRES – St SAUVEUR – AILLY – BREILLY to PICQUIGNY.	
PICQUIGNY	22.10.16		Inoculation of Brigade resumed – cleaning out new billets. Parting visit PICQUIGNY – billet SO – Need of maintcial.	
"	23.10.16		Cleaning Billet. cleaning and mending kit + saddlery. cleaning waggon sorting out equipment &c. Inspection of Transport by I.O.M. at 2 p.m.	

Army Form C. 2118

WAR DIARY
or
INTELLIGENCE SUMMARY.

(Erase heading not required.)

Instructions regarding War Diaries and Intelligence Summaries are contained in F.S. Regs., Part II. and the Staff Manual respectively. Title pages will be prepared in manuscript.

Place	Date	Hour	Summary of Events and Information	Remarks and references to Appendices
PICQUIGNY	24.10.16		Lieut Irwin Capt Kennedy, Taylor & Lt. Relf - Curran arrive.	in 2 men
			reports missing. 2nd Lieut Irwin taking Owens Report to H.Q.M. 2 missing men	
	25.10.16		Capt Kennedy to relieve Capt Stephenson & 11th R.B.	
			Capt Taylor & 2 men on leave	
	26.10.16		Pt Kelly & Pt Bagley approved by Police in Amiens - absent	
			without leave - on the line & march - remanded to await trial - trial recd	
	27.10.16		R.A.M.C. visited ambulance -	
	28.10.16		2 pm Instruction for Stretcher Bearers from Brigade.	
			4 groups daily inspection of billets by Interpreter + Caretaker & owner)	
	29.10.16		Capt Watson returns from leave	
	30.10.16		Sgt Armitage & Pte Brown awarded Military Medal	
	31.10.16		Orders to move recd - Gas Cancelled	

A.C. Osborn
Capt.
Commanding 60 D.T. Amb.

Army Form C. 2118.

WAR DIARY
or
INTELLIGENCE SUMMARY.

(*Erase heading not required.*)

Instructions regarding War Diaries and Intelligence Summaries are contained in F. S. Regs., Part II. and the Staff Manual respectively. Title pages will be prepared in manuscript.

Place	Date	Hour	Summary of Events and Information	Remarks and references to Appendices

1577 Wt.W10791/1773 500,000 1/15 D. D. & L. A.D.S.S./Forms/C. 2118.

Army Form C. 2118

WAR DIARY
or
INTELLIGENCE SUMMARY.
(Erase heading not required.)

WAR DIARY
OF
60th 7th Amb.
FOR
Novr 1916.

Vol 16.

COMMITTEE FOR THE
MEDICAL HISTORY OF THE WAR
Date −3 JAN. 1917

Army Form C. 2118

WAR DIARY
or
INTELLIGENCE SUMMARY.
(Erase heading not required.)

Instructions regarding War Diaries and Intelligence Summaries are contained in F.S. Regs., Part II. and the Staff Manual respectively. Title pages will be prepared in manuscript.

Place	Date	Hour	Summary of Events and Information	Remarks and references to Appendices
PICQUIGNY.	1.11.16		POSITION OF Unit. Billet No. 50. N side of Main Street (chateau). Transport lines ch factory near Parcel N side. Present with unit O.C. Capt KIRTON McARTHUR Lt Edwards & A/Cpl Curran Cpl TAYLOR on leave Mullan on leave KENNEDY Temp? July 11 4RB Maintenance & Sgt Major — (Vacancies). 2nd Major Brennan sums Lt A/Cpl Curran took over charge ? 11th R.B from Cpl Kennedy	
	2.11.16		Marched to billets in FOUDRINOY. — inspected on route by E.O.C. 20th Bgm. — D. McGuinnis — returned to Unit from F.S.C.M.	
FOUDRINOY.	4.11.16		Capt Mullan returned from leave —	

T2134. Wt. W708—776. 500000. 4/15. Sir J. C. & S.

Army Form C. 2118

WAR DIARY
or
INTELLIGENCE SUMMARY.
(Erase heading not required.)

Instructions regarding War Diaries and Intelligence Summaries are contained in F. S. Regs., Part II. and the Staff Manual respectively. Title pages will be prepared in manuscript.

Place	Date	Hour	Summary of Events and Information	Remarks and references to Appendices
FOUDRINOY	5.11.16		O.C. on leave.	
	6.11.16		Capt MOORE reports his arrival returns - Capt Ayre-Curran went to No 23 General Hospital - 11th RB	
	7.11.16			
	8.11.16		Marched to PICQUIGNY.	
PICQUIGNY	9.11.16		2nd Lt Taylor returned from leave - Capt McMillan took over duty Capt McMillan - Capt Townsend proceeding on leave.	
	10.11.16		11th KRR. - Capt Stephenson returns from leave & Capt Moore returned Ambulance from 11th R.B.	
	11.11.16		Lt Gordon Hynes Ambulance - 2 Dent to 60th Division for duty Capt Taylor to 10th RB. - Capt Hanks reports to duty military inspected parade by G.O.C.	
	12.11.16		Inspection by G.O.C. IVth Army.	
	13.11.16			
	14.11.16		Capt Kennedy & 3. OR on leave. - C.M. on Dr McSwiney.	
PICQUIGNY	15.11.16		MARCHED at 8 a.m. to VILLE-SUR-ANCRE. (removed by Bus) arrive at 1.15 p.m. E.25.c.8.3.	
VILLE-SUR-ANCRE	16.11.16		Services of 9 Mls H.L. principals in Dr McGimpsey's H. Transport arrives from PICQUIGNY. - Intercepts Wood - 6 NCO 20 Rm.	

WAR DIARY
or
INTELLIGENCE SUMMARY.
(Erase heading not required.)

Army Form C. 2118

Place	Date	Hour	Summary of Events and Information	Remarks and references to Appendices
VILLE SUR ANCRE	1916			
	18	Noon	Capts KIRTON, HANKS, MOORES & 3 Tent subdivisions sent to 164th Casy M Dressing Stn at CARNOY, with Off. Coy. Dist. relieved from CARNOT. Order from A.D.M.S. 2nd Division	RAMC. 53 others ranks A.S.C. 9 OR 4 S.S. wagons 1 limber 1 Lt. Col.
	20.11.16		2 Talbot cars sent to O.C. 20th div. Supply Column.	
	21.11.16		O.C. returns from leave. Capt Edmunds sent to relieve Capt. Wall with 20th D.A.C. – Capt HENRY on off duty D. M'Gowan sent to M. Person.	
	22.11.16		Capt. Townend M.O. 11th KRR. relieves from leave – Capt McArthur returns to Ambulance from 11th KRR – 3 saddles from Car. F. 20th D.S.C.	
	23.11.16		5 mobile motor ambulance sent in exchange for our Talbots. Keay & Talbot – those sent to us – in very bad repair, 3 unfit to take the road.	
	24.11.16		1 NCO & 2 OR relieves from leave.	
	25.11.16		Mail paid –	
	26.11.16		Q.M. Sgt. DIGBY returns from CARNOY. C.M.D.S.	

Army Form C. 2118

WAR DIARY
or
INTELLIGENCE SUMMARY.
(Erase heading not required.)

Place	Date	Hour	Summary of Events and Information	Remarks and references to Appendices
VILLE-SUR-ANCRE E.25.C.8.3	27. Nov.		M.O. 11th K.R.R. on sick list relieved by Capt McARTHUR. M.O. 10th K.R.R. -"- -"- Capt HENDRY	
	28. Nov.		4 Other Ranks on leave.	
	29. Nov.	16	Capt Hawks despatched to 29th Division for duty as R.S.G. instructors	
	30. Nov.		Medical Board (29th) on P.B. man	

A.C. Osburn
Lieut Col. R.A.M.C.
Comdg 60th - 9th Amb.

Army Form C. 2118.

WAR DIARY
or
INTELLIGENCE SUMMARY.
(Erase heading not required.)

140/903

Vol 17

WAR DIARY
OF
60th Field Ambulance
RAMC
For
December 1916 - [?]

COMMITTEE FOR THE
MEDICAL HISTORY OF THE WAR
Date 31 JAN 1917

20th Div

Place	Date	Hour	Summary of Events and Information	Remarks and references to Appendices
Dec 1/15				

Army Form C. 2118.

WAR DIARY
or
INTELLIGENCE SUMMARY.
(Erase heading not required.)

Place	Date	Hour	Summary of Events and Information	Remarks and references to Appendices
VILLE-SUR-ANCRE	Dec 1st 1916		K.I.A.D.S. (shed 6 2d) T.6 A 45 (Transport lines)	
			O.C. Capt. Mullan - McArthur - 101. O.R. - Capt: Kirton & Moore	61. O.R. at Carnoy – on attacks duty
				6. O.R. detached duty
			Capt Kennedy &	4. Q.R. leave
			Capt Hendry -	10th K.R.R. attacks duty
			Capt Edmonds -	20th D.A.O. " (no reinforcements)
	3.12.16		30 men lent to 25th M.A.C. for fatigue party	
	4.12.16		Visited detachment at CARNOY	
	7.12.16		Detachment returned from 25th A.C.	

WAR DIARY
or
INTELLIGENCE SUMMARY.

Army Form C. 2118.

Place	Date	Hour	Summary of Events and Information	Remarks and references to Appendices
VILLE-SUR-ANCRE				
	9.12.16		60 beans to join Capt KIRTON at CARNOY	
			Supplied C.M.D.S. at CARNOY prior to taking over charge	
	10.12.16		Order Cancelled. Am now to take unit to Div C.M.F. Near Division to proceed for duty at Trones Wood A.D.S. aid posts at LES BOEUFS & GINCHY. Capt Kendry & Lt A Allen returned from detached duty. Finished M.D.S. & Beau Division	
	12.12.16		Col Kendry proceeds to Beau Camp	

Army Form C. 2118.

WAR DIARY
or
INTELLIGENCE SUMMARY.
(Erase heading not required.)

Place	Date	Hour	Summary of Events and Information	Remarks and references to Appendices
DIVE COPSE	13.12.16		Capt Moore arrived from Bearer Camp near GUILLEMONT visited Bearer Division & C.M.D.S.	
	16th 12.16		Lt Edward on leave to England	
	21.12.16		Inspected proposed new site for Corps M.D.S. near Trônes Wood) Bearer division to move to MEAULTE on 22nd — 195 waggon helping to unload Ordnance Stores at the Plateau (loading also 2 horses badly injured	
	22.12.16		Order for unit to take over Corbie Chateau Bearer Division marches from TRÔNES WOOD) to MEAULTE.	
	23.12.16		Capt Keiton & Asst Hendry and Bearer division marches from MEAULTE to CORBIE Chateau. — Capt Kennedy & Hayward's F. Amb. Marches from DIVE COPSE to CORBIE Chateau.	

Army Form C. 2118.

WAR DIARY
or
INTELLIGENCE SUMMARY.
(Erase heading not required.)

Place	Date	Hour	Summary of Events and Information	Remarks and references to Appendices
CORBIE (Chateau).	23.12.16		Town Major informed me that T.M. Battery would chose accommodation in the Chateau which is being used as a hospital ! protested and asked for written orders – He also informed myself & Capt Kennedy that the place was far from empty. O.C. 59th Field Amb Co from whom he took over was only ordered 2 days ago. MANAGE were expected from Tuesday noon. Yesterday! Disinfection carried out my Transport moved. Fairly busy number of miscellaneous fork arriving. Patrol of trini Pond.	
	24-12-16.		Capt Kennedy & 2 O.R. to ½ Tent sub div Equipment & Stones & CITADEL to take over charge of Troops in Lbed area	
	26-12-16.			
	28".12.16		Patrol of trini pond. – very cold. Capt MULLAN returned leave –	
	29".12.16		Inspected Corps A.D.S. Transit Lines – Capt HENDRY to Div Corps made necessary arrangement	

Army Form C. 2118.

WAR DIARY
or
INTELLIGENCE SUMMARY.
(Erase heading not required.)

Place	Date	Hour	Summary of Events and Information	Remarks and references to Appendices
CORBIE (Chateau)	30.12.16		Conference at Div. H.Qrs. 3.30pm 5 O.R. on leave	
	31.12.16		Present with Unit. D.G. Capt KIRTON. At 14 Corps Rest Station (sick camp) Capt MOORE, McARTHUR, HENRY. At CITADEL Capt KENNEDY ON LEAVE OM MULLAN, EDMOND	

A.C. Sturm
Lieut.
Commanding 60th Bn Aus
31/Dec/1916.

20 K.D.W.

140/943

WAR DIARY
of the
60th FIELD AMBULANCE
January 1917

COMMITTEE FOR THE
MEDICAL HISTORY OF THE WAR
Date 13 MAR. 1917

Army Form C. 2118.

WAR DIARY
or
INTELLIGENCE SUMMARY.
(Erase heading not required.)

Instructions regarding War Diaries and Intelligence Summaries are contained in F.S. Regs., Part II. and the Staff Manual respectively. Title pages will be prepared in manuscript.

Place	Date	Hour	Summary of Events and Information	Remarks and references to Appendices
CORBIE (Chateau)				
	1 Jan 1917		(Posting unit 1.1.17) O.C. 20 Officers 140 O.R. at Corbie 3 Officers 53 O.R. at DIVE COPSE	
		8 am	Unit marches from Corbie to MEAULTE	
		8 am	Advance party 1 Officer 12 O.R. march to TRONES WOOD A.D.S. from DIVE COPSE	
MEAULTE				
	2 Jan	8 am	Unit marched to TRONES WOOD DRESSING STATION and took over charge from No 4 Field Amb @ Guards Division	
	3 Jan			
TRONESWOOD			DRESSING STATION Collection of wounded begun (From 17 aus 20 a Divisions) at Noon 2nd	

WAR DIARY
or
INTELLIGENCE SUMMARY.
(Erase heading not required.)

Army Form C. 2118.

Place	Date	Hour	Summary of Events and Information	Remarks and references to Appendices
TRONES WOOD	Jan 4		Dressing station S.30.A.7.4. 8 Cars supplied by MAC (No 25)	
	5		7 " " " " 20 Stretcher	
			6 " " " " 17 " bearers	
			3 motor cyclist	
	2		H.A. wagon attached from Egypt Division	
			wounded received from	
			17 Div. A.D.S. GINCHY cross roads.	
			20 Div. A.D.S. COMBLES catacombs	
			+ HAIE WOOD. T.28.b.8.5	
	5.1.17		Construction of fuel huts - drawing material &c.	
			tarted A.D.S. Coulk Guacky + Hou wood	
	8.1.17		pulling up Nissen huts Curful huts - drawing	
			grounds - drawing plan + Equipment to	
			Daily average sick about 1/3 Officers + 100 OR	
			wounds 2 Officers + 20 OR	
	9.1.17		Capt HORTON - Rot Major - 76 Bears by Hair Coors MDS	

WAR DIARY
or
INTELLIGENCE SUMMARY.

(Erase heading not required.)

Army Form C. 2118.

Place	Date	Hour	Summary of Events and Information	Remarks and references to Appendices
TROMES WOOD. D.S			Colonel Madden Capt Thornber, Colonel Banbury addressed N.C.Os and Officers (as)	
	10.1.17		Officer patrols working levelling up shell holes & making roads - during interval the following friendly - Grenade division - 1 brigade in line - 1 in support	
	14.1.17		17th Division relieved by 29th Division	
	15.1.17		Visited A.D.S. (Campbell.) Genech - Hell wood -	
	16.1.17		Capt. HENDER to 11th K.R.R. - vice Capt Townsend	
	18.1.17		Bt General Banbury admits upon Bronshuk - Bath owents 9 took about 120. wounds 15 since first advance will train	
	20.1.17		Find Hours continued (have been sick eating Jackey yours) - (some from Guns: 2D=Flg 4th Division - Capt. Thorn taking Trotr B scales Coast in Hospital	

WAR DIARY or INTELLIGENCE SUMMARY

Army Form C. 2118.

Place	Date	Hour	Summary of Events and Information	Remarks and references to Appendices
Thornwood	21 Jan 17		Drewy Clothes. Coel HENDRE returns from M.K.P.R in MCARTHUR on loan of them. Capt. KIRTON & Beau Brown returns from HAIG WOOD	
	23.1.17		Work continues. Elephant tent - linen put to improving standing troops - Officer was to QM Store. Laying Down Brick floors. renewing old paths &c. Slabby road to W.S. Camp - Lorry had breakdown & utility vaults for pole destruction fuel labour Stan - K. removing tent replanning block by 9 Camp - + putting up marquee + spading tail for Cairo & trolley platform for Beaunville. Ordered lorry trailer to collect Reports and in (4") in Beaunville Railway & more to Graunvillay training Officer (dawn)	
	24.1.17			

T2134. Wt. W708—776. 500000. 4/15. Sir J.C. & 8.

Army Form C. 2118.

WAR DIARY
or
INTELLIGENCE SUMMARY.
(Erase heading not required.)

Instructions regarding War Diaries and Intelligence Summaries are contained in F.S. Regs., Part II. and the Staff Manual respectively. Title pages will be prepared in manuscript.

Place	Date	Hour	Summary of Events and Information	Remarks and references to Appendices
THOMAS WOOD. ADS				
	24.1.17		Packing + arranging for landing over on 25th and 6 O.C. 87th F.Amb	
	26.1.17		Advance party Capt Mullan + 10 men to FRANVILLERS. Capt Moore + 74 men on base	
		6pm	Handed over Bussy camp equipment to O.C. 85th F.Amb.	
FRANVILLERS	26.1.17		Marched at 8.10 am to FRANVILLERS arrives at 2 pm. 1 Officer + 30 men sent "6 25th M.A.C. for fatigue party	
	29.1.17.		Capt Mullan to Divisin Capt Wall to Corps 20. OR.Q Men employed Road making, orderly &c	
	30.1.17		Fatigue party returns. Sick daily about 75. evacuations 25.	
	31.1.17		MMP 56 Lt EDMOND Capt KIRTON-HENDRY + Lt EATES Q.M Detached duty Capt KENNEDY, MULLAN, Lt LEAVE CoL MCARTHUR MOORE	

Major [signature]
Lt Col RAMC

140/1991

20th Divn.

60th Field Ambulance

Feb. 1917

COMMITTEE FOR THE
MEDICAL HISTORY OF THE WAR
Date 4 APR. 1917

Army Form C. 2118.

WAR DIARY
or
INTELLIGENCE SUMMARY.
(Erase heading not required.)

96/19

WAR DIARY

OF

60th FIELD AMBULANCE

FOR

FEBRUARY. 1917. Lieut.

Major J. McLaurin

Army Form C. 2118.

WAR DIARY
or
INTELLIGENCE SUMMARY.
(Erase heading not required.)

Place	Date	Hour	Summary of Events and Information	Remarks and references to Appendices
FRANVILLERS (AMIENS MAP)	Feb 1st 1917		Officers / Board with ambulance, O.C. Qr Master, Capt^s KIRTON, HENDRY & Lt (EDMUND). Route marching, drill	
-,,-	2.2.17		Parade orders by 9.O.C. 55th Regt. Intense cold continues. Route marching drill	
-,,-	3.2.17		Parade cancelled at 10.45 a.m. Route marching & drill	
Feb 4. 1917 BONNAY			Unit paraded 9 am & marched to BONNAY. Billets poor. Still intensely cold. Continued training	
-,,-	6.2.17		Advance party Capt KIRTON, Qr Mr, Mr G, 5 Cpls & 76 men. to TRONES. WOOD. Drancy Ctn. 6½ at 8 a.m. also L.G.S. waggons. Taking over from 89th 7th Amb. 29th Divn.	
TRONES. WOOD	7.2.17		Unit marches (Reserved by Lorry) to TRONES WOOD arrived 11.30 am. Capt HENDRY & 55 O.R. to Beaver Camp at S. 24. d. 5.5. night 9. 6"/7" Dublin Trench, 29 Divn. Wounded on telus	

Army Form C. 2118.

WAR DIARY
or
INTELLIGENCE SUMMARY.
(Erase heading not required.)

Place	Date	Hour	Summary of Events and Information	Remarks and references to Appendices
TRONES WOOD	8.2.17		Capt Graham +15.O.R. from 87th Field Amb. arrives for duty. S.30.A.5.5. (Sheet 57C.S.W. 1/20,000) Capt McCullagh + 15 O.Rs 14 Field Amb joined for duty. O.C. Qr. Mast. Capt. KIRTON + Lt EDMOND, Capt McARTHUR (returns from leave) chem duty Attack by 17th Divn on line near Sailly-Saillisel.	
— " —	9.2.17		Motor Ambulances on Duty. 25 MAC 6. 20th Divn 6. 17–Divn 7. daily Wounded admitted 237. Visited A.D.S. Ginchy Sick 150 daily. — about 40 C.R.s 110 C.C.S. Capt Graham +15.O.R. returns to 87th F. Amb from 52nd 7. Amb. S/Sgt Major SEABORNE A.S.C. reports for duty from 20th Divl Train Capt. McARTHUR to 11th KRR to relieve Capt TOWNSEND - transferred to R.E.	
— " —	9.2.17		Wounded 109. Admitted & Capt RUDDLE admitted sick. Dr HARDY 12th R.B. Capt KIRTON	

Army Form C. 2118.

WAR DIARY
or
INTELLIGENCE SUMMARY.
(Erase heading not required.)

Instructions regarding War Diaries and Intelligence Summaries are contained in F.S. Regs., Part II. and the Staff Manual respectively. Title pages will be prepared in manuscript.

Place	Date	Hour	Summary of Events and Information	Remarks and references to Appendices
TRONES WOOD (S.30.A.5.5.)	10.2.17		Coll SUTHERLAND R.A.M.C. stands by daily when needed. M.O. Great Pioneer Bttn. wounds admitted 76. Continuing enlargement of hut arrangement Kitchen, Operating Theatre, Personnel huts &c.	
-"-	11.2.17		wounds admitted 28	
-"-	13.2.17		Capt MOORE returns from leave. wounds admitted 43	
-"-	14.2.17		Completed lining house-huts. wounds admitted 46	
-"-	15.2.17		Surplus funds distributed amongst 20 men (specially good workers) (War Savings Certificates). wounds admitted 38	
-"-	16.2.17		-"- -"- -"- 69	
-"-	17.2.17		Capt HENDRY returns on 17/15 -"- -"- -"- 15. Lt EDMOND to Bonn Camp. visited R.O.S. Guidsby. Capt TURNBULL & REEVES reported for duty. Capt McCULLOGH returns to No 4 F.O. Amb.	

WAR DIARY
of
INTELLIGENCE SUMMARY.
(Erase heading not required.)

Army Form C. 2118.

Instructions regarding War Diaries and Intelligence Summaries are contained in F.S. Regs., Part II. and the Staff Manual respectively. Title pages will be prepared in manuscript.

Place	Date	Hour	Summary of Events and Information	Remarks and references to Appendices
TRONES WOOD	18.2.17		Capt GATTY admitted with Schwein Cramero — Capt FAHY & C.A.F. 7th Stevens ⎬ interviews	
			Capt TURNBULL &72 min D.R. to Bean Camp wounds admits P.U.	
-"-	19.2.17		Capt McARTHUR proceeds to AMIENS sick — Capt REEVES send in M.O.	
			visited to 11th K.R.R.	
			Capt THOMAS returns 632 n/7 Amb wounds admits 46	
			2 Lays Ambulance Cars 1 Ford and 5 O.R, reports from 88 n/7 Amb	
-"-	20.2.17		to duty — visited A.D.S. Guedy	
			Lt PEARSE reports from 88th 2oTrub for duty	
			4 boys and Cars & given from 87 n/ F.A. ⎬ reports for duty	
			2 " " " " " 89th F.A. ⎭ wounds admits 41	
-"-	21.2.17		visited Aid post at FLANK AVENUE. T.9.6.8.4. wounds —"— 31.	
			Capt JONES & Capt TURNBULL	
-"-	22.2.17		4. O.R. reports for duty from 88th 7. Amb	
-"-	23.2.17		Continuing during month clearing ground, wounds —"— 37.	
			Salvage, Improvement, enlargement of Camps + Hospital.	

Army Form C. 2118.

WAR DIARY
or
INTELLIGENCE SUMMARY.
(Erase heading not required.)

Instructions regarding War Diaries and Intelligence Summaries are contained in F.S. Regs., Part II. and the Staff Manual respectively. Title pages will be prepared in manuscript.

Place	Date	Hour	Summary of Events and Information	Remarks and references to Appendices
TROIS-VAAST	24.2.17		2 Amb Car + 4 O.R. returns to 87" 9 Amb for duty. Reinforcements	28.
--	25.2.17		Cpl McARTHUR returned from Hospital Cpl EDMOND " - " - Bearers	wound returns 60.
--	26.2.17		A.D.M.S visits Dressing Station	
--	27.2.17		Attended Sewing Services at 34 C.C.S. 15 O.R. returns to No 4 Fd Amb Lt ESMOND returns to Bearers Coy for duty. Arrangements made for dealing with wounded as large numbers Uncerous Ambulance, Charings, &c.	

Army Form C. 2118.

WAR DIARY
or
INTELLIGENCE SUMMARY.
(Erase heading not required.)

Place	Date	Hour	Summary of Events and Information	Remarks and references to Appendices
TRONES WOOD DRESSING STATION — S.30.A.5.E.	28. Feb 1917		At 5. A.M. attack opened — at 9.30 a.m. wounded began to arrive. 150 wounded 5 Officers had arrived by 2.30 p.m. Capt Hensley & Capt Graham 37th Field Amb (stretcher case) Capt Mortl & McArthur (walking wounded) Capt Bloxam, Ryan, Sutherland & Price arrived with feet and hit the wounded for 2 or 3 hours. M.D.U.S's & Guards Divn 29th Divn & 20th Divn evacuated ambulance wounded mainly 29th Divn. All wounds clean when 4. p.m. ACS Burn Lieut Col comdg 60th Fred Amb	

Army Form C. 2118.

WAR DIARY
or
INTELLIGENCE SUMMARY.
(Erase heading not required.)

Instructions regarding War Diaries and Intelligence Summaries are contained in F. S. Regs., Part II. and the Staff Manual respectively. Title pages will be prepared in manuscript.

Place	Date	Hour	Summary of Events and Information	Remarks and references to Appendices

T.J.134. Wt. W708-776. 500000. 4/15. Sr. J. C. & S.

140/2042

20th Div.

60th Field Ambulance.

Mar. 1917

S

COMMITTEE FOR THE
MEDICAL HISTORY OF THE WAR
Date   11 MAY 1917

WAR DIARY OF 60th FIELD AMBULANCE FOR MARCH 1917.

Vol 20

Army Form C. 2118.

WAR DIARY
or
INTELLIGENCE SUMMARY.
(Erase heading not required.)

War Diary of 60th Field Ambulance for March — 1917.

Army Form C. 2118.

WAR DIARY
or
INTELLIGENCE SUMMARY.
(Erase heading not required.)

Place	Date	Hour	Summary of Events and Information	Remarks and references to Appendices
TRONES WOOD Dressing Station – S.30.A.7.4.	March 1st		Steady stream of wounded being admitted 228 in last 24 hours here all going satisfactorily – a certain number of cases of 29"Divn" are coming in very indifferent cases for – 96, 89" 2"Amb (inform) They will be sent evacuating the sick (wounded) of 20 & 29 & VGuard Divisions also any Corps (Army) Troops in COMBLES, GUYOT, MONTAUBAN area – about 120 sick are sent daily to this about 40 are wounded to C.R.S. & C.C.S. V" nurses also supplying all drugs & discomforts' dressings for divisions & Corps Troops	
	March 2nd		Wounded 112. Lt. Graham returns to 87" F"Amb	
	— 3rd		— " 75. Some 7 Cases opened here one evening	
	— 4th		wounded 62 Lt MOORE to 10"FB	

T2134. Wt. W708—776. 500000. 4/15. Sir J.C. & S.

WAR DIARY
or
INTELLIGENCE SUMMARY

Army Form C. 2118.

Place	Date	Hour	Summary of Events and Information	Remarks and references to Appendices
Trones Wood	March 6th	S. 30 A.7.4.	A.D.M.S. saw Lt. Monk & gave him room to rest pending his application	
	March 7th		Capt. Mullan returned from D.A.C. wounds 25.	
			Lt. Turnbull rejoined 6. No. 61 F.A.	
	10th		Capt. Peare returns to 88th D.A April 19	
March 12th			wounds 29.	
			visited A.D.S. Guichy & Combles	
	16th		Sgt. Godley 8th to Temp. Commission in R.F.A. wounds 49.	
	17th		inspected roads to Le. Transloy - very bad - ground recovery from frost - impassable even for pack-animals.	
March 18th			Capt. Kirton to Bearer division. Lt. Edmond returned.	
	19th		Capt. Moore to Bearer division	
	20th		Bowman	
			Sgt. Major transferred to D.M.S. L.of C. for instruction.	
			Sgt. Major Andrews reported for duty.	

Army Form C. 2118.

WAR DIARY
or
INTELLIGENCE SUMMARY.
(Erase heading not required.)

Instructions regarding War Diaries and Intelligence Summaries are contained in F.S. Regs., Part II. and the Staff Manual respectively. Title pages will be prepared in manuscript.

Place	Date	Hour	Summary of Events and Information	Remarks and references to Appendices
TROUES WOOD	S.30.A.7.4			
	March 20th		Visited area evacuated by enemy as far as BARASTRE. Shell still falling in YTRES. — Ground very foul — roads impassable — many dead — mostly German. Wells filled with rubbish & filth	
	22nd March		Lt. Edmonds to Labour Battalion for duty as M.O. i/c — made further visits to line — having over to move.	
	23 march			
	24.3.17.		baggage being repacked — order re 5th Cavalry division recd. A detachment Indian Hosp! Establishmt to report tos G.C.M. near Killin Bruge. Bougues-maison O.C. & Capt Hendry.	
	26.3.17			
	27.3.17		Visited LE TRANSLOI — moral area — many unknown dead — French & few British & German — ground very foul. Capt Mellon to XII XVth Corps M.O.L. Marcourt for duty.	

WAR DIARY or INTELLIGENCE SUMMARY

Army Form C. 2118.

Place	Date	Hour	Summary of Events and Information	Remarks and references to Appendices
TOSMES (Wood) S.30.A.7.4.	28/3/17.		Painting, packing waggons &c., preparing camp for allotation under a C.C.S. & preparing camp for C.C.S.	
	29/3/17.		With O.C. 62 Dn.Fnd. visited all the area in front of Rocquigny and Sailly Nghs. ? 57's & 61's Bgds. — country foul, weeks almost unmanned Le Mesnil, Bus-k. — ground's clean toward Bus billage very much destroyed.	
	30/3/17		Capt. McArthur to Beaver Division — 85 O.R. (174 O.R.) on detachment Beaver division — Rocquigny — Borastre — Le Mesnil. area under OC 61.7 A. Continued painting &c. very heavy rain. Medical Board O.C. Capt. Hendry + Lt. Townsend M.O. 20 Sn. R.E. on L'Hivington.	
	31.3.17.	S.30.A.7.4		Beaver Division Officers Present Capt. KIRTON "MOORE Capt. McARTHUR OC. Capt. KENDRY & 185 O.R. Tent Sun Detachment 1 Off. McLean KENNEDY & Lt. ESMONS & 14 men 185 O.R.

A.C. Osburn Lt.Col.

149/2086

20ᵈ Div.

No. 60. J.A.

Army Form C. 2118.

WAR DIARY
or
INTELLIGENCE SUMMARY.
(Erase heading not required.)

Vol 21

WAR DIARY
OF
60TH FIELD AMBULANCE
FOR
APRIL 1917

Army Form C. 2118.

WAR DIARY
or
INTELLIGENCE SUMMARY.
(Erase heading not required.)

Place	Date	Hour	Summary of Events and Information	Remarks and references to Appendices
TRONES WOOD — S.30.A.7.4. (with Brown)	April 1st 1917		Present with unit O.C. Capt HENDRY — QM. Capt KIRTON, MOORE, McARTHUR Capt MULLAN, EDWARD KENNEDY Continues practising trenching, bavouet & weapons &c	▽ 735 OR ▽ QM ▽ 85 OR ▽ 150 R
	April 2nd		2nd & 4th Left Scouts reported bivouac for duty Orders received preliminary moving to LECTELLES	
	April 3rd		Lt EATE 141 OR to LECTELLES	

Army Form C. 2118.

WAR DIARY
or
INTELLIGENCE SUMMARY.
(Erase heading not required.)

Instructions regarding War Diaries and Intelligence Summaries are contained in F. S. Regs., Part II. and the Staff Manual respectively. Title pages will be prepared in manuscript.

Place	Date	Hour	Summary of Events and Information	Remarks and references to Appendices
TRONES WOOD	D.S.		Slung Advance party road to LECHELLE and small Dressing station	
	3.4.17		Established there at P.25.c.5.5.	
LECHELLES.	4.4.17		Remainder of Unit marched to LECHELLE via Rocquigny + Bus. CAPT HENDRY to LECHELLES. Capt KIRTON to charge O.C. on leave Capt MOORE i/c Trans wood D. station 148 wounded passed through A.D.S. at LECHELLE (5 officers)	
	5.4.'17		56 wounded	
	7.4.17		Improving billets at LECHELLES.	
	8.4.17		Capt McARTHUR relieves Capt Mullin at 15th Corps M.D.S. A.D.S. wounded to to 62 T. Amb.	
	9.4.17		Unit moves to U.30.D. MOISLAINS — Transfer to Combles	

T2134. Wt. W708—776. 500000. 4/15. Sir J. C. & S.

WAR DIARY
or
INTELLIGENCE SUMMARY.
(Erase heading not required.)

Army Form C. 2118.

Place	Date	Hour	Summary of Events and Information	Remarks and references to Appendices
MOSS LANES			U.30.d.	
	10.4.17		Started work in new Camp M.D.S. – roads &c. Capt Wills reported for special duty.	
	11.4.17		Capt Kirton relieves Capt Moore at Tara Wood. Capt Moore to A.D.M.S. 19 Division. Capt Stockham & Capt Rouse permanent staff appointed to Rgt.	
	12.4.17		Working party 9 137 P.F. arrived	
	16.4.17		Footballer 9 O.Rs & 1 Whe? to Gas Cases (Cay Gas H.Pruo Centre)	
	22.4.17		Capt Wills H.E. Esmond & Rouse Division 116 OR Attend to 186 62M Division at NEUVILLE – BOURTENVAL	
	23.4.17		16 returned from leave. Capt Wills & Rouse Division returns.	
	24.4.17		41 Marquees Pitched 5 Opening tents 2 Shelter 16 Bell tents Kitchen & Cook. in Horse Lines be ready.	
	26.4.17		*teros nearly completed – order recd to stop all work. Capt Wills & Revere Subaltern to 62 Front	

WAR DIARY
or
INTELLIGENCE SUMMARY.
(Erase heading not required.)

Army Form C. 2118.

Place	Date	Hour	Summary of Events and Information	Remarks and references to Appendices
U.30.D.	25.4.17		Lt. EATE to CMDS seek. All tents to check - Also some Inf	26.6 R
V.18.C.28. (Shw157c)	26.4.17		to new site. Capt HENDRY L/CMDS seek 59 G.R. to New Camp	
	27.4.17		All work held work preparing ground making roads putting up Marquis + starting twr - took U/30 d. — D.D.M.S. camp up in afternoon	
	28.4.17		To 15th Corp M.D.S. to see Col Mulw. Thompson re camp, also ruled Terus. Woods. D.D.M.S. left a note re camp stating my absence OC 15 Cot MDS came to see Camp — understand he is to take over. Enlistment I took prisoners him on 30th inst — prouded out Mot Camp was not hardly tris rate supply. Saw D.D.M.S. for confirmation. All ranks hard at work making road putting up marquees & taking stone to from U.30.D. There was I Marceval to get twn. over 60 marquees & tents now up —	

WAR DIARY
or
INTELLIGENCE SUMMARY
(Erase heading not required.)

Army Form C. 2118.

Place	Date	Hour	Summary of Events and Information	Remarks and references to Appendices
V18.C.2.8			FINS, XV Corps Main Dressing Station	
	29.4.17		CE XV Corps Main Dressing Station also SDMS — 13 men & 26 26 7/8 Amb arrived at 1.30. Men & a further 10 men arr 2 Officers at 4 pm. Hands over 4th Hutches + 1 large Marquee & Blankets (450) Tents Above stores + 43 Buildings & Tents at 6 pm to O.C. Evacuations 28" J. Amb. 4 large Marquees	
	30.4.17		XV Corps Commander, 9.D.D.I + D.D.M.S. visited Dressing Station. Continues putting up Nissen Huts making roadway drains labour is 7 Kitty trod carries from Twins Wood 1 from Grove Town — 33 Hospital Marquees 8 Elim Tents 3 Nissen Huts 5 Operating Tents 17 Bell Tents 2 eph stores Tents Operating Theatres be erected — 26 = 7. Amb. take over at 6 pm tonight all sick (wounded) evacuating Treatment of Gas Cases	

ACB [signature] WJC
[signature]
Comdt 66 DMS
RMMC

20th Div.

No. 60. F.A.

COMMITTEE FOR THE
MEDICAL HISTORY OF THE WAR
Date 10 JUL 1917

Army Form C. 2118.

WAR DIARY
or
INTELLIGENCE SUMMARY.
(Erase heading not required.)

Vol 22

War Diary
of
60th Field Ambulance
for
May 1917

WAR DIARY
or
INTELLIGENCE SUMMARY.
(Erase heading not required.)

Army Form C. 2118.

Place	Date	Hour	Summary of Events and Information	Remarks and references to Appendices
V18.C.2.8.	June (FINS) XV Corps M.S.S			
	1st May 1917		Present unit strength 06 Capt Mellor. Mills. L'Esmond 198 men	
			CATTERTON + 9 O.R. at Trois Tours	
			INCO 1 8 O.R. at V.30.D MORLAINS	
			Continued bookmaking - putting up MOZEN hut tents	
			enclosing Mineral Water Lahore etc.	
	2nd May		Note from C.C.S. Capt HEHJRY + L'ENTE evacuated 273 men.	
	3. May 17		Further work continued on XV C.M.S.S	
			D.T.M.S XV Corps & B.9. G.S. I CE XV Corps making	
			daily visits	
			Tents pitched to accommodate 26° 25 7m/G	
	4. May 17		D.M.S IV Army Inspected work done by Unit trans Junt.	
			to Expert	

Army Form C. 2118.

WAR DIARY
or
INTELLIGENCE SUMMARY.
(Erase heading not required.)

Place	Date	Hour	Summary of Events and Information	Remarks and references to Appendices
V 10 C 28 (Fins)	5. May 17		Further work on C.M.O.T. (about 400 scrub. posts through 39 my Ottawa) Capt. Mellor Willis & 2nd Lieutenant & 14 Sh. infantry. 26 & 9 Mol? Rect & hurt have all work making roads, and the tele bearing fatigues &c.	
	6. May 17		Visited HAVRINCOURT WOOD & frontarea A.N.S. &c.	
	8. May 17		Nothing d? important. Nr 2nd nd 4th D Corps visited ambulance for the work on C.M.O.T. Road all material from forw wood & Neuville (V.30.d) ha now been brought ½ to trains - personnel being carbonising lower making drains roads pitching tent & erecting nissen huts.	
	9. May 17		Visited 62" 7. Aml/9 & MET2. NEUVICORT & front area.	

WAR DIARY or INTELLIGENCE SUMMARY

Army Form C. 2118.

Place	Date	Hour	Summary of Events and Information	Remarks and references to Appendices
V.18.a.2.8	10th May 17		arranged to take over duties of ADMS 20th Div during his absence. Saw O.C. 61st, 162nd F.A. & O.C. 136th 9th F.Amb. & O.C. 138th Field Amb. – Capt Kenton to take over charge of front by 20th Div – Capt Mullen relieves Capt Shuter [?]. Camp & Trenwan [?] & ambulance. Lost Mullen & men at Trones Wood – Capt Mullen & 6 men at general fatigues for XV Corps but continued to carry on general fatigues between detaching M.O.S. digging septic tank, making weed, removing tents & tent, laying duckboards, & erecting nissen huts. There tents & now over 100 Hopital Marquees Nissen Huts [?] & about 1000 palliasses. Started accommodation at 8 a.m. Took over duties of A.D.M.S. 20th Div at 8 a.m.	
	11th May			

Army Form C. 2118.

WAR DIARY
or
INTELLIGENCE SUMMARY.
(Erase heading not required.)

Instructions regarding War Diaries and Intelligence Summaries are contained in F. S. Regs., Part II. and the Staff Manual respectively. Title pages will be prepared in manuscript.

Place	Date	Hour	Summary of Events and Information	Remarks and references to Appendices
V.15.c.25.			FINS (SHEET 57E)	
	11 May 1917		Took over temporary command of Ambulance at 9 AM during absence of Lt Col Oshorn A/ADMS XX Division. Unit continued with the general fatigues of XV C.M.D.S. — roadmaking &c.	
	12 May 1917		Capt. Mulhan H.F. proceeded to No 232 Army Troop Coy. R.E. to take over medical and sanitary charge of that unit in relief of Capt GRAY. Lt EDMOND J proceeded to 26 F.Amb (XV C.M.D.S) for duty in relief of Capt McARTHUR G.A.D, R.A.M.C. who returned to H.Q. 60 F.Amb. Sgt Bolton and 4 O.R. proceeded to O.31.b.5.1 (Sheet 57C) to locate dead Cookie in the LE TRANSLOY, LESBOEUFS, MORVAL, SAILLY-SAILLISEL Area, in accordance with instructions from A.D.M.S. XX Div. Unit carried on the general fatigues of XV C.M.D.S.	
	13 May 1917		Capt GRAY J.P., R.A.M.C. returned to H.Q. 60 F.Amb. from 232 A.T.Cy R.E. Capt McARTHUR R.A.M.C. came 31.O.R. reported to 62m F.Amb. for duty — A.D.M.S. instructions. Usual fatigues of XV C.M.D.S. carried out by unit.	

Army Form C. 2118.

WAR DIARY
or
INTELLIGENCE SUMMARY.
(Erase heading not required.)

Instructions regarding War Diaries and Intelligence Summaries are contained in F. S. Regs., Part II. and the Staff Manual respectively. Title pages will be prepared in manuscript.

Place	Date	Hour	Summary of Events and Information	Remarks and references to Appendices
V.18.c.2.8. (SHEET 57c)			FINS.	
	14 May 1917		Usual fatigues to FW C.M.D.S. carried out by unit. A.D.M.S. G.O.C. XX Div. visited the camp at 2.50 p.m. for inspection. Owing to hostile shell fire the camp had to be evacuated about 3 P.M. and in accordance with instructions of A.D.M.S. XX Division with reference to (SHEET 57c) Casualties to Personnel – one A.S.C. Dr. slightly wounded.	
V.24.a.6.3.	15 May 1917		Two Cacs Ambulance Cars returned to above unit from 61st F. Amb. complete with Sgt Pateman and 5 other ranks. S.O.R. Rent + A.S.C. H.T. with 2 Horse Ambulance wagons returned from 63rd F. Amb. for duty. Sgt Bothin + 74 O.R. returned from O.31.B.5.1 after completion of duties. Carried on the general fatigues to M.D.S.	
	17 May 1917		Lieut G. N. MONTGOMERY R.A.M.C. having been posted to this unit for duty is taken on the strength accordingly. Usual fatigues to M.D.S. carried on.	

Army Form C. 2118.

WAR DIARY
or
INTELLIGENCE SUMMARY.

(Erase heading not required.)

Instructions regarding War Diaries and Intelligence Summaries are contained in F. S. Regs., Part II. and the Staff Manual respectively. Title pages will be prepared in manuscript.

Place	Date	Hour	Summary of Events and Information	Remarks and references to Appendices
V.24.a.6.3	19 May 17		O.C. Ambulance car with Driver & Orderly returned to unit from 61st Amb., for duty.	
	20 May 17		Capt. McARTHUR, R.A.M.C. and 31 O.R. returned to unit from 62nd F. Amb. Pte Crofoot returned to unit after completion of duties with XX Divven [Division] Sanity [Sanitary]. Jno. Ambulant Cars and A.O.R. reported to 61st F. Amb. for temporary duty. Usual Fatigues and at M.D.S. - pulling up tents, roadmaking, etc.	
	21. May 17.		Capt McARTHUR and GRAY proceeded to 61st F Amb. for temporary duty. Lt EDMOND proceeded for temporary duty as M.O./c 11 KRRC. Lt. MONTGOMERY, 4 O.R. Ram, 2 Bearers, 1 WaterCart, and 30R ASC M/T proceeded to H.16.d.9.5. 2 Motor Ambulances + 4 O.R. returned to this unit from 61st F Amb. 1 Motor Ambulance with Driver & Orderly returned to this unit after completion of duties with ADMS XX Div.	
	22. May 17.		Lt. EDMOND returned to this unit from 11 KRRC. Capt Mullen reported from completion of duties as M.O./c 232 Coy R.E. & proceeded as M.O. to 11 to h.I. Unit with Transport moved to H.16.d.9.5. Capt McArthur & GRAY rejoined unit at H.16.d.9.5	

WAR DIARY / INTELLIGENCE SUMMARY

Army Form C. 2118.

Place	Date	Hour	Summary of Events and Information	Remarks and references to Appendices
H.16.D.9.5			60 O.R. arrived on the following posts from 8th Australian Fd Amb.	
also 15 7c to 10000	23/5/17		M.D.S. at H.16.a.95, A.D.S. - H.16.d.2.8, Advanced Collecting Post - C.10.c.7.7, Leading Post - C.9.d.5.5, Relay Post C.11.a.5.2. J. Martin Capt	Acting A.D.M.S. confirms
	24/5/17	11 pm	Maj ASBURN relieved to command Lent from acting A.D.M.S.	
		9 am	A.D.S. - work arrangd - Labour party organised - Visited visitors new (Rear) D Station - in a very good condition to be used as a Gas Centre for shell gas cases except to be used as a Gas light cases. To recover to following point H.32.d.7.7, aviation - to ambulance for ANZAC Corps A.D.M.S. I marshalled on a M.D.S. - points rd DDiMS organisation to use 1 C.20 and C.20 and 1 other objection - In change of Observation than 1 other objection - Recon route to new MDS	
		2 pm	Inspection new MDS	
		4 pm	to view MDS. All personnel + 80% of both dressing station on work at both dressing station	
	25/4/17	9 am	to view MDS. Carry up Lorries + carry up further arrangements made ordered by D.Australian Division commander Genl	
		2 pm	to new MDS orders J.D.Australian Division commence

Army Form C. 2118.

WAR DIARY
or
INTELLIGENCE SUMMARY.

(Erase heading not required.)

Instructions regarding War Diaries and Intelligence Summaries are contained in F.S. Regs., Part II. and the Staff Manual respectively. Title pages will be prepared in manuscript.

Place	Date	Hour	Summary of Events and Information	Remarks and references to Appendices
H.Q.9.5. Sheet 57C 10000.	26.5.17		Division now under orders of 16 Corps. A.D.M.S. G.O.C.	
		9 a.m.	to new A.D.S. labour party erecting 6 E.P. tents, 68 men + 3 officers at C.20.	
			Work continued at both Dressing Stations.	
		9 p.m.	to new M.D.S. (C20) from there to loading post, relay post & walking wounded post, to R.A.P. (Reft) Offrs House – fairly heavy shelling in area in front of walking wounded – 20 officers 9.62.B. relieved Capt Prinsen & attending post – platform & lorry	
	27.5.17.		Work continued at Loft (new) Dressing Station – platform & meds – operating tent &c.	
		9 a.m.	to new M.D.S. C.20. D.2.8. 50 men working on encumbrians installed new M.D.S. C.20. D.2.8. 50 men working at shelling not serious – Removal of material at shelling M.D.S. Shelling store material at M.D.S. New up scheme for reserve of R.A.P. materials in a R.A. Pat.6.	
			2 Relay posts Collecting & Refng in front. A.D.M.S. visited (Rear) D.S.	
		11.0 a.m.	A.D.M.S. observer forward to see R.A.P.S. + Relay post up to front & C.S.C. 7.B. – said way up & Dressed at C.15. C.O.6. Shrapnel over path	
		1.15 p.m.	to M.D.S. C.20 observer forward to see R.A.P.S. + Refs M.O's 12 R.B. D.R.B. M.O. 12 R.B. D.R.B. + coffee at C.11. a.3.9 & C.15. C.0.6. Shrapnel near C.11 a.3.9	
		2 a.m.	Shelling near C.11.a.3.9 on C.10.B.	

WAR DIARY
or
INTELLIGENCE SUMMARY.
(Erase heading not required.)

Army Form C. 2118.

Place	Date	Hour	Summary of Events and Information	Remarks and references to Appendices
A.16.D.9.S Sheet 57C Tepee. to C.20.D.3.6	28.5.17	9 am 9 am 10 am 11 am	to C.20. New M.D.S. – heavy shelling of ypres about 300 yd N.W. worked parties on further work on L.M.R. Decoy Station. Visited R.A.P. Reserve Batth in VAULT C.25.b.5.9. M.D.S. rain shells – no casualties. Later saw us – G. Rehan 62nd & New R.P. at C.50.2.3. to C.20 (MDS) all down Cap. Kuntz Loke Liver in observing dig out /heavy shelling (27 wounds) of MDS area 6 Canadian R.A.M.C. at Loft (Roar) Dressing Station	
C.20.D.3.6	29.5.17.	10 am	DDMS IV Corps works inspected Ambulances at following Seems quite satisfied: Visited 4 wounds of Civil in No 3 C.C.S. MDS – Laundries &c. building new M.DS. Units work in cleaning camp – Laundries &c.	
	30.5.17	9.bm 10.bm 1 am	To MDS at C.20. Further shelling in night – within 200 yard Ford Car damaged g 1 mile (water cart) wounded – slight. – protection for patients thrown over being pressed on with. Lo Kensung post & Relay posts – fairly steady shelling To MDS & Prisons C9 & C.15 – C9 & C.7.9 superiority of valleys in C.9 & C.15 – return Ambulance	
	31.5.17. 11 km 2 pm		ADWS inspected Ambulance visited MDS work progressing satisfactorily – No 7 Cars reduced (6 worts) others being collected	

Army Form C. 2118.

WAR DIARY
or
INTELLIGENCE SUMMARY.
(Erase heading not required.)

Place	Date	Hour	Summary of Events and Information	Remarks and references to Appendices
H.16.D.9.5. Sheet 57.C		MIDNIGHT 31/5/17	Supplies 11/5/West HdQuarters at 15ft. (Read Dressing Station) H.16.D.9.5.	H.16.D.9.5
40000	31.5.17	H.16.D.9.5.	O.C. Casually. Montgomerie, McARTHUR. A. Tent subdivision B Tent subdivision A. Beare Intervision (ready horse club in line). 62nd F.A. to Beaux 62nd F.A. Capts KIRTON, EDMOND, GENY.	
			MAIN Dressing Station C. 20.D. 3.6 C Tent subdivision ½ Bearer subdivision 62 nd ½ to horse say. ½ Bearer subdivision	
			Loading Post C.15.A.9.9. 1 NCO 6 men	Let R.A.P. 1 NCO 18 men C.5.D.78 Right R.A.P (Relay point) C.11.A.76 available
			Collecting post C.10.C.7.9. 2 NCO +15 men	Supernumy C.S.A.2.3 1 NCO 18 men 50's own R.M.O.
			Relay post C.11.a.3.9. 1 NCO +12 men	A.C.Brown Col.

14c/2210

No. 60. F.a.

June, 1917.

COMMITTEE FOR THE
MEDICAL HISTORY OF THE WAR
Date -7 AUG. 1917

Army Form C. 2118.

Vol 23

WAR DIARY
or
INTELLIGENCE SUMMARY.

WAR DIARY OF 60th FIELD AMBULANCE FOR JUNE 1917

Army Form C. 2118.

WAR DIARY
or
INTELLIGENCE SUMMARY.
(Erase heading not required.)

Place	Date	Hour	Summary of Events and Information	Remarks and references to Appendices
H.16.D.9.b. Sheet 57C 1/40000	June 1st 1917		Nr BAPAUME Left (Rear) Dressing station. Disposition at H.Q.K. O.C., Capt Lello, Lt Mullen, Lt Montgomery 2 Tent subdivisions & Nursing Bearers (60). Capt Keith, Edward, Gray & 1½ bow half C.20.B.3.6. at M.D.S. 1 Tent subdivision & 42 men. at Loupart Post C.15.a.9.9. 1 NCO & 8 men at Collecting Post C.10.C.7.9. 3 NCOs & 14 men at Relay Post C.11.A.3.9 2 NCOs & 12 men at Infirmary ("cream") C.5.A.2.3. 1 NCO & 8 men R.A.P. (5th") C.5.C.7.8. 1 NCO & 8 men at No 1 Left Batt 2/H 11st	

Army Form C. 2118.

WAR DIARY
or
INTELLIGENCE SUMMARY.
(Erase heading not required.)

Instructions regarding War Diaries and Intelligence Summaries are contained in F. S. Regs., Part II. and the Staff Manual respectively. Title pages will be prepared in manuscript.

Place	Date	Hour	Summary of Events and Information	Remarks and references to Appendices
H.16.d.9.5		1 p.m.	Coraille R'bain - Nil	
sheet 57.C.			R'bain - 9 p.m.	Coraille R'bain Nil
40/50			250 lamps kept sent up to Loosy pits Shelley? Ave near M.D.S. - continuin	Loosy av. 9.
		9 p.m.	Brau Surgeon ? 62nd F.A. wanting to relieve Co. 7 M. Sgt. Capt Mills to collecting post - no further stretchering ? pots R.	
	9th June	noon	- unable to reach VAUX on account ? shelling	
		6 p.m.	to M.D.S. - work proceeding	
		7 p.m.	Cpl. McArthur to M.D.S. to relieve Cpl Gray.	
	3rd June	to M.D.S with D.D.M.S. D=Stop VAUX LX.		
		10 a.m	heavy shelling Ave road VAUX LX.	
		2 p.m.	Capt REEVE admitted from 11th K.R.R. with ruptured muscle R.A.M.C.	
		7 p.m.	Capt BENNETT 62nd F. Amb arrived for duty vice Capt REEVE. (sick)	

WAR DIARY
or
INTELLIGENCE SUMMARY.

Army Form C. 2118.

Place	Date	Hour	Summary of Events and Information	Remarks and references to Appendices
H 16 D	9.5		New Field Medical Cards A.F. W.3118 issued. Extra cards in use.	
	4.6.17		A daily visit is being made to M.O.S. — it is possible to reach I. Park by day. I see Inners Park — Collecting posts by night.	Casualties Rt. Ors. 2 Lt. 20.
	5.6.17.		Capts KENNEDY & MULLAN — posted to Battalions. Capt McARTHUR hopes to 1/5 K.R.R.s. Shelling continues fairly heavily near A.D.S.	Casualties Rt. Or. 9 Lt. o. 19.
	6.6.17		54 N.C.Os & Men of 60 & 6.9 Mont sent up to Graham Reserve & 62nd Mont further work continues as L.R.D.S. rp.o8. Conville Bolen Orr debris to Benham Luper & B6 towards Bolen.	Casualties Rt. Ors. 6 Lt. 11.
	7.6.17			Casualties Rt. Ors. 7 Lt. 14.
	8.6.17		R.Bolls. R.A.P. moves to C 10 c 8.7.	Casualties Rt. Ors. 5 Lt. 20.

WAR DIARY or INTELLIGENCE SUMMARY

Army Form C. 2118.

Place	Date	Hour	Summary of Events and Information	Remarks and references to Appendices
H.16.d.9.5.	8 June		R.E. to see Collecting Post - in view of phosphorus + gas and the constant shelling little better 5 wounds. Rifle in 20. 6 M.D.S. blocked by Cralon. 16 wd shell bursting in Mannequin 2/11 a.m. - 2 wounds, remainder through B.30 cavity N.Y.D. CCS MRNS ran separately am I.19 in F.Amb. CCS MRNS ran separately. Ford Cars to be stationed in Boy opposite C.P. C10C7.9 Shed 579 twice at Cross road C.11.A.1.6 between 10.30 + 3.30 am - F.S. Convent obtained. This was the evacuation of badly wounded can pass a long, 2 rows, stretch carry Road 6 G.11.7.1.6. Remember R.S., asked to know material from opposite M.D.S. also to Clister and Dugout built which one would be built from Gognicourt M.D.S. shelled at 2 A.M. Ry W Belo 5 tall 12 wounded. Reports 5 left 12. A.D.M.S. visited an advance Headquarters. Dug out has been about arrange for further materials. HIRONDELLE belong - the has been about willing to continue continuous heard our armour B.M.Oh + R.A.P.s 2 Battln on Cine.	
10½ MPS			Visits R.P.nt - Collecting Pt.Colhery Post. it being warmer to walk on the by day - fair hours shelling - but ground in just enough gives. MMD was whole skeleton	
MMPA			Cog. 2 cc. grown	

Army Form C. 2118.

WAR DIARY
or
INTELLIGENCE SUMMARY.
(Erase heading not required.)

Place	Date	Hour	Summary of Events and Information	Remarks and references to Appendices
H.Q. D.Q.S.	10.6.17		Captn. R.S.C. reported on an inspection of horses - question sent to Division re horse inspectors. Further returns handed down for Enlarging A.D.S. further Gurka sent. Wounded Reptd to be patients in Hospital averaging 80 averages about 5 Sept 15.	Gourock Railway Wellesley
	11.6.17		Pte Jno Connellor 1. arrived with C.R.E. re trump with M.D.S. — as this is left.	
	12.6.17		Visited A.D.S. walks & headsupt. Lt MARBURY & KANE United States (Army) joined as MEDICAL Officers reinforcements from 50th Division & arrived in surveying. 12 O.R. attached to our A.T.S. & march in commbs Pt Nil 58 turn wounded. Support Balls R.M.O. rmvd C16.B.3.B to K.7. In View Lick reserves. CRE revamps at C20. & CRE re cable at NOREUIL also. Saw CRA re camouflage at C20. CRE received U.S.R. to C.20 D.A.Q.M.G. re Horse inspections re Lt MARBURY & KANE U.S.R. Wellsby	
	13.6.17	9.30 AM	Took 2 new American Officers to Loading post - took necessary Stations & walks them. A Drainage doing good work there - Continues of M.D.S. & A.S.P.22 Cpl Batho improving & rebuilding shifts & C.S.P.22 left Ballu. Compar 58 ston Rmpa. C.S.A 23. 100 yards 2.3 Connelly Pt 2. Connelly Pt 7.	

WAR DIARY or INTELLIGENCE SUMMARY
Army Form C. 2118.

Place	Date	Hour	Summary of Events and Information	Remarks and references to Appendices
H.16.D.95			Lieut Fulmer RAMC evacuated (sick) ?	
	14.6.17		Lieut Butler RAP moves to C.S.9 B.3. Pt Lola ML killed. ?	evacuated
	15.6.17		Made loading M.L & Collecting tent at R.A.P. about noon. Collecting pit with shuts work in further improving. Collecting pit with a view to the day evacuating cases also at R.A.P.	Rt 3 letter. 16
	16.6.17		A considerable number of casualties are brought in from 68 Division in our right.	Pt ML left 15. Pt ML K/E 39
	17.6.17		Orders from G.S.M. — Stone situated to our main from 7 port ill chance of M.D.S. † from the heavy shelling — evacuate to M5	Pt ML left 7
	18.6.17		Further heavy shelling — created M5 60 at 69 & ? and Bearers are taken today Relief in left section.	
	19.6.17		Made today hut & M.D.S work necessary satisfactory — L.R.O.S M.D.S has now a command of ? 150 patient in 40 hrs can	Pt L. left 16
	20.6.17		Inspection by D.M.S. 14 Army + DDMS. W Corps — very many ? + S.M.S. Welcome — very satisfactory — no criticism of all.	

WAR DIARY or INTELLIGENCE SUMMARY

Army Form C. 2118.

Place	Date	Hour	Summary of Events and Information	Remarks and references to Appendices
H.16.d.9.6. Sheet 57.C.	22/6/17		ASTWD informed me that be considered himself & supports to Captn. Lathgate to defend the Ambulance G2 Brown - absent G2 64 F.A. arrive to obtain government R.B.	
		10.00	A.D.W.S. 62nd Divn & O.C. 2/3 went asking F.A. arriving at A.23.c.2.8. Reconnoitred road to near F.L.A. Ambulance (Tent Subdivision) Equipment packed. B. & C. Section. 94 BUDNER, R.A.M.C. killed & P.6 ELLIOTT & HARPER wounded by 96 ELLIOTT & HARPER - slight shell shock N.Y.D.(N)	
	23.6.17		H.E. twenty near L.R.A.P. (C.5.a.2.3.) p6 CHELMSFORD shelling soon ceased - Enemy artillery becoming more active -	
	24.6.17		F.A. O.C. 2/3 waiting orders - problems of committee re w present shelter of evacuation re. Enemy artillery becoming more active again 11. O.R. 2/3 W.R. F.A. and Ammunition wd at M.D.S. 2 O.R. do do do attached too Wind and 7.50 am - Shell in on evacuating team - skyles about 900 yds to N.N.W.	

WAR DIARY or INTELLIGENCE SUMMARY

Army Form C. 2118.

Place	Date	Hour	Summary of Events and Information	Remarks and references to Appendices
H.16.d.9.6	25.6.17		33 men +1 N.C.O. & 62 nd Fld Amb's relieved Capt KIRTON arrived from A.D.S.	
			Lt. MONTGOMERY + 3 O.R. to DOMESMONT (LENS-1-100000 B.5) as an advance party 1 Tent Subdivision & transport marches in rear 59 th Bgde Group	
		4 p.m.	GOMIECOURT. A.23.c.28.a. an advance party Capt KIRTON in charge & medical arrangements of 59 th Brigade – with aux.. man, body. 2 Officers wet thing and those to M.O.'s to talk over 2/3 w.w. Redan 2/32" wet thing own (tracks) to the house) over to	
			Present arrangement George TUSON Field Ambulance Front Line R.A.P. 1 C.S.a.3.3 R.A.P. 1 C.S.d.5.6. 7th Bn R.A.P. (No longer under our care) Forward Relay Post C.11.A.3.9. A.D.S. C.10.c.7.9 Loading post C.10.d.1.7 wgt C.10.c.7.9 C.25.a.9⅟₂x9⅟₂ Waggon Exchange	men NCOs 8 1+ 8 1 — — 12 2 16 3 6 1 1 — 1 —

WAR DIARY or INTELLIGENCE SUMMARY

Army Form C. 2118.

Place	Date	Hour	Summary of Events and Information	Remarks and references to Appendices
H.16.D.9.5	25/6/17		Foot inspection held.	
	26.6.17		Regiment marched to GOMIECOURT. Inspection revisits at GOMIECOURT. 4 Officers and 100 other ranks arrived by Bus from R.A.P. 2½ hrs. being taken over to 2½ hrs. One left side of line	Field ambulance 2/7
Sheds C to N GOMIECOURT	27.6.17		Front line evacuation arrangements handed over to 4 pm. Left MARCHED 2 pm for GOMIECOURT arriving at 4 pm. O/C was very J. And at noon and O/3 was patient house on 6 o'/3 war moving 7. And at noon Hospital at H.16.d.9.5. & 30 patient house on 6 o/3 war Amiens x airings	
GOMIECOURT	28.6.17		Transport with Lt EDMOND & MAROONY marches at 7am. for Amiens x airings. at 2.15 PM Major & Pannant 8 pm buses & bus blown down by heavy storm, rained at 10am and reached CANDAS EXCHANGE; Unit entrained at ACHIET-LE-GRAND at 10am. and reached CANDAS of DOMESMONT. Marched via BEAUVILLE & DOMESMONT and via BEAUQUESNE & CANDAS of	
DOMESMONT Sheet 8 LENS 10,000	29.6.17		at 2.15 pm and reached DOMESMONT at 7pm. Transport arriving at 10 pm.	
	30.6.17		Route march to all ranks 10-12 a.m. Training begun. Heavy rain in afternoon. Cleaning billets - company hospital &c.	

Lt. Col. Nicholl
DOMESMONT.

A.C.Osburn Lt.Col. RAMC
Comg. 6 Co. Field Amb.

COMMITTEE FOR THE
MEDICAL HISTORY OF THE WAR
Date 10 SEP. 1917

No. 60. 7. O.

B.E.F.

SUMMARY OF MEDICAL WAR DIARIES FOR

60th F.A., 20th Divn. 14th Corps, 5th Army.
from 21.7.17.

WESTERN FRONT July- Sept. 1917.

O.C. Lt. Col. A.C. Osburn.

SUMMARISED UNDER THE FOLLOWING HEADING.

Phase "D" 1. Passchendaele Operations July-Nov. 1917

(a) Operations commencing 1st July 1917.

B.E.F.

<u>60th F.A. 20th Divn. 14th Corps, 5th Army.</u>   WESTERN FRONT.
<u>O.C. Lt. Col. A.C. Osburn.</u>   July-Aug. '17

<u>Phase "D" 1. Passchendaele Operations July-Nov. 1917.</u>
(a). Operations commencing 1/7/17.

1917.	<u>Headquarters.</u> At F.10.c.8.6.(27.)
July 21st.	<u>Moves and Transfer.</u> Unit transferred with 20th Divn. from 4th Corps, 4th Army to 14th Corps, 5th Army and arrived at F.10.c.8.6. (27)
24th.	<u>Moves Detachment:</u> 2 and 18 to 61st C.C.S. Dozinghem for duty.
30th.	<u>Moves:</u> To A.16.b.8.8. Concentration Area (28)
31st.	<u>Operations:</u> Zero hour 3.50 a.m. Bombardment till 7.30 a.m.
	<u>Medical Arrangements:</u> 2 and 151 sent to W.W. Coll. Post (62nd Field Ambulace) to assist with casualties.
	<u>Casualties Evacuation:</u> About 300 wounded waiting to be cleared at 3 p.m.
	<u>Operations Enemy.</u> Area N.E. of camp shelled at 4 p.m.

B.E.F.

60th F.A. 20th Divn. 14th Corps, 5th Army.   WESTERN FRONT
O.C. Lt. Col. A.C. Asburn.   July-Aug. '17

Phase "D" 1. Passchendaele Operations July-Nov. 1917.
(a). Operations commencing 1/7/17.

1917.	**Headquarters.** At F.10.c.8.6.(27.)
July 21st.	**Moves and Transfer.** Unit transferred with 20th Divn. from 4th Corps, 4th Army to 14th Corps, 5th Army and arrived at F.10.c.8.6. (27)
24th.	**Moves Detachment:** 2 and 18 to 61st C.C.S. Dozinghem for duty.
30th.	**Moves:** To A.16.b.8.8. Concentration Area (28)
31st.	**Operations:** Zero hour 3.50 a.m. Bombardment till 7.30 a.m.
	Medical Arrangements: 2 and 151 sent to W.W. Coll. Post (62nd Field Ambulace) to assist with casualties.
	Casualties Evacuation: About 300 wounded waiting to be cleared at 3 p.m.
	Operations Enemy. Area N.E. of camp shelled at 4 p.m.

Army Form C. 2118.

WAR DIARY
or
INTELLIGENCE SUMMARY.
(Erase heading not required.)

Vol 24

CONFIDENTIAL

War Diary
of
60 Field Ambulance
for
July 1917.

Army Form C. 2118.

WAR DIARY
or
INTELLIGENCE SUMMARY.
(Erase heading not required.)

Instructions regarding War Diaries and Intelligence Summaries are contained in F. S. Regs., Part II. and the Staff Manual respectively. Title pages will be prepared in manuscript.

Place	Date	Hour	Summary of Events and Information	Remarks and references to Appendices
DOMESMONT.			Unit in billets	
LENS SHEET No. 11. 100.0.0			Convoy Present O.C. & Capt Gray, Kirton, Solomons, 2nd Lts. Montrouy, KANE MARBURY U.S.R U.S.R and 203 other ranks	
	1st July 1917.		Work proceeding cleaning - whitewashing draining removing manure h.k. from billets, constructing ablution benches - latrines incinerators &c. Carpenters employed making Seat Inspection room, weather proof. Training scheme continues.	
	July 15th & 16th 1917		During the period 15th to 18th" The unit was employed in drawing, refitting & overhauling equipment. A small detention hospital was organized of about 6 beds at the circle of the Brigade Group, been treated. Daily route marches, drills, lectures on first aid sanitation, sports.	

Army Form C. 2118.

WAR DIARY
or
INTELLIGENCE SUMMARY
(Erase heading not required.)

Place	Date	Hour	Summary of Events and Information	Remarks and references to Appendices
DOMESMONT LENS SHEET No 11	July 1st-10th (cont'd) 1 p.m.		Kit inspections, equipment inspections, parades, lectures & general refitting were carried out.	
	July 4th 1917	9 a.m.	The unit was inspected by S.D.C. Bream. He was favourably impressed by the unit & done but thought that some steps should be taken to improve the personnel of the A.S.C. attached to the unit. A reinforcement of one QM and 8 men from Sqd. on base depot joined the unit.	
	July 7th 1917		Lt Kane U.S.R. evacuated to No 3 Canadian Gen Hosp. Boulogne with Cerebral Jaundice.	
	July 10-20		The programme of training was continued — lectures, drills, route marches carried out regularly. The rehearsing of gas masks & general refitting was completed. Sports were held, & interaction competitions in football & cricket carried through. An excellent concert — the performers all being men of the unit was held in an orchard on the night of No 18th. The strength of the unit on 29.6.17 (the day we came to Domesmont) was 21 officers — 708 men & 204 O.R. The strength was 22.3 — 60 officers & 274 O.R. on army the day we moved North — 21st inst. We had in the interval Reinforcements of RAMC & 3 reinforcements A.SC. There were three inoculations done. 1 Sergt N.C. went on leave on 11th July.	

11/7/17

WAR DIARY or INTELLIGENCE SUMMARY

Army Form C. 2118.

Place	Date	Hour	Summary of Events and Information	Remarks and references to Appendices
PROVEN	19.7.17			
Belgium Rantif France Sheet 21 1/40,000			Capt Edmond & 2.O.R. went forth as advance party on 19/7/17 The unit marched out of Louvenant at 11.15 a.m. 21.7.17 and arrived at Trouilles-Cantos station at 1.30 p.m. The men fell out & lunched in the Leave camp beside the station while the entraining of the transport was being done. This was accomplished without a hitch & the men were all on board by 3.30 p.m. — 191 men & 4 officers. The C.O. left in here 2nd Batt. by Motor Ambulance. The train left punctually at 4.51 a.m. & accomplished an uninterrupted journey according to schedule as far as Hazebrouck, which was reached by 10 p.m. Thereafter owing to congestion of traffic, progress was slow & intermittent, but Proven was reached without mishap at 3 a.m. on the morning of the 22nd July. The men were detrained & marched to our Camp — situated in a wood at Shot 27 Fld. H.O. — which they reached at 4.45 a.m. & after tea had been served out, they lay down for a much needed rest.	
	21/7/17			

Army Form C. 2118.

WAR DIARY
or
INTELLIGENCE SUMMARY.
(Erase heading not required.)

Instructions regarding War Diaries and Intelligence
Summaries are contained in F.S. Regs., Part II.
and the Staff Manual respectively. Title pages
will be prepared in manuscript.

Place	Date	Hour	Summary of Events and Information	Remarks and references to Appendices
PROVEN Belgium (Partly) France Sheet 27 1/40,000			F.16.D.4.0 - sheet 27 1/20,000	
	22.7.17		Sunday was spent & the men were allowed to rest after their long journey, after the ordinary tents were put up & camp arrangements made.	
	23.7.17		Anti-gas respirators for horses were issued, & a demonstration of their application was given. Before the whole unit. Two hospital tents were erected & recpt'd of the sick of the Brigade. Capt. Willis, Lt. Hanbury & 18 O.R. were attached for duty at 61 C.C.S. Dozinghem.	
	24.7.17			
	27.7.17		Capt. Kenton returned from leave.	
	28.7.17		The past week has been a quiet one. The men daily underwent drill — squad, contour, & gas-helmet drills etc. The sick of the Brigade were collected daily, either picked up in our wards, or evacuated as circumstances dictated. We were at no time under shellfire. On three occasions enemy aeroplanes passed over us during the night, dropping bombs in the neighbourhood, but not in no case nearer than ten kilog'rammes, with the exception of two new performances	
	29.7.17.		Orders received to be ready to march to Canada Farm area on the night	
	29.7.17.		O.C. visited 3 A.D.S. on Canal Bank & Coy. L. Lowrie's C.P. at MOUTON FORM. B.14.A.6.2. sheet 28 NW.

30/31 July
Will A.S.m.p 38½ Division

T2134. Wt. W708—776. 500000. 4/15. Sir J. C. & S.

Army Form C. 2118.

WAR DIARY
or
INTELLIGENCE SUMMARY.
(Erase heading not required.)

Instructions regarding War Diaries and Intelligence Summaries are contained in F.S. Regs., Part II. and the Staff Manual respectively. Title pages will be prepared in manuscript.

Place	Date	Hour	Summary of Events and Information	Remarks and references to Appendices
Sheet 28 N.W. 20000	30.7.17.	9.a.m	Bn. H.Qrs. 62 2nd Lieut. & C. Red Station WATOU - also A.16.B.8.8 & H. Camp.	
F.10.D.4.0 Sheet 27 Hooge			Bn. marches to concentration Area A.16. at 10.25 p.m. via Route A. Chemin Militaire, International Corner A.9.a.r.3. Sheet 28 N.W.	
A.16.B.8.8 sheet 28 N.W. 20000	31/7/17		Zero Hour 3.5.A.M. Our bombardment started & continued until 7.30 a.m. after which it gradually diminished until perhaps about normal at noon. 6.30 a.m & 9 a.m visited Bn. H.Qrs. Message from A.D.M.S. that 62 2nd Lieut. Corp. L/Cp. were taking it easier. Visit told Edward Kirton & Lt. Montgomerie & assist Lieut. Montgomerie & assist Lieut. Rutherford 157 O.R.	
		11.30	walked back at 3 pm - still about 300 wounded waiting. Enemy friends divisions about 4 pm. Enemy began shelling area N.E. of Camp.	A.C.O'Brien Lt. Col

140/2364

No. 60. 7. A.

COMMITTEE FOR THE
MEDICAL HISTORY OF THE WAR
Date -1 OCT. 1917

B.E.F.

SUMMARY OF MEDICAL WAR DIARIES FOR

60th F.A., 20th Divn. 14th Corps, 5th Army.
from 21.7.17.

WESTERN FRONT July- Sept. 1917.

O.C. Lt. Col. A.C. Osburn.

SUMMARISED UNDER THE FOLLOWING HEADING.

Phase "D" 1. Passchendaele Operations July-Nov. 1917

(a) Operations commencing 1st July 1917.

Aug. 1st.	<u>Moves</u>:	To Copper Nolle Cabaret A.17.a.2.6.(28)
5th.	<u>Moves Detachment</u>:	1 T.S.D. to take over Mordacq Farm B.17.c.9.3. 1 T.S.D. to take over Sussex A.D.S. C.19.c.2.3.
	<u>Operations Enemy.</u>	Heavy shelling of area around Mordacq Farm.
	<u>Casualties:</u>	0 and 30 mostly from R.F.A. in vicinity.
6th.	<u>Operations Enemy.</u>	Mordacq Farm still being shelled.
11th.	<u>Moves:</u>	To B.15.c.5.3. (28.)

B.E.F. 2.

60th F.A. 20th Divn. 14th Corps, 5th Army. WESTERN FRONT.
O.C. Lt. Col. A.C. Osburn.   Aug. Sept. '1

Phase "D" 1. (a) (Cont.)

1917.

Aug. 11th. (Cont.)	Medical Arrangements: Div. W.W.Coll. Post formed at Cheapside B.17.d.8.8. as original post at B.12.c.2.3. became untenable through shell fire.
12th.	Operations Enemy. Hostile shelling of area near unit
13th.	" " Further shelling.
16th.	Operations: Casualties: Zero 4.45 a.m. About 720 cases passed through W.W. Coll. post up to 1 p.m. many having to be made into lying cases.
19th.	Moves: To F.10.c.5.5. Priory Camp.
30th.	Decorations. Sgt. Barker awarded M.M.

Aug. 1st.	<u>Moves:</u>	To Copper Nolle Cabaret A.17.a.2.6.(28)
5th.	<u>Moves Detachment:</u>	1 T.S.D. to take over Mordacq Farm B.17.c.9.3. 1 T.S.D. to take over Sussex A.D.S. C.19.c.2.3.

<u>Operations Enemy.</u> Heavy shelling of area around Mordacq Farm.

<u>Casualties:</u> 0 and 30 mostly from R.F.A. in vicinity.

6th.	<u>Operations Enemy.</u>	Mordacq Farm still being shelled.
11th.	<u>Moves:</u>	To B.15.c.5.3. (28.)

B.E.F.

60th F.A. 20th Divn. 14th Corps, 5th Army. WESTERN FRONT.
O.C. Lt. Col. A.C. Osburn.   Aug. Sept. '1

Phase "D" 1. (a) (Cont.)

1917.

Aug. 11th. (Cont.)	<u>Medical Arrangements</u>: Div. W.W.Coll. Post formed at Cheapside B.17.d.8.8. as original post at B.12.c.2.3. became untenable through shell fire.
12th.	<u>Operations Enemy.</u> Hostile shelling of area near unit
13th.	" " Further shelling.
16th.	<u>Operations: Casualties:</u> Zero 4.45 a.m. About 720 cases passed through W.W. Coll. post up to 1 p.m. many having to be made into lying cases.
19th.	<u>Moves:</u> To F.10.c.5.5. Priory Camp.
30th.	<u>Decorations.</u> Sgt. Barker awarded M.M.

Army Form C. 2118.

WAR DIARY
or
INTELLIGENCE SUMMARY.
(Erase heading not required.)

Vol 25.

WAR DIARY
OF
60th FIELD AMBULANCE
FOR
AUGUST 1917

WAR DIARY
or
INTELLIGENCE SUMMARY.

Army Form C. 2118.

Place	Date	Hour	Summary of Events and Information	Remarks and references to Appendices
A.17.A.2.6 sheet 28 / Yprès			Near COPPER NOLLE CABARET (WOESTEN - POPERINGHE area) Proceed with Head Quarters — O.C.: Capt. KIRTON - EDMOND - MONGOMERY 2 C of R Subalterns - Bearer Serains & Transport. Attached { 1 officer 114 *R.B. } for Training. 49. OR 59th Brigade 20. Officers. 10 men at 61. C.C.S.	
	1.8.17		Heavy rain all day — Billet being shared with 130 & 129th Sea Forth: 38th Division. Camp in a very bad state - many used & sleeping elsewhere - Men employed in cleaning camp - men employed in attending Camp	
	2.8.17		Heavy rain all day — 8. O.R. returns from C.M.D.S	
	3.8.17.		Heavy rain all day — Camp flooded - Training continues } attacks men as far as health permits.	

WAR DIARY or INTELLIGENCE SUMMARY

Army Form C. 2118.

Place	Date	Hour	Summary of Events and Information	Remarks and references to Appendices
A.17.A.2.6.			Sheet 28	
	4/8/17		Cpl Grey/O.R. returns from Prisoner Cage duty. Nurse from O.C. 61 CCS that Fred Culverwer are not to be returned.	
	5/8/17	Noon	Capt Gray + 1 Fred Culverwer sent to take over MORBECQ Farm (13. O.R.) & 1 Fred Culverwer sent to take over Sussex A.D.S. Cpl KIRTON + EDMOND + 18 O.R. C.19.c.2.3. B.17.c.9.3.	
		2 PM	Inspected MORBECQ Farm & Sussex A.D.S. having 30 admissions including R.F.A. from Shelley MORBECQ FARM area Hounge pattern in vicinity.	
	6/8/17		Lt T. JOHNSTONE R.A.M.C. arrived as Quarter Master relief me. to find 2 motor clerks to C.M.D.S — sent Pars vas & Km 20 Mitchell beams (Refinery) to 6.15 PM H.Quarter B.21.A.3.0 sent 2 extra clerks Isala clerk + 8 9.O.S. and Sussex farm & Sussex A.D.S.	
		4 PM	took MORBECQ FARM & Sussex A.D.S. being shelled — MORBECQ FARM still	

WAR DIARY
or
INTELLIGENCE SUMMARY.
(Erase heading not required.)

Army Form C. 2118.

Place	Date	Hour	Summary of Events and Information	Remarks and references to Appendices
A.17.A.2.6. Sheet 28 Ypres	7/8/17		"Train" sent a/s.m. Cross R.S.C. to relieve S/S Major SEABORNE. walk reports to D.A.D.M.S. as S.M. Cross has only been 3 weeks & has all division of this never previously been with a/s M/S in the Field. Orders No 2 to send 12. Stretcher Brs. to each Regt of 59th Brigade 12 and 12. Stretcher Brs. to each Regt of 59th Brigade – Count ? Supply ? Guards Division – Pte Taylor in collision with motor cyclist. Field proceeded up to Advance HQrs (80.R.) to B.15.c.5.3 Sheet 28 & advance party & Advance HQrs (80.R.) to B.15.c.5.3 Sheet 28 & Advance party, and to RAMC personnel all 4 large motor ambulances from Sandbag, and to RAMC personnel all 4 large motor ambulances 4. M.T. personnel and Canada Farm A.10.A.2.B. to duty to XIV Corps MDS Chouse ? MORDACH Farm military wounded	
	8.8.17		Lt Montgomery to Chouse ? MORDACH Farm divisional Capt Gray to D/ army prisoners Cage at F.10.outsk (27) took over about 15 wounds & 30 sick men 39 Q.R. Bearers under O.C. 61 form 1 by 20 bearers along the Klul 64 division under O.C. 61 form by 20 bearers along the b continue work 90 R. proceded to B.15.C.5.3 61 F.Amb. (reported at Frezcher R.A.P.)	
	9.8.17.	16	O.R. bearers proceeded to O.C. 61 F.Amb. up to 80. Hurry Bean division, up to 80. Lt Brotts U.S. Army reported his arrival on duty	

Army Form C. 2118.

WAR DIARY
or
INTELLIGENCE SUMMARY.
(Erase heading not required.)

Instructions regarding War Diaries and Intelligence Summaries are contained in F. S. Regs., Part II. and the Staff Manual respectively. Title pages will be prepared in manuscript.

Place	Date	Hour	Summary of Events and Information	Remarks and references to Appendices
A.M.A.2.6. Sheet 20				
	9.8.17	10000	A.M. T.R. Wilson R.A.M.C. reports for duty. R.S.M. Osborne relieved to 20 Reinforcement Camp. M/55829 Cpl Cross reports for duty. Lt Brooks, Lt Johnston & Lt Clarke (39th Royal Sussex) + 28 O.R. (Reinforcements) to Reserve Bn. 15. C.S.3. to new reinforcements.	
	10.8.17	17	Lt Trotter posted to 38th Division. Capt Wills, Lt Manbury + 70 O.R. returned from 61 C.C.S. 10.R. to the Base. U.S. Army. Lt Manbury proceeded to Sussex A.P.S. New bed to R.C. Post to be built at B.12.d.3.2. Following sent to O.C. 6th Bn 1 water cart. 2 H.A.M. carts 8 H.D. Horses. 1 whole thatcher carrier. 4 L.D.R. 4. whole thatcher covers. + 8 O.R. O.C.6. +7.O.R. Total 81. Capt Kirton posted to Reaux Swain camp.	
	11.8.17		Capt Ash reports his arrival for choice duty. 1 O.R. sent to 14 Corps H.Qrs for choice duty. Lt Clark + 25 riflemen sent to O.C. Beaux Brown (to help in corrunches work at New Rn W.W. C.P.) Capt Wills + 10 O.R. +tent +equipment — dung, rubgin, staking, alignment damage to proceed to look over cookery shape? the XIV Corps Scrub Collecting Point at A.12.C.3.3.	

WAR DIARY or INTELLIGENCE SUMMARY

Army Form C. 2118.

Place	Date	Hour	Summary of Events and Information	Remarks and references to Appendices
B.15.c.5.3. Nw 20 troops S.E. of ELVERDINGHE	11.8.17		All quiet to Wieprecht Area & Bn Headquarters. Dis. W/Cpl at B.N.C.2.3. shell 20 found unexploded from shell fire – construction work abandoned. Near Pd. Pelerin – CHEAPSIDE. B.17.d.8.6. & took 4 enemy Tanks away. very heavy	
	12.8.17		3. O.R. to MORACQ FARM – work thru the enemy wire over 100 wounded daily. 2 O.R. to "Sussex" Post work burying bodies, being carried out daily. 1st Lt. KANE reports to arrive in duty. 2nd Lt. KING – posts to 62nd Field Amb 19. U.S. Army. area was heaguarters beginning. Hostile shelling? area near heaguarters beginning.	
	13.8.17		5.O.R. to CHEAPSIDE to duty – 2000 sandbags repaired road to men on with the work. Daily visits to CANAL BANK to MORACQ & CHEAPSIDE also to XIV Corps. the D.W.W.C. Pots at CANADA FARM – personnel now working Post C. Pot at 80 Beaver & 50 Tent Division personnel now working in 4 separate detachments with rations, dungs, greene, equipment, personnel to 7. ram to bed daily. Heaguarters constants (shells) 4.O.R. to Reinforce Joined. ELVERDINGHE 3 officers & 23 Other Ranks returned from MOUTON FARM B.14.A.2.7 Staff Captain to Army HqQuarters to 5.8.16 Tell Three in charge of flow	

WAR DIARY or INTELLIGENCE SUMMARY

Army Form C. 2118.

Place	Date	Hour	Summary of Events and Information	Remarks and references to Appendices
16" Pozyn(?)19|7			Relieving stores sent back ink & room 6 to A.17, A.2.6. heavy shelling Roof at C. 15.A.5.3. collapses into store - number of heavy shelly wall being shelley at B.14.A.2.7.	bombing
B.14.A.2.7. C.15.A.5.3.			16 O.R. sent from BRUTON FARM (B.14.A.2.7) to join Brown detachment to Brown Division on detachment to room. 1 Officer	
			Strength a Brown Division	
			↑ 96 O.R.	
			Capt ASH I.O.R. to CHEAPSIDE	
			p Brown. 1 Girl Guide.	
14.8.17			p Brown 1 Girl Guide to join Brown Division at 61° 9° Mar 69	
15.8.17			1 H.D. Horn & 2 O.R. A.S.C. to join CHEAPSIDE	
			(wale car to CHEAPSIDE)	
16.8.17			(Capt GRAY reported at 3 p.m.) Visit to CHEAPSIDE remains them at work until	
			Zero hour 4:45 p.m. 4:30 p.m. 1 p.m.	
			about 720 cars passed through — many having the road only lying	
			cars — many German wounds about 8 or 10 being a Cretican to C.S	
			dump the day visiting Survey 4.159 lying can should with many	
			spent over to the day visiting Sunset 4.159 lying can should seen at Canada Farm	
			Seven wounded about 200 that were at Canada Farm 97 all work	
			Disposition of Unit as follows, Brown in front line 20	
			R.A.M.C "Sunset" A.D.S 20	
			"CHEAPSIDE" D.W.M.C.P 6	
			XIV Corps Book Cp 10	
			XIV Corps M.D.S 15	
(Report of operations attached)			Another detachment at Hoogenacker(?) fallen on Cans	10

Army Form C. 2118.

WAR DIARY
or
INTELLIGENCE SUMMARY.
(Erase heading not required.)

Instructions regarding War Diaries and Intelligence Summaries are contained in F.S. Regs., Part II. and the Staff Manual respectively. Title pages will be prepared in manuscript.

Place	Date	Hour	Summary of Events and Information	Remarks and references to Appendices
B.14.A.2.7.	17.8.17.		3 O.R. wounded 1 H.O. Horse killed. Concentration begun at 9.17.A.2.6. Coppernole Farm began. Capt Grey + 8 O.R. to F.10.C.5.5 to take over camp at Prior Camp - Louie Woods - in 59th Bgde group area. Being at Maton Farm struck store at Elverdinghe grounds Dump made at Moulin 1=0 PM	
	18.8.17		2 O.R. severely wounded - "Sussex" relieved at 4 pm "Cheapside" " " noon Moesacq : Twomoolam at 8 km Cpl Wilks at Conrad Farm relieved at 11 pm All ranks concentrating at Coppernole preparatory to attachments to F.10.C.S.S.	

Army Form C. 2118.

WAR DIARY
or
INTELLIGENCE SUMMARY.
(Erase heading not required.)

Instructions regarding War Diaries and Intelligence Summaries are contained in F. S. Regs., Part II. and the Staff Manual respectively. Title pages will be prepared in manuscript.

Place	Date	Hour	Summary of Events and Information	Remarks and references to Appendices
F.10. C.S.S. LOUIEWOODS Sheet 27	19.8.17		Capt Montgomery took over in charge of 11th F.R.B.	
	20.8.17		Capt Solomon & 20 R on leave 6 cartons	
			Capt Solomon & 20 R & 10 O/Rkns	
	21.8.17		Capt ASH sent to Tents & marg class & 10 O/Rkns	
	22.8.17		G.O.C. 59th Bde inspects camp	
			G.O.C. 5 Division visits camp	
			Recommend alarm for D.C.M. & 2 military medals sent in	
	23.8.17.		6 O/Rs returned to Mob Vet Section in 29th Division	
			4 Reinforcements arrived	
	24. 1917 Aug		6 O.R. on leave	
			Staff captain veterinary re training up 6 32 Cheshire leave per	
			& remaining in hospital	
			battalion	

Army Form C. 2118.

WAR DIARY
or
INTELLIGENCE SUMMARY.

(Erase heading not required.)

Instructions regarding War Diaries and Intelligence Summaries are contained in F. S. Regs. Part II. and the Staff Manual respectively. Title pages will be prepared in manuscript.

Place	Date	Hour	Summary of Events and Information	Remarks and references to Appendices
F.10.C.5.5. PRIORY CAMP LONGUEVAL (WOOD).	25.8.17		Detachment to Army School of Cookery Lt MARBURY en route to Paris - 24-31st	
	27.8.17		Capt GRAY to 5730g R.H.A. Tennis Sn.5	
	30.8.17		Sgt BARKER military medal.	
	31.8.17		Visited MOTORS 3d K Btys at New route of evacuation in how linch Capt TAYLOR. M.O. 11" R.B. arrivals will Gas poisoning. Present with Unit O.C. Capt KIRZON WILLS. Lt JOHNSTON.	Capt ASH with 115 KRR Lt Mongomery. 11" R.B. Capt Edmond Crystford leave in Paris Lt MARBURY 5" R.H.A & Dr. Capt GRAY

A.E. Osborne
Capt
O.C. 10th Manch.

Army Form C. 2118.

WAR DIARY
or
INTELLIGENCE SUMMARY.

(Erase heading not required.)

Instructions regarding War Diaries and Intelligence Summaries are contained in F. S. Regs., Part II. and the Staff Manual respectively. Title pages will be prepared in manuscript.

Place	Date	Hour	Summary of Events and Information	Remarks and references to Appendices

A 5834 Wt. W4973 M687 750,000 8/16 D. D. & L. Ltd. Forms/C.2118/13.

Details not placed with Inv. no 10/15/38.
8/140/2438

No 60 7.a.

COMMITTEE FOR THE
MEDICAL HISTORY OF THE WAR
Date -5 NOV. 1917

<u>60th F.A., 20th Divn. 14th Corps, 5th Army.</u>   <u>WESTERN FRONT.</u>
<u>O.C. Lt. Col. A.C. Osburn.</u>   <u>Sept. '17.</u>

<u>Phase "D" 1. (a) (Cont.)</u>

1917.

Sept. 24th.   <u>Operations Enemy:</u> Fusilier Camp bombed and gas shelled.

28th.   <u>Moves:</u>   To Hopoutre.

<u>Appendices</u>:-

1. Evacuation arrangements.

2. Report on evacuation arrangements:

Sept.	8th.	<u>Moves Detachment</u>: 1 and 56 took over Fusilier A.D.S. on Canal Bank.
	10th.	<u>Moves</u>: To Pelissier Farm B.21.a.3.0.
	16th.	<u>Operations Enemy.</u> Heavy shelling of A.D.S. and advanced posts.
	20th.	<u>Operations Medical Arrangements: Evacuation</u>:- Zero hour 5.50 a.m. Attack on Eagle Trench. Appendix 1 (Marked Paras only) and Appendix 2 Attached. Evacuation worked smoothly.
	22nd.	<u>Operations Enemy. Casualties:</u> Bombing in vicinity of Fusilier Camp. Stream of wounded still coming down from the line. Relay post at Galwitz had to be evacuated owing to heavy shelling.
	23rd.	<u>Operations Enemy.</u> Pelissier Farm bombed.

Sept.	8th.	<u>Moves Detachment:</u> 1 and 56 took over Fusilier A.D.S. on Canal Bank.
	10th.	<u>Moves:</u> To Pelissier Farm B.21.a.3.0.
	16th.	<u>Operations Enemy.</u> Heavy shelling of A.D.S. and advanced posts.
	20th.	<u>Operations Medical Arrangements; Evacuation:-</u> Zero hour 5.50 a.m. Attack on Eagle Trench. Appendix 1 (Marked Paras only) and Appendix 2 Attached. Evacuation worked smoothly.
	22nd.	<u>Operations Enemy. Casualties:</u> Bombing in vicinity of Fusilier Camp Stream of wounded still coming down from the line. Relay post at Galwitz had to be evacuated owing to heavy shelling.
	23rd.	<u>Operations Enemy.</u> Pelissier Farm bombed.

60th F.A., 20th Divn. 14th Corps, 5th Army.   WESTERN FRONT.
O.C. Lt. Col. A.C. Osburn.   Sept. '17.

Phase "D" 1. (a) (Cont.)

1917.

Sept. 24th.   Operations Enemy: Fusilier Camp bombed and gas shelled.
     28th.   Moves: To Hopoutre.
              Appendices:-
              1. Evacuation arrangements.
              2. Report on evacuation arrangements:

Army Form C. 2118.

WAR DIARY
or
INTELLIGENCE SUMMARY

(Erase heading not required.)

Vol 26

WAR DIARY
OF
60th FIELD AMBULANCE
FOR
SEPTEMBER 1917

M/Andrew
Lt Col
Commanding
60th Field Ambulance
A.M.C.

Army Form C. 2118.

WAR DIARY
or
INTELLIGENCE SUMMARY
(Erase heading not required.)

Place	Date	Hour	Summary of Events and Information	Remarks and references to Appendices
PRIORY CAMP.			F.10.C.5.5.	
	1/4/17		Distribution of Unit	
			At Headquarters O.C. Capt KIRTON — WILLS — Lt(QM) JOHNSON	
	1.9.17		Attached to 10th KRR Capt ASH	
			11th RB Lt MONTGOMERY	
			5th Bgde RHA Capt GRAY	
			Capt EDMONDS	
			M. ZOUGON (Civilian) Lt MARBURY	
			Paris Capt. Wills to 10 K.R.B.	
		6 p.m.	Capt. Wills to 10 K.R.B.	
			Capt. Wills to 5th Bgde on intervals	
	2.9.17		Sgt HANDY; BICKERTON; BROWN; BARRIT; Col FREEMAN returned from Schools Clubs	
			Lt MONTGOMERY returned "	
			Capt ASH returned "	
			Capt GRAY returned to 11th KRR Vice Capt McARTHUR	
			Lt MARBURY returned from leave	
	4.9.17		6 P.B. arm'd to Asst. Batman proceed to MTIS Depot IMYRE	

2449 Wt. W14957/M90 750,000 1/16 J.B.C. & A. Forms/C.2118/12.

WAR DIARY or INTELLIGENCE SUMMARY

Army Form C. 2118.

Place	Date	Hour	Summary of Events and Information	Remarks and references to Appendices
PRIORY CAMP	4.9.17		1st Advance party 13 NCOs men to PELUSIER FARM	
	5.9.17		Lt HORNEY joined for duty. 2nd Advance party 21 NCOs men to PELUSIER Fm	
	6.9.17		CAPT EDMUNDS returned from leave. 3rd Advance party 13 NCOs men to PELUSIER Fm. O.C. 1/9th 2nd Mont Co. Views on front line posts with O.C. 129th 2nd Mont Co	
	7.9.17		Lt MONTGOMERY took over charge of 10th R.B. CAPT WILLS returned to duty. CAPT WILLS took over charge of 10th R.B. Training perfecting – annul	
	1.9.17 to 7.9.17		Unit in Rest. – Hospital Statistics.	
	8.9.17		Visited front line posts & began to take our share in Front line work. 156 O.R. took over from FUSILIER A.D.S. CAPT KIRTON & WILLS on CANAL BANK	

WAR DIARY or INTELLIGENCE SUMMARY

Army Form C. 2118.

Place	Date	Hour	Summary of Events and Information	Remarks and references to Appendices
PRIORY CAMP	10.9.17.		Usual marches at 8 a.m. to PELISIER FARM B.21.A.3.0	
			Took over EVACUATION ARRANGEMENTS	
			3 Officers 151. O.R. Bat. Visiting Company reported for duty	
			58. Rank & 61st F.Amb. " " "	
			22. " " "	
			79. Rank & 62nd F.Amb. Ø " " "	
			19. " "	
	11.9.17		CAPT. JACOB reports his arrival	
			& relieves Lt. MAPHURYAL FUSILIER — who proceeds to CEMENT HOUSE FORWARD MDS	
			1.O.R. from 61st G.R. for duty	
	14.9.17		12.O.R. from 61st F.A. A.D.S. and one a officer of ADVANCE posts	
	16.9.17		Daily visits paid to A.D.S. Lt Zimmerman reports his arrival	
			Very heavy shelling	
			5.O.R. from 6th F.A. for duty	
			6th 7th — for duty CAPT BENNETT returns to Zimmerman	
	18.9.17		3.O.R. " " " be arrived from H.C.R. 61.0 P.M.	
			Capt GRAY reports his arrival & will 20 O.R. from Brig. Band.	
	19.9.17		CAPT J.H. ELLERS arrived for duty and 26.O.R. armours from Brig. Band.	

Place	Date	Hour	Summary of Events and Information	Remarks and references to Appendices
FUSILIER A.D.S.	20/9/17		2nd Headquarters moved to Fusilier during night 19th/20th Sept.	
		Zero Hour 5.50 AM		
			1. Report on Evacuation arrangements } attack 2. " " Operations (medical) }	

Army Form C. 2118.

WAR DIARY
or
INTELLIGENCE SUMMARY

(Erase heading not required.)

Instructions regarding War Diaries and Intelligence Summaries are contained in F. S. Regs., Part II. and the Staff Manual respectively. Title Pages will be prepared in manuscript.

Place	Date	Hour	Summary of Events and Information	Remarks and references to Appendices
PELUSIER FARM. FUSILIER A.D.S.	20.9.17		Zero hour 5.50 a.m. Report on arrangements & preparation attached with map. Report on the Attack on EAGLE TRENCH & Detail as on attached report. Somewhere during operations	

Army Form C. 2118.

WAR DIARY
or
INTELLIGENCE SUMMARY.

(Erase heading not required.)

Place	Date	Hour	Summary of Events and Information	Remarks and references to Appendices
FUSILIER & PELISSIER FARM.	21st Oct		Report of Operations continued — wounded arriving fairly steadily during night — stretcher cases per Hans Salvage from Bellery Order Ain Ford Car & MO's Wagon Trolley. GALWITZ & CORNER HOUSE route.	
		At 4 A.M.	Decauville made its first journey from TAMWORTH only about 3 landaus completing & shelter cars & about 8-12 stretcher cases & about 20-25 walking wounded came down — as far as W bank sunk to shelling wounded but damaged tree & a tractor being sent up to Brunchirn then to another than & 3 trucks & Con Cb to SOLFERINO shelter than was informed that the train waited until daylight by & taken to C to SOLFERINO.	
		At 9 A.M.	was informed that it was bomb on the 24. The morning journey was more or less then it 16 shell Cars run out & action for Tamworth led to further by cause had been primed to late & Tamworth had already been evacuated. Women came for lots of wounded since I am pressure they were collected.	
	8:30 am		Both Cars CROAPOD & SOLFERINO can evacuate to a certain road running to GALWITZ Area — TAMWORTH Anne down — Tamworth road would C put into CEMENT	
	9 a.m		Sends TAMWORTH car convey down to STRAY FARM — would C put into CEMENT wh Cmd Mot & present car coming down STRAY FARM — would C run the portion	
	11 a.m		Visits TAMWORTH GALWITZ & party stably all round the pouches - Horses away & having everything. Meet GOE Dunn & explain everywhere until & keep plainly 1 interrupter Decauville works to supersede Decauville Trolley	

WAR DIARY
or
INTELLIGENCE SUMMARY

Army Form C. 2118.

Place	Date	Hour	Summary of Events and Information	Remarks and references to Appendices
PELISSIER FARM.	22.9.17		Bn¹ Stretcher Squad gradually reduced to 20 in front line – remainder to reserve at S¹ JOHN, and PELISSIER.	
FUSILIER A.D.S.			Capt EDMONDS went up to relieve Capt KIRTON at CEMENT HOUSE to return & STAND BY. Bennett went up.	
		1.a.m.	1.O.R. killed. (6½ Bgde sent Stretcher Bearers Fusilier & Pelissier Farm. Enemy active. Bombing near Cork House coming down – but number unknown. Stream of wounds & sick coming down at midnight from Fusilier to Cork House. Enemy kept up [illegible] shelling – Squad will down to continuous heavy [illegible]	
		11.a.m.	Further things hum by with dummy genades with dummy forces by Enemy at 6.30 pm last night 21st included Counter attack by Enemy from ENCORE (& Fury ch) to their mounted	
		4.p.m	Call for 6 more Squad in front of Au Bon Gite, CORNER HOUSE from our in front of Au Bon Gite, (further report as per Typed pts attached).	

+ S¹ JOHN.

Place	Date	Hour	Summary of Events and Information	Remarks and references to Appendices
PELLISIER FARM.	23.9.17		SOLFERINO evacuated by 2 OR BN a Caretakers LYNPHURST to FUSILIER. 25 O.R. and Band returned to Bn. HdQrs. 25 O.R. was moved on line Capt WILLS proceed to "HORNET" known as "Fusilier 6" Capt ARH, KIRTON, 1st Fusilier Capt ARH, Capt GRAY 6 Fusilier Hd Qrs. 1st WORD received from CEMENT HOUSE Capt BOURKE 5 hrs killed in adjacent field 200 yds NE of building From Brigade RCL legends retaliates line in response to enemy arty	

Army Form C. 2118.

WAR DIARY
or
INTELLIGENCE SUMMARY.
(Erase heading not required.)

Place	Date	Hour	Summary of Events and Information	Remarks and references to Appendices
PELUSIER FARM B21.A.3.6. Sheet 20 1/20,000	24.9.17		O.C. No.11. 76th A.C. Taken round account hot. Fusilier Post. Bowles to recall all but sketchy Company. Carnot orders issued. to return to Fusilier. Capt. ASH returning to Fusilier. Capt. Wiles in hour from 232.W.Fopp.	
	25.9.17		No.11. – No.12. – No.11. – 75 Aust. & 45 Division 3 Officers – 180 men relieved Beyond Sketchy Company (Relief) reconnaissance to their end all Casualty rolls 1 Roleng. Dunlop.	
	26.9.17		Capt Pollard & 38. O.R. 61st Fusiliers & 61st F.Amb. Reserve Carly Took over SOLFERINO. 11th 9 Aust A. –	
	27.9.17		48. O.R. H.A. waggons – to returning to 61st 9 Pen (?) 61 57. OR & 1 h 62 9 Aust D. Unit in course of relief & advance Park & Fusilier.	

WAR DIARY
or
INTELLIGENCE SUMMARY.

Army Form C. 2118.

Place	Date	Hour	Summary of Events and Information	Remarks and references to Appendices
PRIORY CAMP	28th Sept 1917		F.10.C.5.5. - Handing over completed	at 11am. 28th
			Unit moved from B.21. A.3.0 Pelissier Camp	
			Lt. Hornsey to being charge 7" S.C.R.D.	
			Report rec'd in a.m. Brit Reave Company Pionnery 62nd Sqnd.	
			Unit paid at 6pm. Capt BENNETT Pionnery 62nd Sqnd. Gnr view	
	29th Sept 1917		Warning order rec'd to move at 3.45 pm from HOPOUTRE	
			to BAPAUME for BAPAUME.	
	30th Sept 1917		Unit leaving –	
			Orders to entrain at 3.45pm on Oct 1st	

A.C. Steven
H.A.M.C.
COMMANDING

O.C. on special leave
Capt KINTON Bn in command 89th Field Company T
Capt'/s ASH. EDMONDS (temp attd)
Lt. MARBURY + Lt. HORNSEY (army attd)
to duty.

SECRET.   1   *War Diary*
EVACUATION ARRANGEMENTS
During Active Operations - 20th DIVISION.

A. **POSITION OF OFFICERS**

1.	CEMENT HOUSE; Forward A.D.S. U.28.c.1.3. and "WEEDON" Siding U.28.c.5.5.	Capt. KIRTON " WILLS Bearer Officer	60 F.Amb. 60 " 61 "
2.	Fusilier A.D.S., C.13.c.1.3.	Capt. ASH Lieut. HORNSEY	60 F.Amb 61st "
3.	SOLFERINO B.22.b.8.4. (Lying Wounded Loading Post)	Capt. EDMOND Lieut. MARBURY	60 F.Amb. 60 "
4.	Galwitz (Relay Post) C.8.a.8.5.	~~Lieut. ZINKHAM~~ *Capt. BENNETT.*	62 F.Amb.
5.	PELISSIER FARM.	Capt. GRAY (if available)	60 F.Amb.

REGIMENTAL AID POSTS.

I. Right Brigade.

1.	Joint Aid Post for two attacking Battalions	AU BON GITE ~~LANGEMARCK~~	~~U.29.a.4.2.~~
2.	Support Battalion Aid Post:	CEMENT HOUSE	U.28.c.1.3.
3.	Reserve Battalion Aid Post:	Cork House.	C.3.a.15.35.

One of the M.Os. at Joint Aid Post is prepared to move forward if necessary to a suitable R.A.P. selected by Battalion Commander.
He will notify the M.O. Support Battalion who will take his place at Joint Aid Post after having himself notified Reserve Battalion M.O., who then moves up to CEMENT HOUSE.

II. Left Brigade.

1.	Joint Aid Post for two attacking Battalions	"PIG & WHISTLE"	U.28.b.4.2.
2.	Support Battalion Aid Post:	CEMENT HOUSE	U.28.c.1.3.
3.	Reserve Battalion Aid Post:	CORK HOUSE	C.3.a.15.35.

One M.O. at Joint Aid Post will be prepared to move forward to U.22.d.7.6. when this has been evacuated by Battalion Headquarters. M.Os. of Support and Reserve Battalions move up on being notified by the M.O. in front of them of his change of position.

All R.M.Os must notify by runner, O.C. of CEMENT House of all changes in their position, and take with them the R.A.M.C. stretcher bearers allotted to them.

DISPOSITION OF R.A.M.C. STRETCHER SQUADS AT ZERO.
Joint Aid Post.

Left Brigade.	Right Brigade.
* 8 Squads 60 F.Amb. (U.28.b.4.2)	* 8 squads 61 F.Amb. ~~(U.29.a.4.2)~~ *Au Bon Gite*

Support Aid Post

U.28.c.1.3.

2 squads 60 F.Amb.   2 squads 61 F.Amb.

Reserve Aid Post.

C.3.a.15.35.

2 squads 60 F.Amb.   2 squads 61 F.Amb.

Forward A.D.S., CEMENT HOUSE.

U.28.c.1.3.

Left Reserve.	Right Reserve.
4 squads 60 F.Amb.	4 squads 61 F.Amb.

Relay Duty.
4 squads 62 F.Amb.
(carrying to WEEDON & CORNER HOUSE.
to be increased if necessary)

CORNER HOUSE Relay Post.

C.2.c.5.7.

2 squads 62 F.Amb.   Relay Duty.
4 squads 62 F.Amb.   Reserve.

GALWITZ Relay Post.

C.8.a.8.5.

2 squads 62 F.Amb.   Relay Duty.
4 squads 62 F.Amb.   Reserve.

FUSILIER A.D.S.

C.13.c.1.3.

4 squads 62 F.Amb.   Reserve.

* 4 squads may be retained at CEMENT HOUSE if insufficient room for them at R.A.P's.

DIVISIONAL STRETCHER ~~PARTY~~ COMPANY.
Disposition Four Hours After Zero.

Joint Aid Post.

Left Brigade	Right Brigade.
U.28.b.4.2.	U.29.a.4.9. *au bon Gito*
2/Lieut. KELLY	2/Lieut. MIDDLEBROOK
4 runners (59 Bde.)	Sgt. LAW.
Cpl. GOLDSTONE.	4 runners (60 Bde.)

CEMENT HOUSE.
(U.28.c.1.3.)

1 L/Corpl. and 6 squads of 59 Bde.
1 L/Corpl. and 6 squads of 60 Bde.
Cpl. HAYHURST and 4 runners from 61 Bde.

GALWITZ.
(C.8.a.8.5.)

Cpl. GODDAIR and 2 runners 61 Bde.

FUSILIER.

Lieut. HARGREAVE.   9 squads 61 Bde.
5 squads 59 Bde.   5 runners 61 Bde.
5 squads 60 Bde.   Sgt. HAYCRAFT and Cpl. TITHERINGTON.

NOTE: The runners are available to form 4 additional squads.

Solferino.
(B.22.b.8.4.)
1 N.C.O, 10 squads (Div. Headquarters Section.) *will arrive at 4 p.m.*
Y DAY at SOLFERINO.

Every No. "4" in both R.A.M.C. and Divisional Company will carry a Shell Dressing Haversack with 8 shell dressings. These haversacks must be returned and the shell dressings economized.

DECAUVILLE.

Loading Post: WEEDON. (U.26.c.5.5.)

1st Train for CHEAPSIDE (Div.W.W.C.P.) & Solferino.
              Lying wounded, leaves 3½ hours after ZERO.
2nd   -------do------   4 hours after zero.

These trains return and continue working. The journey each way takes about ¾ hour. Each train holds 8 lying and 25 sitting.

    Bearer Officer, 61st Field Ambulance will control the DECAUVILLE arrangements and superintend the bearers of 61st Field Ambulance.

    One N.C.O. will be stationed at WEEDON to superintend loading.

    Should a break occur on the line near WEEDON the trains will come up as far as HANLEY LOOP at C.3.central (500 yards south of IRON CROSS and should a break occur there the trains will come as far as BROAD STREET, the siding at GALWITZ. In the above circumstances lying cases will be taken from CEMENT HOUSE to HANLEY on track from IRON CROSS and to BROAD STREET, GALWITZ by road on wheeled stretcher.

    One N.C.O. will be stationed on DECAUVILLE at CHEAPSIDE to take off all Walking Wounded.

A. **LYING WOUNDED** will be brought into R.A.P's by Regt. Stretcher Bearers assisted if casualties are numerous by the Divisional Stretcher ~~Bearers~~ COMPANY.

2. From R.A.P's they will be carried by R.A.M.C. stretcher squads to Forward A.D.S. at CEMENT HOUSE.

3. From CEMENT HOUSE they will be carried to WEEDON SIDING, and sent down by Decauville train to SOLFERINO, and from there by Motor Ambulances to C.M.D.S (CANADA FARM) and C.C.S.

4. If DECAUVILLE line is unusable, Lying Cases will be taken by wheeled stretcher to GALLWITZ, and sent on from there by Ford Cars or Horse Ambulances to FUSILIER A.D.S. or may be sent by Trolley line from C3.c5.5 to FUSILIER or via CORNER HOUSE and Duck-board track to TAMWORTH, and there by Motor and Horse Ambulance to FUSILIER, and from there to C.M.D.S. and C.C.S.

B. **WALKING WOUNDED** - will proceed by DECAUVILLE train at WEEDON SIDING to Divisional Walking Wounded Collecting Post at CHEAPSIDE B17.d9.9 . If room is not available by DECAUVILLE trains, walking wounded will proceed to CORNER HO. or GALLWITZ and via Duck-Board tracks and Cactus Pontoon to CHEAPSIDE. H.A. Waggons will carry from GALLWITZ to CACTUS PONTOON and on to CHEAPSIDE if possible.

LYING SICK - will be disposed of in the same way as Lying Wounded.

WALKING SICK as for Walking Wounded. On arrival at CHEAPSIDE by lorry C.S.C.Post.

All sick will eventually be sent to C.S.C. Post at CANADA FARM.

8 Trolleys will be kept at GALLWITZ under the care of the N.C.O i/c of the Relay Post, 4 to be sent up to C3 c5.5 at ZERO

4 wheeled stretchers are to be kept on the roadside W. of the Steenbeck.

10 at CEMENT HO.

2 at GALLWITZ.

The O.C. CEMENT Ho. should detail an N.C.O. to see that wheeled stretchers and trolleys are returned to these posts by Relay Squads on their return journey.

N.C.O's on Relay Posts &c. are responsible that Stretcher Squads on their return journey take back a fresh stretcher, and a blanket , also that empty petrol tins are brought down from the front line for each full tin sent up by the returning squad.

All stretcher squads have a number, each bearer wearing a "Tally" on the top button of his jacket with the number written on.

"No.4" (the Leaders) tally has the squad no. written in red, the other 3 men's tally written in blue.

RMOs should distinguish each of their Regimental Squads by a letter.

IT IS ESSENTIAL -

That the squads are kept intact (casualties will be made good as far as possible from squads kept in reserve)

That the squads are always sent forward or back with a note stating the tally numbers of the squads as well as how many squads are being sent.

IT IS ESSENTIAL (contd)

That when demanding squads it is stated whether R.A.M.C. or Divisional squads are required.

That Divisional squads and Reserve R.A.M.C. are not called for unless the casualties are heavy or the Bearers already working are exhausted.

R.M.O's should bear in mind that if demands for many additional stretcher squads are made, it must inevitably lead to many casualties amongst the Bearers, who must themselves then be evacuated, thus materially adding to the difficulties of all concerned.

The call for Divisional Stretcher COMPANY to work in the front line should be with the assent of a Staff Officer of the Brigade concerned.

Every Bearer will go up into the line in "Battle Order" - as follows:-

1. Service dress and puttees.

2. S.B. or Geneva Cross armlet.

3. Skeleton equipment - haversack and cleaning material.

4. Ground Sheet.

5. Steel helmet.

6. Iron ration.

7. Unconsumed portion of day's ration.

8. Box Respirator and P.H.Helmet.

9. Tally with squad number.

10. 1st. Field dressing.

11. Water Bottle full.

12. A shell dressing attached to each shoulder strap.

The No.4 of the Divisional Stretcher Coy's Squad will have a shell dressing haversack complete, Medical water bottles full and books of tallies issued to them before operations begin.

N.C.O's and Nursing Orderlies should have a pair of scissors attached to their lanyards, and all N.C.O's should have note book and pencil.

AS FAR AS POSSIBLE

    60th. Field Ambulance Bearers will work between Left R.A.P. and CEMENT Ho.

    61st. Field Ambulance Bearers will work between Right R.A.P. and CEMENT Ho.

    62nd. Field Ambulance Bearers will work back in relays from CEMENT Ho. to CORNER Ho. and from there via TAMWORTH Loading Post to FUSILIER or via GALLWITZ and Loading Post there to Fusilier A.D.S.

In the event of the Regt. Stretcher Bearers being unable to bring in all the wounded to the R.A.P's, the Divisional Stretcher Bearer Compy. will be brought up from FUSILIER and employed in bringing cases in to the R.A.P.

Unless specially ordered, the Divisional Stretcher Bearer Co. squads will work in front on the R.A.P's. They will not in any case work behind the Forward A.D.S. at CEMENT Ho.

All cases must be seen and tallied by a Regt. M.O. if possible. After being seen at CEMENT Ho. they will be carried to the DECAUVILLE Loading Post at WEEDON between CEMENT Ho. and the STEENBECK and loaded on the DECAUVILLE trucks there.

As WEEDON SIDING is about 200 yards of CEMENT Ho. it will be permissible if Regt. Officers so directs, for a limited number of suitable cases to be carried there direct from the R.A.P.

The N.C.O. in charge of WEEDON SIDING will not allow any cases to be kept there if the train is not in, and will send them on to CEMENT Ho. to wait.

Stretcher Bearers must be particularly careful to keep in their squads of four and to report to the Checking Sergt. at each post when either arriving with a case or returning.

They should be careful to bring back Box Respirators and Rifles of the patients whenever possible.

Squads of R.A.M.C. Stretcher Bearers will be allotted a duty between different posts, and should not go beyond their posts in either direction unless given a written order by an N.C.O.

Nos. 4 of each squad will be held responsible for keeping their squads together and reporting to the Checking Sergt.

O.C. Bearer Divisions   Lt. Colonel R.A.M.C.
COMMANDING
60th Field Ambulance

7

The following will be the Checking Sergts, at the various posts. -

	R.A.M.C. Squads		DIV. Stretcher Coy.
	i/c		
RIGHT R.A.P.	Sgt. Bailey	Cpl. Adcock	Sgt. Low.
LEFT R.A.P.	Sgt. Barker	L/c Gorman	Cpl. Goldstone
CEMENT HOUSE	Sgt. Hardy	Sgt. Davis	Cpl. Hayhurst 2L/cs
	Sgt. Williams	Cpl. Lynch	
WEEDON	S/S Cash	L/Cp. James	
GALLWITZ	Cpl. Freeman	Sgt. Currie	Cpl. Goddow
CORNER HOUSE	Sgt. Rollo	Cpl. Benstead	
FUSILIER	Sgt. Armitage	Sgt. Glancey	Sgt. Haycroft
	Sgt. Bickerton		Cpl. Titherington
	Cpl. Garside		
	Cpl. Chuter		

C O O K S

CORNER Ho.	62nd.
GALWITZ	62nd.
CEMENT Ho.	60th.
LEFT R.A.P.	60th.
RIGHT R.A.P.	61st.

A.C. OSBURN
Lt. Colonel R.A.M.C.
O.C. 60th. FIELD AMBULANCE
& BEARER DIVISIONS,
20th. DIVISION.

SEPTEMBER 17th. 1917.

War Diary

REPORT ON THE ARRANGEMENTS FOR THE EVACUATION
OF WOUNDED DURING ACTIVE OPERATIONS
20-21st. SEPTEMBER 1917.
- EAST OF LANGEMARCK.

Disposition of Personnel of 60th. Field Ambulance and Bearer Divisions of 61st, and 62nd, Field Ambulances and Divisional Stretcher Compy. at Zero hour was as in my No.20-27 attached of which copies have been distributed to all R,M,O's and the Staff Captains of the 3 Brigades with the following modifications:

a. Joint Aid Posts for the Right Brigade had been transferred to JONES POST-U 28.d.1.7 Sheet 20. During the night 18-19th.

b. It was considered advisable to keep the first reinforcement of 12 Squads of Divisional Stretcher Compy. at SOLFERINO in order to reduce congestion at CEMENT HOUSE.
The Head Qrs. of O.C. Bearer Divisions was moved to FUSILIER A.D.S. C.13.c.1.3 Sheet 28 N.W. During the night 19-20

I. A few minutes before Zero hour I was informed that the Road Junction at TAMWORTH C.7.d.2.3½ had been destroyed during the night by hostile fire, thereby blocking the evacuating line by road between the Front Line and both CACTUS PONTOON and BARD CAUSEWAY. I visited the spot shortly after Zero and made arrangements to have cases hand carried past this point, 4 Ford cars were despatched from FUSILIER via CACTUS PONTOON to form a circuit on the far side of the obstruction, to be prepared to evacuate Lying Cases from that point to SOLFERINO should the DECAUVILLE break down.

II. At Zero + 2 hours I received information that the DECAUVILLE had been destroyed between TAMWORTH and GALLWITZ, and also between GALLWITZ and HANLEY LOOP, and also between TAMWORTH and BLETCHLEY, thus breaking my other principal line of Evacuation.
At this hour the Walking and some of the Stretcher Cases had begun to arrive at my Forward A.D.S.
Runners were despatched with orders to change evacuation arrangements back to the trolley line and Hand carriage via GALLWITZ and CORNER HOUSE. To prevent congestion at TAMWORTH, Horse Ambulance Wagons were also sent up to a point on HUDDLESTONE ROAD just South of the obstruction at TAMWORTH.

III. It was found possible to evacuate the bulk of the Lying Cases by the circuit of Ford Cars established E. of CACTUS PONTOON, the remainder arriving at (BARD CAUSEWAY) FUSILIER A.D.S. via the trolley and Horse Ambulance Wagons.

IV. About 3 p.m. when the damage at TAMWORTH had been repaired Ford Ambulance cars were pushed up to GALLWITZ. Owing to further breaks in the lines, the DECAUVILLE which it had been hoped, would work as far as the break near TAMWORTH, remaining completely out of

(1)

action until 4 a.m. on the 21st., when one train loaded with 16 Stretcher Cases left for BLETCHLEY. Owing to an oiled tractor having become derailed at BLETCHLEY the wounded had to be transferred to an ordinary train which took them on to SOLFERINO. 4 more trips were made in this fashion from TAMWORTH between 4 a.m. and 2 p.m. on the 21st., bringing about 50 Lying Cases in all. Owing to the uncertainty as regards the DECAUVILLE, the bulk of the cases were evacuated by Motor and Horse Ambulances, and the trolley line from GALLWITZ. Owing to the trolley line being a considerable distance from the road and Forward A.D.S., it was not found of much advantage to use the trolley line N. of the point at which it crosses the road near GALLWITZ.

V. DIVISIONAL STRETCHER COMPY.

The Divisional Stretcher Compy. had been provided into permanent squads of 4, and it was found that they worked very well when needed. The first call for their assistance came about 5 p.m. of the 20th. inst., from the Left Brigade for 8 squads to clear the line at dusk. 12 squads were immediately despatched to the Left Brigade Aid Post, the 4 additional squads to be held in readiness for the use of the Right Brigade. Shortly afterwards a request arrived from the Right Brigade for 6 squads. These were despatched immediately and additional squads were then sent up as further calls arrived until by 8 a.m. on the 21st. 34 squads were working on the Divisional front bringing down wounded to the R.A.Ps. The Divisional Headquarter Party of 6 squads being held in reserve at SOLFERINO and later on brought up to the CANAL BANK. It was not found necessary to employ these latter in the Front line, but they were found very useful in acting as a Loading Party both at SOLFERINO and FUSILIER and also in assisting for a few hours the Relay Party at GALLWITZ.

VI. The area at GALLWITZ was very heavily shelled intermittently during the 72 hours ending at 8 a.m. on the 23rd. Owing to two direct hits on the dug-outs there, this post had to be abandoned for several hours during the night 20-21st, the wounded being sent round by CORNER HOUSE where a portion of the Personnel from GALLWITZ were also sent to assist.

VII. Very heavy shelling took place in the Front Area between JONES' HOUSE and AU BON GITE and round ALOUETTE and also at intervals round the Forward A.D.S. at CEMENT HOUSE. Cases came down extremely well in spite of the obstacles caused by the breaking of the rail and roadway and the shelling of the GALLWITZ area, it being reported from the Aid Posts that practically all the casualties known to be due to the fighting on the 20th. were clear by 4 a.m. on the 21st.

VIII. About 9 a.m. on the 21st. it was found possible to withdraw about one third of the Divisional Stretcher Bearers and give them a rest, but further casualties occurred later on in the day made it necessary to send up fresh squads.

IX. At Zero + 14 hours as arranged, the R.M.O. of the Ox. & Bucks.L.I. moved forward from JONES' POST to PUFF HOUSE U29.b.599. Sheet 20 taking the 4 R.A.M.C. squads allotted to him. At the same time the Support R.M.O. 6th.K.S.L.I. moved from CEMENT HOUSE to JONES' POST with 2 squads. No other changes took place in the position of the R.A.Ps.

X. CASUALTIES,
    a. The wounded cleared to SOLFERINO (including 15 very severe cases needing immediate evacuation to C.C.S.) was 166 Lying and 36 Sitting cases of which number 47 Lying and 11 Sitting cases arrived by train, the remainder by

Motor Ambulance.

b. The number cleared to FUSILIER (including 48 very severe cases needing immediate evacuation to C.C.S.) was 204 Lying,- including 13 Officers - and 126 Sitting Cases; about an equal number of the Lying Cases arrived there by trolley and by Motor Ambulances. The total wounded cleared, including 21 Officers was 370 Lying (of these 63 were very severe cases and sent direct to C.C.S.)and 162 Sitting cases. Owing to the night of the 20-21st. being extremely dark, a large number of the Walking Wounded came direct to FUSILIER; a good many of them were picked up near GALLWITZ and TAMWORTH by Horse Ambulance Wagons, and all of them were despatched from FUSILIER by Horse Ambulance Wagon to CHEAPSIDE.

XI. Although the DECAUVILLE was out of action, SOLFERINO was found very useful not only for the cases brought via CACTUS PONTOON, but also for the overflow cases from FUSILIER where the accommodation for dressing wounds is limited.

XII. Casualties during 20-21st.and 22nd. to the R.A.M.C. and Divisional Stretcher Party were under the circumstances not as numerous as might have been expected in view of the very heavy shelling in front of the area, the total being -

R.A.M.C.   2 killed and 22 wounded.

Div,St. Brs.   3 "   11   " & 2 gassed.

Owing to the constant sniping and very heavy shelling, especially in the Left Brigade area, the Regt. Stretcher Bearers found great difficulty in getting the cases in.
The destruction of the DECAUVILLE and the blocking of the road by hostile fire were the additional factors in preventing the evacuation being speeded up,
The formation of a Dump of 400 stretchers at CEMENT HOUSE close to the R.A.Ps before Zero was found to lighten the work of all concerned very considerably.
The only difficulties experienced in getting the wounded away being due to the military situation, especially the heavy shelling in the Forward Area during daylight.
The work of the Bearers has been most exhausting and difficult, and their work has been most creditably carried out in spite of constant shelling and fairly heavy casualties. 40 men have been lost from casualties and this necessitated a good many squads being reconstructed. All ranks did extremely well under very difficult circumstances.

As the whole of the 3 Bearer Divisions are still working in the Line as well as all Divisional Compy. Squads, a further report will be made, but Capt, Edmonds,Capt, Kerton, and Capt. Ash have all done extremely well.

140/2499

No. 60 7. O.

COMMITTEE FOR THE
MEDICAL HISTORY OF THE WAR
Date -8 DEC. 1917

B.E.F.

SUMMARY OF MEDICAL WAR DIARIES OF

60th F.A., 20th Divn. 14th Corps, 5th Army.

To 3rd Corps, 3rd Army on 2/10/17.

WESTERN FRONT. Oct. 1917.

O.C.

SUMMARISED UNDER THE FOLLOWING HEADINGS.

Phase "D" 1. Passchendaele Operations July-Dec. 1917.

(b) Operations commencing 1/10/17.
Canadians attacked Passchendaele Oct. 30th.

Canadians took Passchendaele Nov. 6th.

60th F.A. 20th Divn. 14th Corps, 5th Army. WESTERN FRONT.

O.C. Oct. 1917.

3rd Corps, 3rd Army from 2/10/17.

Phase "D" 1. Passchendaele Operations July-Dec. 1917.

    (b) Operations commencing 1/10/17.
        Canadians attacked Passchendaele Oct. 30th.
        Canadians took Passchendaele Nov. 6th.

1917.   Headquarters. Priory Camp F.10.c.5.5. (Sheet 28)

Oct. 2nd.   Moves and Transfer. Unit transferred with 20th Divn. to 3rd Corps, 3rd Army and moved to Beaulencourt en route for new area.

B.E.F.

SUMMARY OF MEDICAL WAR DIARIES OF

60th F.A., 20th Divn. 14th Corps, 5th Army.

To 3rd Corps, 3rd Army on 9/10/17.

WESTERN FRONT. Oct. 1917.

O.C.

SUMMARISED UNDER THE FOLLOWING HEADINGS.

Phase "D" 1. Passchendaele Operations July-Dec. 1917.

(b) Operations commencing 1/10/17.
Canadians attacked Passchendaele Oct. 30th.
Canadians took Passchendaele Nov. 6th.

60th F.A. 20th Divn. 14th Corps, 5th Army. WESTERN FRONT.

O.C. _____   Oct. 1917.

3rd Corps, 3rd Army from 2/10/17.

Phase "D" 1. Passchendaele Operations July-Dec. 1917.

   (b) Operations commencing 1/10/17.
       Canadians attacked Passchendaele Oct. 30th.
       Canadians took Passchendaele Nov. 6th.

1917.   Headquarters. Priory Camp F.10.c.5.5. (Sheet 28)

Oct. 2nd.   Moves and Transfer. Unit transferred with 20th Divn. to 3rd Corps, 3rd Army and moved to Beaulencourt en route for new areas.

Army Form C. 2118.

WAR DIARY
or
INTELLIGENCE SUMMARY

(Erase heading not required.)

Vol 27

WAR DIARY

60TH FIELD AMBULANCE

OCTOBER 1917

Confidential

Army Form C. 2118.

WAR DIARY
or
INTELLIGENCE SUMMARY
(Erase heading not required.)

Instructions regarding War Diaries and Intelligence Summaries are contained in F. S. Regs., Part II. and the Staff Manual respectively. Title Pages will be prepared in manuscript.

Place	Date	Hour	Summary of Events and Information	Remarks and references to Appendices
	1/10/17		Unit moved from PRIORY CAMP F.10.C.5.5 Sheet 28NW. at 10.15AM and arrived at HOPOUTRE at 9.15PM.	
BEAULENCOURT	2/10/17		Unit detrained at BAPAUME at 10pm and marched to BEAULENCOURT arriving at 12 noon	
	3/10/17		Capt EDMOND J. RAMC. who had at various behind in PRIORY CAMP rejoined unit with one Corps Ambulance Car. 1st D. MARBURY W.B. U.S.M.C assumed temporary medical charge of 119 RR vice Capt MACARTHUR evacuated sick 5 men granted the Military Medal Pte BELLINGHAM, M.T.A.S.C, COLLINS, BRIDGEMAN G, HUMPHREY, FORSYTH RAMC. S.Sgt CORGIN and 25 OR. proceeded to FINS to take over ADS. GOUZEAUCOURT taken over A.D.S. and Bearer Posts from 135 F. Amb.	
	4/10/17		Capt EDMOND RAMC. and 70 OR. proceeded to FINS to take on ADS. GOUZEAUCOURT taken over A.D.S. and Bearer Posts from 135 F. Amb.	
	5/10/17		Unit moved from BEAULENCOURT to FINS V.12.C.5.4 Sheet 57C S.E. Bearer Capt GREY & 20 OR. behind to attend 659 Brigade Sick	

2449 Wt. W14957/M90 750,000 1/16 J.B.C. & A. Forms/C.2118/12.

WAR DIARY
or
INTELLIGENCE SUMMARY

Army Form C. 2118.

Place	Date	Hour	Summary of Events and Information	Remarks and references to Appendices
F.M.S	6/10/17		Capt GRAY and 20 O.R. rejoined unit from BEAUREN COURT	
	9/10/17		T/Capt J KIRTON, RAMC evacuated Military Cross. Walterius came with me at 1 P.M. on this day - checks they put each I know them.	
	10/10/17		24 O.R. proceeded to F.A.O.S. + Bearer Posts relieving 24 O.R. who returned to H.Q.	
	11/10/17		Ptes See, Brown R. Adams are church of the strength, evacuated to 63 C.C.S. from XIV C.M.D.S. Lt.Col. A.C.Osborn, D.S.O. R.A.M.C. granted 30 days special leave 1 – 30 Oct. D. MARBURY U.S.M.C. returned H.Q'rs from 11 KRR on completion of temporary duty. Capt Wells C.R., R.A.M.C. returned from leave.	
	12/10/17		Capt GRAY R.A.M.C. proceeded on leave 15 – 25 Oct Capt Wells proceeded for duty to A.D.S.	
	14/10/17		Capt. EDMUND Rent. rejoined H.Q. from A.D.S.	
	15/10/17		M. HORNSEY rejoined unit from temporary duty with Y.D.C.L.I.	

Army Form C. 2118.

WAR DIARY
or
INTELLIGENCE SUMMARY
(Erase heading not required.)

Place	Date	Hour	Summary of Events and Information	Remarks and references to Appendices
FINS	16/10/17		23. O.R. to A.D.S. for duty and 20 other ranks returned to B.M.Q.	
	17/10/17		C/H Hurst and Pte Robbins R.A.M.C. reported their arrival from 3rd Corps Sage Park for duty.	
	18/10/17		Lt Marbury proceeded to A.D.S. for duty. This proceeded to treatment & evacuation of casualties of D.C.M. and M.M. for A.D.M.S. XX Div.	
	19/10/17		Ct Jones R.A.M.C. reported for duty from Calais Base Depot.	
	20/10/17		Pte Cotrell reported from duty with XIV Corps H.Q. R.F.A.	
	23/10/17		Capt. Edmond. R.A.M.C. proceeded for temporary duty with 91st Bde R.F.A. Major General W. Douglas Smith, G.O.C. XX Div. inspected H.Q. & word	
	24/10/17		D.M.S. III Army inspected unit	
	25/10/17		20 O.R. proceeded to A.D.S. for duty, 19. O.R. returned to H.Q.	
	26/10/17		Lt Hornsby R.A.M.C. proceeded Water and medical charge of 92nd Bde. R.F.A.	
	27/10/17		Lt Marbury U.S.M.C. assumed temporary duty with 110.L.I Capt P.H. Zinkham U.S.M.C. reported for duty from 61 F. Amb. 91st Bde R.F.A.	
	28/10/17		Capt Edmond R.A.M.C. returned from temporary duty with and proceeded to A.D.S.	

Place	Date	Hour	Summary of Events and Information	Remarks and references to Appendices
FINS	29/10/17		Capt T.A. GRAY returned from Court. Lt & Qmr JOHNSTONE T RAMC proceeded to ALBERT to attend a Catering Course for 3 days to be held at 3rd Army Schools School of Cookery	
	31/10/17		Capt C.R. WILLS RAMC taken over temporary medical charge of 10 RB vice R. MONTGOMERY RAMC on leave.	

J Kinlen
Capt RAMC
a/o.c 60 F Amb.

No. 60. F.A.

140/2576

COMMITTEE FOR THE
MEDICAL HISTORY OF THE WAR
Date 17 JAN. 1918

Army Form C. 2118.

WAR DIARY
or
INTELLIGENCE SUMMARY

(Erase heading not required.)

Vol 28

War Diary
of 60: Aus: Ambulance
R.A.M. Corps
for
November 1917

A/J.M.Brown
Lt.Col
Commdg.

Army Form C. 2118.

WAR DIARY
or
INTELLIGENCE SUMMARY
(Erase heading not required.)

Place	Date	Hour	Summary of Events and Information	Remarks and references to Appendices
FINS V12c8.8 57c S.E. 20.000	1/12/17		Disposition of Personnel.	
			At H.Q. O.C., Capt Rob, Gray, Hilton, Zuckham, Lt Johnston, + 180 O.R.	
			At A.D.S. GOUZEAUCOURT Q36 d.3.9., Capt. Edmond. + 20 O.R.	
			On Leave. Lt. Montgomery.	
			On Detachment. Capt Wills 10th R.B. At Aveluy bookg school Lt Johnstone	
			" Lt Markng 11th D.L.I.	
			" Lt Murray 91st Bde. R.F.A.	
			At Left Aid Post. (Q18 d 9.9) 8 O.R.	
			At 16 Ravine (R20 a 1.9) 8 O.R.	
			At 15 Ravine (R19 a 8.3) 6 O.R.	
			At Quarry (R25 d 3.9) 8 O.R.	
			At Right R.A.P (R32 b 5.9) 6 O.R.	
			At Relay Post (R25 a 9.5) 4 O.R.	
			O.C. returned from leave	
	2/12/17		Lt Johnstone returned	
	3/12/17		Secret Instructions received to prepare for operations. 58 O.R. Infantry arrived for training in Stretcher Aid	

WAR DIARY
or
INTELLIGENCE SUMMARY

Army Form C. 2118.

(Erase heading not required.)

Place	Date	Hour	Summary of Events and Information	Remarks and references to Appendices
	3/12/17		Material drawn to enlarge & improve bearing accommodation for A.D. Posts & Relay Post. Ambl. engaged motor transfer duties, & in evacuating all wounded from Divnl. front, & in receiving sick from the Corps area; sick averaging from 180 to 210 daily; wounded very few in number.	
	4/12/17 – 10/12/17		Continued construction work on dugouts & routine duties. D.M.S. III Corps requested that a plan be made for 30 cars at H.Q. Notice received ADS Aid Post near Beaucamp; 15 Ravine, somehow would be relinquished by the Divn. before the operations. New Relay Post site chosen & new R.A.P. at R19d2.6 & Partridge Rd (R20d7.3) respectively, material drawn & construction of these two places proceeded with, also feed accommodation made at A.D.S. & 16 Ravine (3 Elephant Huts) Capt Gray proceeded to 46th Labour Group as M.O. in charge.	
	11/12/17		Lt Stormley & 2 Dt. Marting returned.	
	12/12/17		32 O.R. IIIrd Corps Traffic Control arrived for accommodation. Bearer Divn. of 61st Div commenced to assemble for training & organization for the operations. Detachments from Sq 60th, 161st Bdes, Divnl. Sketcher Coy, Divnl. Sketcher Coy, began to arrive for training & formation into Divnl. Sketcher Coy, 1800 Sketchers, 2900 Mankels, 350 petrol tins for water, 1400 reserve rations (1000 obsoleting eva being gradually drawn for formation of dumps in forward area. 28 Marquees, 29 Bell tents,	60 FIELD AMBULANCE 3 DEC 1917 ORDERLY ROOM

WAR DIARY or INTELLIGENCE SUMMARY

Army Form C. 2118.

(Erase heading not required.)

Place	Date	Hour	Summary of Events and Information	Remarks and references to Appendices
	13/12		Orders received to keep two tent sub-divisions back. Capt Kirton proceeded to A.D.S. on the 7th inst.	
	14/12		Between Nov 2nd & 14th visited all R.A.P's, & Relay Posts frequently; construction proceeding satisfactorily. Visited Sector trenches in front of Beaucamp. Horses held clean & well stabled. Arranged with C.R.E. for repair of Kulley line up valley in R20. Branched with Decauville to Cable oaks & trams. Preliminary instructions for M.O's & R.M.O's issued. Secret thing maintained as far as possible by the use of verbal orders. Conferences held frequently with D.D.M.S. IV Corps & A.D.M.S. also has personally G.O.C.'s of H.Qs of 59th, 60th & 61st Bdes. on two or three occasions. Saw personally all R.M.O's of Divn., O.C. of 210 Ambls., & their Bearer officers. O.C. Decauville Railway & Q. branch of Divn., A.P.M. &c.	
	15-19/12		Continued preparations in Front Area; formations of advanced dumps, transport very heavy worked. 61 & 62 Ambls. sent each 9 men, 3 officers, 3 H.d. wagons, limbers, water carts. Divnl. stretcher bay, forms into squads & killed to Beaucamp. Divn. ditto ditto Lucrey Ravine, R8 e 9.0 La Vacquerie at R10 central, selected as forward R.A.P's. R.M.O's to remain with Battns.	

60 FIELD AMBULANCE
No. 2
7 DEC 1917
ORDERLY ROOM

WAR DIARY or INTELLIGENCE SUMMARY

Army Form C. 2118.

Place	Date	Hour	Summary of Events and Information	Remarks and references to Appendices
	19/11/17		Advd. W.H.C.P. formed at GOUZEAUCOURT Baths, Lt. Harvey & Lt. Brookes U.S.A. in charge. Lt. Montgomery & 6 O.R. proceeded to take charge of 16 Ravine. Capt. Whelo t/b to be M.O. 10th K.R.B. M.D. 10/6 Ravine. Capts. Quinn & Jones & Mallam, Bearer Divn 61st F. Amb. with transport towards Lebine Left Bole. forward towards R3. Capts. Chandler & Bennett, Bearer Divn 62nd F. Amb. & transport to R.A.P. Partridge Road & New Relay Post in R19. to work forward with Centre Bole. Capts. Riches & Jackson, remainder of 60th F.A. Bearers & necessary transport held in readiness to proceed forward with Right Bole. via Bonnavis at R21.d.3.3. & R21 central. Sqd. Bole. party D.S.C. to be handed over at Zero hour to Staff Capt. Sqd. Bole. 60 & 61st Bole parties in reserve at the Baths. Band 29 O.R. also in reserve at H.Q. Fins. 5 Bans in reserve at H.Q. Fins. Arrangements made & parties detailed for 8 stretcher bearers to proceed to each Battn. of the Divn. 4 to No.2 of Sqd. Bole, Sgt. standy in charge. 1 having orderly to each Bole. H.Q. for 1st Aid & Liason. Dril front has been narrowed to width of 2000 yards, A.D. Posts in Gonnelien, Beaucamp, & 15 Ravine area having been given up.	

REPORT ON WORK AT A.D.S. AT GOUZEAUCOURT
AND OF THE BEARER DIVISIONS.
20 - 25th. NOV.1917.

Disposition at Zero Hour. 20/11/16

At Right R.A.P. Capts. Chandler & Bennett & Bearers of 62 F. Amb.
At Left R.A.P. " Quinn, Jones & Stallard & Bearers of 61st.F.A.
Lieut. Montgomery and detachment from Tent Div.of 60 F.A.
in charge of this post with a view to it becoming a Forwd.
A.D.S.
Relay Posts at R.25.a.8.4. R.19.d.5.7. detachments 60 F.A. Tent Div.
Reserve Bearer Posts at the Quarry R.25.d.4.9. & at Partridge Rd.
& detachment 60 F.A. Tent Div.
Divl. W.W.C.P. Lieuts. Hornsey & Brookes & detachment 60th; F.A. Tent
Div.
A.D.S. CeO. Capts. Ash, Edmond & Lieuts. Marbury & Johnstone &
remainder of Tent Div. 60 F.A. less detachment at Fins H.Q.
Reserves of Bearers of 60,61,& 62 F.Ambs. & Bgde. Stret.
parties of 60 & 61 Bgdes.

59 Bgde. Party of D.S.C. in reserve at the Quarry under the orders of
G.O.C. 59 Bgde.
Large reserves of stretchers,blankets,dressings,rations,water & medical
comforts &c. had been pushed up as far as Support Line on both flanks
in order to facilitate formation of Forwd. A.D.S's. as required on the
Advance.
Bearer Transport of each Fd.Amb. Horse Amb. Wagons, water ct. & limbers
with stores had been kept intact with their respective Bearer Officers
to facilitate breaking up into independent Bearer Divs.

Work at A.D.S.
Accommodation had been increased as far as the short notice allowed
while but proved very inadequate for the large no. of cases brought in
from the 20,29,12,6,Cavalry,51,& 40 Divs.,Army Troops,Tank Corps,Corps
Troops,Wounded prisoners &c.

Lying Cases
Lying Cases began to arrive shortly before 8 o'clock a.m. & from that
hour onwards a steady stream of cases arrived. About mid-day they began
to arrive in very large nos. The rapidty of their arrival being accounted
for by the fact that the cars were working up to the front line on both
flanks & also large nos.(50 or more at a time)were brought in by German
prisoners (the first German wounded arriving at the W.W.C.P. at 8 a.m.)
During the afternoon of Zero day a stream of cases which at times was
very heavy continued to pour into the Dressing Station quite exceeding
the accommodation in the motor ambs. and amb. trains. At one time over
120 Stret. patients were lying in the open awaiting Motor Ambs. & Trains
to remove them to C.CSS. The limit of accommodation at the A.D.S. which
allowed not more than 3 serious cases than to be dressed at a time &
the fact that between 3 & 7.30 p.m. only 2 motor ambs; returned from
C.C.S. accounted in some degree for the block, which was aggravated by
the sudden influx of patients brought down by German prisoners.
The Decauville trains proved unreliable. It was understood that it
would arrive at Hospital Siding at 6.40 a.m.; it actually arrived at
8.45 a.m. It was at once loaded & left, but only managed to complete
2 journeys by 18 hours after Zero. It was therefore left out of the
calculations as regards the disposal of Lying Cases,the majority of
which were despatched by Motor Ambs. to either Ytres or C.M.D.S.
To prevent further congestion at the A.D.S. about 40 or 50 car loads of
patients were passed straight through to M.D.S. & 7 of the 10 cars working on the Forwd. Circuit were withdrawn to the Rear Circuit to help to
clear the A.D.S.
The names of 400 stret. cases were taken in the first 24 hours but owing
to the congestion, heavy rain, darkness &c. the attempt to keep complete
records was abandoned.

It was hard to give definite figures but about one half of the cases appeared to be from the 29th. Div.

Nature of Wounds

There was a larger proportion of machine gun bullet wounds including fracture femur, penetrating abdomen & chest, & a fair no. of men of the Tank Corps with H.E. wounds & many Heavy Artillery patients. With the exception of 4 Gas cases which arrived at the W.W.C.P. & were evacuated as Lying cases, no other Gas cases were seen.
There was a marked absence of S.I. wounds, & "shell shock" were infrequent. During the 24 hours ending midnight 21 - 22 the situation grew easier owing mainly to the more regular running of the motor ambs. & Amb. Train, but a large no. of cases went through of whom about 300 had their names taken.
It was found however that the taking of the names seriously delayed the evacuation of those cases not requiring redressing at the A.D.S.
As many as possible F.M. cards were made out & Invariably in the case of those who passed through the rooms reserved to the dressing of serious cases.
22nd. - 25th. Conditions gradually returned to nearly normal, cases diminishing rapidly after 10 a.m. on the 22nd., the nos. being increased by batches of men arriving from the 51st. & other Divs. from the Corps on the Left & from Heavy Artillery, Cavalry &c.
At the lowest estimate considerably over 1000 Lying cases passed through the A.D.S. during the more active period of the operations.

Walking Wounded

The use of the Baths at Gouzeaucourt was found of a great convenience in dealing with the large no. of W.W., the Canteen & good supplies of hot tea &c., adding materially to the comfort of the patients. During the first 24 hours 900 W.W. cases were treated; here again a very large no. being from the 29th. Div.
In addition to the above a large no. of sick were loaded up & despatched in lorries & trains to the C.S.C.P. at Fins.
A no. of the trivial cases, roughly about 300, were loaded up without passing through the W.W.C.P in addition to those counted.
On the 21st. inst., 692 cases were treated & a certain no. in addition passed through direct.
In the 3½ days ending 6 p.m. on the 23rd. 2753 W.W. had been actually counted & treated, but the total no. evacuated including large nos. from the 40th. & 51st. Divs. & Army Troops was very considerably in excess of this figure. probably nearer 3500.
All ranks at the A.D.S. & W.W.C.P. worked exceptionally hard & to this alone was due the fact that it was possible to care for & evacuate such large nos. with such very limited accommodation.
The work was rendered all the more arduous by the fact that the Tent Div. of the 60th. F.A. was finding the permanent staff for 6 detachments at Aid Posts & Relay Posts in addition to working single handed what was practically a C.A.D.S. & a Corps W.W.C.P., including the Cavalry & the bulk of the casualties of 7 Divs. in addition to Army Troops &c.

Bearers

The Bearer Divisions working under the most adverse possible circumstances carried out their work with the greatest possible despatch & efficiency, cases being got back from the front line in an extraordinary short time; Aid Posts & Relay Posts being established in the Sunken Rd. at La Vacquerie. The swinging to the right of the Div. causing this line to become as had been anticipated the principal route for evacuation.
The 60th. Bgde. Party of D.S.C. was called for early in the operations. Owing to the advance North & the exhaustion of the bearers, it was found necessary to open an A.D.S. in Masnieres which though exposed to a very considerable fire both from Machine Guns and Artillery was found to considerably diminish the length of the carry.

A. C. Osburn
Lt Col R.A.M.C.
O.C. 60. Field Amb.

SECRET.   INSTRUCTIONS RE- OPERATIONS.

INSTRUCTIONS FOR O.Cs. BRIGADE PARTIES OF DIV. STRETCHER COMPY.

59TH. BRIGADE 2nd. Lieut. Smith & 30 O.R.

This party will parade in full marching order at 5 p.m. on "Y" afternoon, & march to their rendezvous at the Quarry R25 d.3.9. Each pair will take a stret. & 1 blanket. On arrival at the Quarry one will be detailed to act as Storeman, and packs & rifles &c. will be left under his charge should the party be ordered to assist Regt. Stret. Bearers. At the Quarry O.C. will get his party into Battle Order less rifle, bayonet, S.A.A. and entrenching tool, and with tallies on each man & 2 shell dressings tied to their shoulder straps. When this has been done he should report for orders to Staff Capt. 59th. Bgde. (rear Hd:Qrs.) at R19 d.3.5.
Rations will be issued up to and including "Z" day, after which they will be rationed by the 59th. Bgde.

60th. & 61st. Bgde. Parties

Lieut. Pritchett & 38 O.R.   2nd. Lieut Acton & 38 O.R.

These parties will parade at 5 p.m. "Y" day as for 59th. Bgde. with same equipment &c and march under their own Officer to the Baths at Gouzeaucourt; on arrival there they will store in a convenient place under a guard to be found by the 60th. party, their packs, rifles, S.A.A., entrenching tools & bayonets.
When each O.C. has got his party into Battle Order minus the above he should report to O.C. S.D.S. Gouzeaucourt and await further orders. They will be rationed by 60th. F.A.
It is essential that all ranks understand that they must return to the front line with a stretcher (and a blanket, if possible) between every 2 men and unless specially detailed for "Relay" duty, O.Cs. should see their men do not pass further back than the Regt. Aid Post of their Bgde.

TRANSPORT

30 M.A.C. cars will arrive on "Y" day; 6 of these will proceed at dusk and park in the lane N.W. of A.D.S., also 2 charabancs for W.W.
Sergt. Paterson will be in charge of the Div. Cars, ie- 6 Fords & 4 large cars for evacuating cases from the Forwd. A.D.S's back to Gouzeaucourt. He should see that these cars are not mixed up with M.A.C. cars evacuating from A.D.S. to Ytres M.D.S.
The road between Fins and Gouzeaucourt from "Z" plus 4 and onwards is likely to be blocked; all movements must therefore take place before "Z" if possible.
3 H.A. Wagons of 61st. F.A. will work forwd. on the left, 2 H.A. wagons from 62nd. F.A. & 3 from 60th. F.A. with 20 mules fitted with pack saddles &c. and drivers will rendezvous in rear of the Baths at Gouzeaucourt in Q36 a. at dusk on "Y" day. 10 of the mules will carry petrol tins full of water; also a limber wagon packed with supplies to form a Forwd. A.D.S. which will move off with Capt. Birton & 60th. F.A. Brs.if necessary. Water carts and additional limbers of 61st & 62nd. Bearer Divns. may also rendezvous here.
2 H.A. wagons of 59th. Div. will report at Hd.Qrs. in Fins on "Y" day. Sergt. Bennett and Cpl. Chuter will take charge of these and see that all W.W. are taken off the trains in Fins at W7 a.1.4 and carried by these H.A. wagons up to the W.W.C.P. at V18 c.9.5 near 61st. F.A. about 800 yards along the Fins-Hurlu road. The greatest care will be taken that all W.W. are directed to this point; they will also be arriving by charabancs and on foot.
3 H.D. 4 mules & a cob of the 61st. F.A. & 3 A.S.C. Personnel, 4 H.D, 6 mules and a cob of the 62nd. F.A. and 5 A.S.C. Personnel and 3 H.D. of the 59th. Div. will be rationed by the 60th.F.A. from & including "Z" day. The forage for the 61st.F.A. will have to be taken to the R.A.P. at 16 Ravine daily.

(2)

AMBULANCE TRAINS

L/cpl. Weemyss and Pte. Griffiths will be in charge of the Amb. train which will arrive at Hospital Siding at Gouzeaucourt at "Z" plus 2. They will take charge of all the patients on the train and of the necessary drugs, splints, tourniquets &c. sufficient for a 4 hrs. journey and see that all H.W. bottles, splints, blankets, strets, &c. are duly returned by C.C.S. The former will arrange with the Qr.Mstr. for extra H.W. bottles and for a few spare rations to be kept on the train at Fins at N9 a.1.4. He will report to-day the 18th.inst. to Capt. Phillips at Fins Yard in order to get thoroughly conversant with his duties. He will remain in charge of the train until further orders.

See that all will have it as

WALKING WOUNDED

W.W. will be directed E. of Gouzeaucourt to the Baths; <u>only really severe cases</u> will have their dressings changed if necessary. They will not have either A.T.S. or F.M. cards until their arrival at Fins. A rough record of nos.only will be kept.
After having tea they will be passed <u>without delay</u> in batches to the Hospital siding opposite the A.D.S. and loaded there on to -
(a) Amb. Trains. (b) returning ammunition trains (c) charabancs; the more serious being loaded on the charabancs.

Sergt. Blow will be in charge of the Hospital siding and have under him 3 squads from the Div. Band for loading and Police duty.

L/cpl. Cuthbertson will be on Police duty outside the Baths and will have 1 squad of the Div. Band under him & will work in conjunction with Sergt. Blow.

All W.W. loaded on the trains must be warned that they are to get off at Fins and exchange into the H.A. wagons working from there under Sergt. Bennett & Cpl. Chuter.

LYING WOUNDED

L.W. going by train to the C.C.S. will have to have F.M. cards & A.T.S. given to them if possible at the A.D.S. If a block occurs this will have to be omitted. Cases sent to the C.C.S. need have neither. Lying cases will be loaded on Amb. Train or M.A.C. cars.
Sgt. Blow will see that both drivers & orderlies are warned that they are to see that all H.W. bottles,splints,blankets & strets. are returned and report those who fail to do so.
Sergt. Major Cross & Sergt. Paterson will arrange with the Qtr.Mstr. for dumps at the A.D.S. of petrol, forage &c.

RATIONS

61st. & 62nd. F.A. have each brought a limber wagon for rations.
The following will be rationed by 60th.F.A.
61st. F.A. :3 Officers & 65 O.R. R.A.M.C.
8 R.D. horses,4 mules & 1 cob.
6 A.S.C. Personnel.
Rations for above will be sent daily to 1S Ravine.

62nd. F.A. 3 Officers & 58 O.R. R.A.M.C.
4 R.D. horses,6 mules & 1 cob.
5 A.S.C. Personnel.
These will be rationed daily; the R.A.M.C. rations being sent to New R..R. and the A.S.C. rations & forage being sent to Baths by arrangement with Transport Sergt. of A.S.C. of 62nd. F.A.

20 O.R. Div. Band will be rationed at the Baths and 2 Officers & 73 O.R. of the 60 & 61 Agds. Stret. parties will also be there.
8 R.D. & 3 drivers of the 19th. Div. and 1 Div. Band will be attached to and remain at Hd.Qrs. in Fins.

POLICE DUTY AT FINS &c.

Cpl. Wallace will form a Control Post in Fins & arrange with M.T.C. that every car reaching Fins is replaced by M.T.C.car at the A.D.S. without delay.
(1 N.C.O. from the Div. Band will be detailed if necessary to act as Policeman at the cross roads N.of Gouzeaucourt to ensure M.T. leaving the main road and proceeding to the Bauks). Cpl. Wallace will see that every empty car returning to A.D.S. will carry rations, dressings &c. from the Qtr.mstr's stores and for this purpose the M.T.C. cars next for duty should remain in the yard opposite the Qtr. mstrs stores.

MOVE OF BEARER DIVISION

5 squads of the 31st.F.A. and 5 of the 82nd. and the remaining squads of the 80th.F.A. will be held as a reserve at the A.D.S. & also the remainder of the Div. Band's the Bgde.Stret.parties of the 30 and 31 Bgdes.
It is hoped that the reserve Battn. of the 95th. Bgde. will establish an Aid Post which will also act as a Bearer & Relay post at or about H10 c.2.8 Sunken cross roads. From this point Sgt.Harey will send back his messenger for mules with water & rations; the same messenger will report to Capt.Kirton at A.D.S.
Capt. Kirton, Capt. Kinkken and 10 squads drawn from the above reserves with Sgt.Harker & Cpl. Hadley & the limber wagon & 5 G.S. wagons of the 80 F.A. (if these have not already gone forwd.) will then proceed forward to establish touch with the reserve Battn. forming a half way house between Partridge Road & the Reserve R.A.P. if necessary or will establish themselves at the R.A.P.
Capt.Kirton will leave Capt.Kinkman & a portion of his party at Partridge Road if not required further forwd. He will notify the Qtr. Mstr. as well as his O.C. of the exact position of this Bearer Post as soon as it is established.
Similar movements will be necessary probably for the 31 and 32 Bearer Divs. a proportion of whose reserves at A.D.S. should be left intact. These Divs. have made their own arrangements as regards the limber wagon of extra stores for an Advanced Bearer Post.
It may be necessary to follow up Capt. Kirton with a second party in charge of Sgt.Davis & an Officer if one is available.
Should these movements take place the Qtr. mstr. will arrange to form a dump of stores, dressings,&c. at the Barricade R21 d.4.4 or at some other suitable point on the Cambrai Road or in La Vacquerie.
In a similar way as long as 31 & 32 Bearer Divs. are rationed by us dumps of water & rations &c,&c. must be pushed forwd. either by mules or wheeled transport.

MOTOR CYCLIST

On "Y"/"Z" night a motor cyclist will report at A.D.S. from 21st. M.A.C., 1 from 31st. F.A. & 1 of the 80th. F.A.(Pte. Walker).
M.A.C. cyclist will be used for fetching cars.
31st. F.A. " " " " " Keeping touch with 18 Ravine & Left area
80th. F.A. " " " " " " " " the Right area.

CAR SERVICES FORWARD

The Divl. cars under Sergt.Paterson will run between the A.D.S. & Villers Plouich on the left and the Barricade in R21 d. on the Right.
If the roads are passable, as the operations advance they will proceed further in each direction.

CASES

Light Lying Cases may be sent to M.D.S. if A.D.S gets crowded.
No A.T.S. at A.D.S.
Gas to M.D.S., severe to C.C.S.
S. I. to M.D.S. unless dangerous.
Prisoners &c., as others.
Indians as others.
Sick to C.S.C.P. (M.D.S.)

RATIONS

At Z plus 2 Two M. Police will report for duty and will be rationed by this Unit. Also drivers & car orderlies of the Divisional Cars.

"A" Form.
MESSAGES AND SIGNALS.

Army Form C. 2121.
(In pads of 100.)

TO: 20th Division / Guards Div

Sender's Number: DF 1
Day of Month: 5
AAA

Can you forward Return of Trench Mortars in possession for ~~fortnight~~ ending 1/12th.

From: 3° Corps Q

Lt Colonel

Army Form C. 2118.

War Diary or Intelligence Summary
(*Erase heading not required.*)

Instructions regarding War Diaries and Intelligence Summaries are contained in F.S. Regs., Part II. and the Staff Manual respectively. Title Pages will be prepared in manuscript.

GOUZEAUCOURT - Q36 d.4.9   30th. Nov. 1917.

6.30 a.m. Heavy Barrage of the enemy in the direction of La Vacquerie, Gonnelieu, Villers Guislain also heavy firing in the direction of Havrincourt.
7 a.m. Warned Sergt. Majors, R.A.M.C. & A.S.C. Adjt. (Capt. Ash) & Qtr.Mastr. that all ranks were to stand to
7.30 a.m. Orders given for all ranks to be prepared to leave at short notice. Barrage increasing in intensity & now falling about 1000 yards to the Eastward of the A.D.S. Heavy firing just to N.W. of the village. All motor Ambs. ordered to have their engines running & to be on the main road heading towards Fins.
8 a.m. Barrage now falling in the valley about 600 yards W. of Dressing Station.
8.30 a.m. Staff Capt.60th.Bgde. arrived stating Northern approaches to Gouzeaucourt had been closed by a very heavy hostile barrage. Firing increasing in intensity, shells bursting in Gouzeaucourt. A stream of wounded were arriving at the A.D.S.
9 a.m. Machine gun firing into village- hostile aeroplanes also firing. Directed Sergt. Major to collect Personnel in rear of the A.D.S. opposite the cars. All lying cases to be passed through direct by car or put on the Decauville train.
9.15 a.m. Despatched some of the Confidential Papers by Motor Amb. cars leaving with wounded. Ordered all cases in the Operating Theatre to be removed by car or train. Train to be started immediately & all Personnel to get on the remaining Motor Ambs. & make for rear Hd. Qrs. in Fins. German Inftry. running towards the village on the East- wards, shelling, machine gun-fire &c getting very heavy. Proceeded with Staff Capt. of 60th.Bgde. to Divsl. Hd.Qrs. to report action taken and enemy's progress. Fairly heavy shelling on the road between Gouzeaucourt & Fins. Enemy evidently attempting to surround Gouzeaucourt - all exits being covered by hostile machine gun fire. German Inftry. seen running down slope in W6 a. & also towards Heudicourt. Reported to Divl. Hd.Qrs. what was happening, owing to lines being cut this was the first intimation they had recd. of the enemy breaking through our lines. Proceeded to rear Hd. Qrs. at Fins & gave orders for the whole of the Bearer Reserves to march in parties of 32 (8 squads) under an N.C.O. along the main road towards Gouzeaucourt with the necessary dressings and stretchers &c. Met Capt. Ash & remainder of Unit who had come direct to Gouzeaucourt. Capt. Ash reported that the Decauville train with all the lying wounded had been cleared & practically the whole Unit including the horse transport in Gouzeaucourt had escaped before the village had been surrounded. He reported they had been heavily fired upon by rifles and machine guns when leaving. Directed Capt. Ash, Capt. Stallard to march back with me and the bearers towards Gouzeaucourt to a point I had selected when leaving Gouzeaucourt about W3 c4.9 as an advanced Dressing Station & Loading Post. Went forwd. with Capt. Ash to see if this point was still safe. Enemy attempting to shell the road but not getting many shells actually on to it. Installed Capts. Ash & Stallard with Brs. at the point selected & made arrangements for the wounded to be evacuated from

there to Fins by Motor Amb. Control Post arranged at the new A.D.S. supplies of stretchers accumulated from Hd.Qrs. [blankets, tea also inserted] Warning given to all Machine Gun Coys. A.S.C. & Transport Details as to what was in progress. Enemy having advanced about 1000 yds. down the Gouzeaucourt-Fins Rd. Owing to the strong wind lorries & Labour parties carrying shovels but no rifles were still proceeding up the road to Gouzeaucourt apparently not having heard the firing going on immediately in front of them. Several urgent appeals recd. from Fd. Officers & others from the 29th.Div. for S.A. ammunition. Ford car sent back towards the firing line from Fins with about 2000 rounds of ammunition taken off from the patients who were now arriving rapidly at rear Hd.Qrs. Later started new line of evacuation for wounded via Metz, Trescault, ~~Villers~~ Beaucamp & Villers Plouich. A great congestion in Fins owing to the arrival of large nos. of unarmed men, labour parties, lorries, limbers, A.S.C. details &c. Capt. Montgomery, Capt. Zinkhan, Lieuts. Marbury & Hornsey employed dressing the wounded at rear Hd.Qrs. About 5 p.m. I found it possible to return to A.D.S. Gouzeaucourt, the enemy having been driven out of the village by Guards & Cavalry &c. Found a number of Guards wounded lying near Dressing Stat. These were all evacuated. Lieut.Marbury & 30 O.R. were brot. up to form a holding party and Forwd. A.D.S. Situation much improved but enemy apparently still within machine gun range of the village. Returned with Capt. Ash to rear Hd.Qrs. after all the wounded had been got away & a portion of the kits. Official documents had been salvaged. Arriving at rear Hd.Qrs. about mid-night 30th. November/ 1st.Dec. 1917.

A.C.Osburn

Hd. Qrs. 60th. Fd. Amb.
in the Field
2nd. December 1917.

Lt.Colonel,R.A.M.C.
O.C. 60th. Field Amb.

Army Form C. 2118.

WAR DIARY
or
INTELLIGENCE SUMMARY

(Erase heading not required.)

Instructions regarding War Diaries and Intelligence Summaries are contained in F. S. Regs., Part II. and the Staff Manual respectively. Title Pages will be prepared in manuscript.

Place	Date	Hour	Summary of Events and Information	Remarks and references to Appendices

2449 Wt. W14957/M90 750,000 1/16 J.B.C. & A. Forms/C.2118/12

No. 60. F. A.

COMMITTEE FOR THE
MEDICAL HISTORY OF THE WA...
Date -1 FEB. 1918

Army Form C. 2118.

WAR DIARY
or
INTELLIGENCE SUMMARY
(Erase heading not required.)

WAR DIARY
OF
60th FIELD AMBULANCE
FOR
DECEMBER 1917

WAR DIARY or INTELLIGENCE SUMMARY

Place	Date	Hour	Summary of Events and Information	Remarks and references to Appendices
FINS	1/12		**Disposition of Personnel.** At Headquarters :- O.C. Lt Montgomery, Capt Zinkhan, Quarter Master. At A.D.S. Tencourt :- Lt Marbury & 30 O.R. At Fiencourt & Beaucamp tank Rds :- Capt Ack. Lt Stornoy, Capt Mullard & Capt Dunn (6th Aust. Amal.) At 16 Ravine :- Capt Chandler, Capt Bennet (61 Welsh) & Capt Jones (61 Welsh) Beam Division of the 3 Pld Ambs. working between 16 Ravine & Fiencourt.	
		10 a.m.	Visited A.D.S. all Cherry Cross; met Capt Ack & Lt Stornoy there & returned with Capt Kirton to Het. Qhs. Zins being shelled intermittently, all ranks standing to preparatory to move off. Shelled become more severe, intended rendezvous Equincourt, Etricourt, & Bohisains 2 Motor Amb. Cars cut off near Cherry Cross, arrangements being made to cut a road out for them. A number of the Officers & mens kits missing or destroyed & a large part of the Amble equipment damaged by shell fire or abandoned.	

WAR DIARY or INTELLIGENCE SUMMARY

Army Form C. 2118.

Place	Date	Hour	Summary of Events and Information	Remarks and references to Appendices
Fins	1/12		Pte. A/Lce Sergt. Bolton wounded in Gouzeaucourt. Lt. Mackay & his party of 30 O.R. had to be withdrawn from Gouzeaucourt, owing to heavy shellfire. A.D.S. at Gouzeaucourt has been again abandoned. Arrangements are being made to evacuate as much as possible of the stores & equipment left there. An entirely new system of evacuation has had to be established via 16 Ravine, Villers Plouich, Beaucamp, Gouzeaucourt, Crater, Charing Cross, Crater in Trescault, & Metz. Large cars are waiting as far forward as Trescault Crater; in advance of this, some Ambulance wagons as far forward as Charing Cross; in front of this, hand carriage. Report received that Sergt Edmond had been killed at 16 Ravine & his body supposed to have been buried somewhere near; also that a number of Bearers are missing from those attached to Bothns. Heavy shelling at Gouzeaucourt & between 16 Ravine & Ribecourt. Report received that Capt. Davidson, Lieut. Willis, & Capt. McArthur were taken prisoners during the opening of the 30th inst.	

Army Form C. 2118.

WAR DIARY
or
INTELLIGENCE SUMMARY.
(Erase heading not required.)

Instructions regarding War Diaries and Intelligence Summaries are contained in F.S. Regs. Part II. and the Staff Manual respectively. Title pages will be prepared in manuscript.

Place	Date	Hour	Summary of Events and Information	Remarks and references to Appendices
FINS	2/7/17		Shelling continued to be heavy in the Villers Plouich, Trescault area. A.D.S. temporarily moved back from Chaney Cross to Trescault crater. Lt. Kinsey returned from Trescault. Capt. Ash sent up again & also Lt. Montgomery. Capt. Rebuck to hand over front line evacuation arrangements to 2/3rd North Midland Fld. Amb. At urgent request of troops, about 30 Infantry Officers & 140 men were pre-concentrated in the Amb. Billets (probably No Pioneers) unit concentrating preparatory to moving off to back area. Bearers of 61 + 62 Fld Ambs. brought back wounded on to their own stations. Transport of 61 Fld. Amb. Cooker also returned. Wheeled stretchers & Stalkes in front line handed over to 2/3rd North Mid. F.A. Dumps formed of tents + stores + Sergt. Talbot + Pte. Dodkin left in charge.	

Army Form C. 2118.

WAR DIARY
or
INTELLIGENCE SUMMARY.
(Erase heading not required.)

Place	Date	Hour	Summary of Events and Information	Remarks and references to Appendices
FINS	3/12/17		Preparations completed for move to RIBEMONT.	
RIBEMONT	4/12/17		Horse transport under G. Pinkney & Capt. Inkster marched via Bapaume to Meaulte; halting one night between Bapaume + Albert. Personnel to proceed by train from Ytres at 3 p.m.: Capt. Kirton + Billeting party proceeded at 5 a.m. to AVELUY + RIBEMONT. Personnel arrived at Ribemont midnight 4/5th. Motor cycle abandoned near Bapaume in charge of M.P.	
RIBEMONT	5/12/17		Transport arrived at Meaulte at 12 noon, ~~transport~~ + proceeded at 6 p.m. via Doullens to Heaolin with Divl. Transport. The following being detached were sent by train from Aveluy to Heaolin at 10 a.m. on the 6th inst: 3 G.S. Wagons, (Supply) (Number), 1 water cart, 3 cooks.	

Army Form C. 2118.

WAR DIARY
or
INTELLIGENCE SUMMARY
(Erase heading not required.)

Place	Date	Hour	Summary of Events and Information	Remarks and references to Appendices
RIBEMONT	6/12/17	6 a.m.	Personnel marched at 6 a.m. to Albert entrained for Heilly, arriving at Berneuville at 6 p.m. Owing to delay in our receiving billeting instructions, did not get into billets at Boubers until midnight 6/7. Billets very poor & limited. Arranged with Town Mayor, Area Commandant, Supply & Agent Officer at Doullens - for rations of 635 Rd Amm transport which was alleged to much from time without supply wagon.	
BOUBERS	7/12/17	3 p.m.	Portion of transport coming by train arrived under Sgt Ridsdale. Capt. Wells & 9 O.R. reported as missing, believed proceeded from Ne 30th Nov.	
BOUBERS	8/12/17		Transport under Lt Marbury arrived	
BOUBERS	9/12/17		Lt Montgomery & advance party left for Wardrecques	
BOUBERS	10/12/17		Capt Jackson & billeting party for transport proceeded to Thiembronne	

WAR DIARY
or
INTELLIGENCE SUMMARY

Army Form C. 2118.

Place	Date	Hour	Summary of Events and Information	Remarks and references to Appendices
BOUBERS	11/12/17		Capt. Kitson, part of Repair Party + 2 Sect. Sub. Divns. proceeded to Strubent + embarked there + proceeded to Wardrecques. Horse transport under Lt. Pulling marched via Thérouanne to Wardrecques, arriving on Rd 12E.	
BOUBERS	12th		Remainder of the Unit proceeded by Anvil to Wardrecques. Sgts Paterson + Freeman + Sgt. Baynske left at Boubers in charge of graphic stores. Great difficulties being experienced owing to breaking down of motor transport. Orders received to take over Ordce Rwy. Station at 8 Rue de Collège, Bailleul.	
WARDRECQUES	13th		Visited Bailleul + prepared to take over site of O.R.S. Hazebrouck being shelled. Many civilian refugees on the roads. Sgt. Cleal + O.R. sent to Bailleul as an advance party.	

Army Form C. 2118.

WAR DIARY
or
INTELLIGENCE SUMMARY

(Erase heading not required.)

Instructions regarding War Diaries and Intelligence Summaries are contained in F.S. Regs., Part II. and the Staff Manual respectively. Title Pages will be prepared in manuscript.

Place	Date	Hour	Summary of Events and Information	Remarks and references to Appendices
WARLOY	14/12/17		Remaining Personnel arrived from Boulogne.	
Do	15/12/17		Transport marched to Bailleul Les Portes cant, Lieuben + 2 G.S.N 1 Sh. Wagon. O.C. proceeded on 6 days leave to Paris. Corpl Ask + further Advance Party moved to Bailleul. 2/Lts Merritt, Copeland + Toy U.S.A.R., reported their arrival for duty	
Do	16/12/17		2/Lt Montgomery posted for duty with 10th R.B. Duty actively taken over on the 26th	
Do	17/12/17		2/Lt Copeland also to 11th K.R.R. Capt Kennedy placed on sick list & sent to Officers Rest Station Bailleul. 2/Lt Toy took over charge of 11th R.B (on the 26th inst.) 2/Lt Harvey posted to duty with 10th K.R.R. on the 11th + permanently transferred on the 16th 20 O.R. 10th R.B + 11th K.R.R under training to Regtl Stretcher Bearers.	
Do	18/12/17			

Army Form C. 2118.

WAR DIARY
or
INTELLIGENCE SUMMARY

(Erase heading not required.)

Instructions regarding War Diaries and Intelligence Summaries are contained in F. S. Regs., Part II. and the Staff Manual respectively. Title Pages will be prepared in manuscript.

Place	Date	Hour	Summary of Events and Information	Remarks and references to Appendices
WARCŒCQUES	20/12/17		Capt. Inkham & Capt. Mulbury on leave to Paris. Unikemployed in cleaning & preparing new D.R.S.	
BAILLEUL	21/12/17		Cleaning & overhauling 13th amb. Equipment & refitting. Patients admitted to the new D.R.S.	
Do.	23/12/17		O.C. returned from leave. Court Martial proceedings promulgated - Pte. Barbery ASC wt.	
Do.	26/12/17		2/Mr. Sergt. sent to Bernaville to give evidence at F.G.C.M. H. Johnstone (RAMC) on the sick list.	
Do.	29/12/17		Q.Q.M.S. IX Corps, Col. J.B. Wilson inspected Ambl. & D.R.S.	
Do.	30/12/17		A.D.M.S. 20th Divn. visited Ambl. Position of Officers O.C. - Capt Roth, Lt Johnstone, Lt Merville at HQ. Capt. Kidson in charge detachment at Wincheepe Capts Inkham & Mulbury on leave in Paris.	
Do.	31/12/17		Patients in Hospital 58. O.R. Deficiency in personnel 2 Officers + 21 O.R.	

2449 Wt. W14957/M90 750,000 1/16 J.B.C. & A. Forms/C.2118/12.

140/2696

COMMITTEE FOR THE
MEDICAL HISTORY OF THE WAR
Date -4 MAR. 1918

No. 60. 7. O.

Jan. 1918

Army Form C. 2118.

WAR DIARY
or
INTELLIGENCE SUMMARY

(Erase heading not required.)

War Diary of 60th Field Ambulance for Jan - 1918

Vol 30

Army Form C. 2118.

WAR DIARY
or
INTELLIGENCE SUMMARY

(Erase heading not required.)

Instructions regarding War Diaries and Intelligence Summaries are contained in F. S. Regs., Part II. and the Staff Manual respectively. Title Pages will be prepared in manuscript.

Place	Date	Hour	Summary of Events and Information	Remarks and references to Appendices
8 RUE DE COLLEGE BAILLEUL (BAILLEUL COLLEGE)	1/7/8		Present with Unit :- O.C., Capt's Cole, Capt Revill, + L.M. Johnstone. Patients in Hospt :- 70.	
	2/7/8		Unit inspected by D.D.M.S, IX Corps. 75 N.C.O.'s + men of the Unit pelected for award with £1. War Savings Certificates from surplus funds of Canteen. Advance party sent to St Joseph's School, 8 Rue de Contye to commence taking over.	Benoit 12.c.4.4 Sheet 28
	4/7/8		Sgt Hardy + 49 O.R. proceeded to Woodcote House for duty as a Return Depot.	
	5/7/8		Capt's Zickham + Harding M.O.R.C., U.S.A., returned from leave to Paris. Unit moved from BAILLEUL COLLEGE to ST. JOSEPHS SCHOOL, BAILLEUL. Capt. Harding joined Return Depot at Woodcote House as O.C. Benoit Depot.	
ST JOSEPHS COLLEGE. BAILLEUL. (8 RUE DE BENOIT CONTYE)	6/7/8		Col. Slater C.M.G., D.S.O., proceeded as D.D.M.S. to VII Corps. Col. B. Wingate D.S.O. took over duties as A.D.M.S., 20th Divn.	
	7/7/8		Capt. Kirton + detachment arrived from WARDRECQUES.	

Army Form C. 2118.

WAR DIARY
or
INTELLIGENCE SUMMARY

(Erase heading not required.)

Place	Date	Hour	Summary of Events and Information	Remarks and references to Appendices
ST. JOSEPH'S SCHOOL BAILLEUL (8 RUE DE BENOIT CARTH)	2/1/18		Unit inspected by D.D.M.S. IX Corps.	
	10/1/18		Capt. Zinkham attached for charge of No 43 Bde R.G.A.	
	12/1/18		Unit has been occupied in cleaning & improving the large building now occupied. Accommodation 200 patients. Average No in hospital 130. Nr discharged to duty daily 8. Principal diseases. Trench feet, P.U.O, Scabies, Diarrhoea, and Septic wounds, Colds, Laryngitis & other minor complaints. Trench treatment for Trench feet is being very thoroughly carried out.	
	13/1/18		Unit inspected by D.D.M.S. IX Corps & A.D.M.S. 20 Div. Capt Zinkham detailed for duty with 7th K.O.Y.L.I, instead of 43 Bde R.G.A. Capt Grenell proceeded to take charge of 43 Bde R.G.A. Capt Munday placed on the Sick list.	
	18/1/18		Capt Zinkham directed to report to G.O.C., L/C., A.E.F.	
	23/1/18		Capt Manbury evacuated to No 4. O.C.S.	

WAR DIARY
or
INTELLIGENCE SUMMARY

Army Form C. 2118.

Place	Date	Hour	Summary of Events and Information	Remarks and references to Appendices
BAILLEUL			Ecole St Joseph Rue Benoit Cortyl	
	27.1.18		G.O.C. 20th Division inspected Tent Statives - Cookery, cooking arrangement + kits - also record & registers shed by unit since 1915. and expressed great satisfaction - Oh much	
			Lt Rigby hospital to be G.O.C. + commanded	
			Patient in Hospital 147. an average of 10 + 12 a day	
	28.1.18		returned to duty	
	29.1.18		Lt Gumbleton QM returned from leave	
	30.1.18		20 division counted to 22nd Corps IX Corps to replace	
	31.1.18		Greenwich Lieut. & Capt A/S Capt Burton on leave	
			+ QM members & present	
			+ 23 Other ranks & present	
			5 Officers	

A. Osborne
Lt Col.
Comm J. Boazphn Amb.

Army Form C. 2118.

WAR DIARY
or
INTELLIGENCE SUMMARY
(Erase heading not required.)

WAR DIARY 60 FIELD AMB.
FEBRUARY 1918
CONFIDENTIAL

60 FIELD AMBULANCE
28 FEB 1918
ORDERLY ROOM

COMMITTEE FOR THE
MEDICAL HISTORY OF THE WAR
Date -8 APR 1918

WAR DIARY
or
INTELLIGENCE SUMMARY

(Erase heading not required.)

Army Form C. 2118.

Instructions regarding War Diaries and Intelligence Summaries are contained in F. S. Regs., Part II. and the Staff Manual respectively. Title Pages will be prepared in manuscript.

Place	Date	Hour	Summary of Events and Information	Remarks and references to Appendices
St Joseph's College BAILLEUL (8 Rue de [Bruat Louge?])	1/2/18		Present with Unit :— O.C. Capt. ASH and Qr. Mr. LEE	
	2/2/18		Unit occupied with D.R.S. 50 O.R. (Nearns) attached to 62nd Field Ambulance at WOODCOTE HOUSE, MDS	
	3/2/18		D.D.M.S. XXII Corps (Col Begg) and A.D.M.S. 20th Div. inspected the Rest Station. Capt. W.H. Brodie R.A.M.C. and Capt. C.A. Boyd R.A.M.C. reported their arrival for duty.	
	4/2/18		Capt. C.A. Boyd took over Temporary medical charge of 11th K.R.R.C. on relief of Lieut J. Wickeland MORE, U.S.A. sick.	
	5/2/18		Lieut. & Qr. Mr. T. Johnstone appointed Trans-Officer in accordance with S.R.O. 3269 para 3.	
	8/2/18		Lieut. C.N. Montgomery R.A.M.C. reported his arrival for duty on completion of duty with 10th R.B. Sgts Barker, Lynch, & Blow proceeded to WARATAH CAMP as Advance Party	

Army Form C. 2118.

WAR DIARY
or
INTELLIGENCE SUMMARY
(Erase heading not required.)

Instructions regarding War Diaries and Intelligence Summaries are contained in F.S. Regs., Part II. and the Staff Manual respectively. Title Pages will be prepared in manuscript.

Place	Date	Hour	Summary of Events and Information	Remarks and references to Appendices
St Joseph's College BAILLEUL (8 Rue Bauvol Lodge)	9/2/18		Lieut. J.W. Copeland MORE, U.S.A. returned to Unit on exchange from C.C.S. 5. O.R. proceeded to WARATAH CAMP as an additional ambulance party. Lieut. C.B. Montgomery R.A.M.C. proceeded for duty with 111 R.R.C. in lieu of (Capt. F.) Boyd who returned to H.Q.	
WARATAH CAMP	11/2/18		H.Q. of the unit moved to WARATAH CAMP and took over a DRS third from 2/3rd East Lancs. Fd Amb. at noon. 6 O.R. returned to HQ upon completion of duty with 62nd Fd Amb. 9 O.R. proceeded for duty from 62nd Fd Amb. to 61st Fd Amb. Capt. Boyd and servant and S/Sgt. Cargill proceeded to DYSENTERY CAMP on a holiday party.	
	12/2/18		Lieut. Copeland U.S.A. S/Sgt. Thiel Hyneman & 38 O.R. proceeded to HAEGEDOORNE DYSENTERY CAMP and took over from 5-0 Fd Amb. Sgt Cooper, Cpl Gambe and 4 O.R. proceeded to CAESTRE STATION as a holiday party. Capt. w. J. Henry R.A.M.C. reported his arrival for duty. Sgt Davis and 24 O.R. returned to HQ on completion of duty with 62nd Field Amb.	SCABIES
	13/2/18		Lieut. Br. Martin Johnston & servant, D.Sgt. Dagby, S.G. Barker, 1 Bloice F/Sgt Dillett and 28 O.R. returned to BAILLEUL from WARATAH CAMP	

2449 Wt. W14957/M90 750,000 1/16 J.B.C. & A. Forms/C.2118/12.

Army Form C. 2118.

WAR DIARY
or
INTELLIGENCE SUMMARY

(Erase heading not required.)

Place	Date	Hour	Summary of Events and Information	Remarks and references to Appendices
WARATAH CAMP	14/2/18		Capt. Henry R.A.M.C. proceeded on 13th inst. to take medical charge of 11th & R.I.B. in relief of Lieut Troy M.O.R.C. U.S.A. sick. Sgt. Blow + 8 O.R. proceeded to HAEGEDORNE CAMP (on duty) H.Q. of the unit returned to BAILLEUL (8 Rue de Bruvot (only)) upon WARATAH CAMP being taken over by 48th & 7th Aust.	
St Joseph's Cothu. BAILLEUL 15/2/18 (8 Rue de Lintzie Brunt)			Capt Brodie and 10 O.R. with necessary transport y material proceeded to EECKHOUT CASTEEL to open an Impulsion Room for sick with 59th Bde. can to be evacuated to CAESTRE. Daily sick evacuated sick. Lieut Copelland M.O.R.C. U.S.A. evacuated sick. One road car and driver 7C 47 Parks A.S.C. M/T evacuated.	
CAESTRE 16/2/18			The Unit moved from BAILLEUL to CAESTRE. Capt J Knox returned from leave Lieut E. P. Troy M.O.R.C. U.S.A. evacuated sick. Lieut J. F. Horney reported unit on completion of duty with 10th K.R.R.R.	
	18/2/18		40 O.R. proceeded to Eeckout Casteel. Sgt Munro + 4 O.R. arrived from No1 N.Z. 7D Amb. to take over CAESTRE D.R.S	

WAR DIARY or INTELLIGENCE SUMMARY

Army Form C. 2118.

Place	Date	Hour	Summary of Events and Information	Remarks and references to Appendices
EECKHOUT-CASTEEL	19/2/18		The unit concentrated at EECKHOUT-CASTEEL. Hazebrouck Dysentery Camp and Captn D.R.S. Henry handed over to No.1. N.Z. F.D. Amb. Also store at St. Joseph's College. Lieut J.F. Horney R.A.M.C. proceeds on leave to U.K.	
	20/2/18		The C.O. proceeded on leave to U.K. Captn Ash assumed command of the unit. The unit marched to STEENBECQUE and entrained for NESLE under command of Capt Kenton.	
OMENCOURT	21/2/18		Capt Ash proceeded to NESLE by motor ambulance with 3 O.R. in advance party. The unit having detrained at NESLE, marched to OMEN-COURT and took over field ambulance set there from 97 F.B.'F.D. Amb.	
	22/2/18		Patients admitted from 3-9 47 Brigade Group.	

Army Form C. 2118.

WAR DIARY
or
INTELLIGENCE SUMMARY
(Erase heading not required.)

Place	Date	Hour	Summary of Events and Information	Remarks and references to Appendices
OMIÉCOURT	23/2/18		One 2O.1 Car with Driver A.H. Smith A.S.C. M.T. reported for duty D.D.M.S. XVIII Corps (Col. PRYNNE) with A.D.M.S. 20th Div. inspected the unit.	
	25/2/18		12 O.R. 11th K.R.R.C. and 8 O.R. 2nd Scottish Rifles arrived for instruction as stretcher bearers. Capt. Brodie proceeded to take over temporary medical charge of 96th & 84th Coys R.E.	
	28/2/18		Capt. Knuton proceeded to take over temporary medical charge of XVIII Corps Reinforcement Camp. Present with unit Capt. Carr, Capt. Argyle & Lt. Fr. (H.Q. Fred Harvey on leave) Capt. Knuton on temporary duty with Reinforcement Camp. 5th Corps Exp. Brigade. Tent Duty with 96th & 94th R.E. 2 Officers & 28 Other Ranks admitted Patients in hospital 30.	

R.V.C. Ash.
Capt R.A.M.C.
Vt O/C 77th Field Ambulance

WAR DIARY
60th FIELD AMBULANCE
MARCH 1918

Army Form C. 2118.

WAR DIARY
or
INTELLIGENCE SUMMARY
(Erase heading not required.)

Instructions regarding War Diaries and Intelligence Summaries are contained in F. S. Regs., Part II and the Staff Manual respectively. Title Pages will be prepared in manuscript.

Place	Date	Hour	Summary of Events and Information	Remarks and references to Appendices
OMENCOURT	1 3/18		Present with unit – CAPT. R.V. CASH. CAPT. C.A. BOYD. Lt. & QM. JOHNSTON. C.O. and Lieut HORNSEY on leave to U.K. CAPT. KIRTON on detached duty – M.O. 4o XXIV CORPS REINFORCEMENT CAMP. CAPT. BRODIE on detached duty as M.O./c 96th & 54th Coys R.E. 2 Offs. + 28 O.R. different Patients in hospital.	
	4 3/18	30	Capt. Boyd detailed to no such of M.C. Coy at MARGNY daily. Must occupied on duties of Divisional Rest Stn. Patients admitted on transfer from 61st & 62nd Fd Ambs. Evacuations to 61 C.C.S. HAM + convalescents G/ARMY CONVALESCENT DEPOT. 10 O.R. category B1 & B11 found unfit as reinforcements. 10 O.R. category A and 10 O.R. category B1 & B11 proceeded to 5th ARMY SCHOOL at 61 C.C.S. S.S. CARGILL, Sgt. COOPER, Pte. WEMYSS & Pte. BEER proceeded to 5th ARMY SCHOOL at 61 C.C.S. for course of instruction as instructors in foot massage. 6 O.R. sent to 54th Bde to be attached to Bns on completion of duty with 96th & 54th Coys R.E.	
	5 3/18		CAPT BRODIE rejoined unit on completion of duty with Officers Rest Stn. at VOYENNES for convalescent	
	7 3/18		Lieut & QM with 15 O.R. proceeded to Officers Rest Stn. at VOYENNES and decorating work there.	
	9 3/18		Summer time came into use this day. 6 O.R. rejoined unit on completion of duty with 54th Bde. Lieut HORNSEY returned from leave to U.K.	
	10 3/18		S.S. CARGILL that, returned from course of instruction at 61 C.C.S. 126 R. 11th KRRC 98 O.R. 2nd Scott Rif. detained to these Bns on completion of course of instruction in stretcher bearing.	
	13 3/18		S. C. Divisional Train unfitted units Transport.	

Army Form C. 2118.

WAR DIARY
or
INTELLIGENCE SUMMARY
(Erase heading not required.)

Instructions regarding War Diaries and Intelligence Summaries are contained in F. S. Regs, Part II. and the Staff Manual respectively. Title Pages will be prepared in manuscript.

Place	Date	Hour	Summary of Events and Information	Remarks and references to Appendices
OMIECOURT	13/3/18		CAPT. R.V.C. ASH M.C. RAMC (T.F.) assumed command of 60th F.D. Amb. on 8.3.18 vice LIEUT COL A.C. OSBURN D.S.O. RAMC on sick leave in U.K.	
			CAPT. C.A. BOYD RAMC assumed the duties of Second in Command on same date by A.D.M.S. Order 10/3/18	
			CAPT. R.V.C. ASH and CAPT. C.A. BOYD granted permission by S.O.O. 20th Div. A/922 6/113 of 13.3.18. to wear the Badge of MAJOR. Authority H.Q. 20th Div. A/922 6/113 of 13.3.18.	
	17/3/18		LIEUT COL A.C. OSBURN D.S.O. RAMC struck off the strength of the unit from 28/2/18 - Authority D.M.S. V ARMY P1/30 of 14.3.18.	
	19/3/18		7 O R reported for duty as reinforcements. Lt & Q.M. JOHNSTONE and party rejoined unit from Off Rest Stn VOYENNES.	
	21/3/18		LIEUT HORNSEY proceeded to take over medical charge of 6th KSLI. On orders from 59th Bde the unit marched to VGNY January 11.30 and established HQ there and A.D.S's at LANCHY & FORESTE with holding posts at R. Received A.D.S's at QUIVIÈRES and DOUILLY. Sheet 66D. 59th Bde HQ at VILLIERS-St-CHRISTOPHE.	
VGNY	22/3/18	6 a.m	message received from 5-9th Bde HQ that the Brigade was occupying a line as follows. Reference Sheet 66D.	
			11 KRR on the Rester- Beaun - 2 Coys holding forward trenches including VAUX village - 1 Coy in counter attack immediately N.W. of VAUX - 1 Coy in BEAUVOIS.	

WAR DIARY or INTELLIGENCE SUMMARY

Army Form C. 2118.

Place	Date	Hour	Summary of Events and Information	Remarks and references to Appendices
UGNY	22/3/18		2nd Scott R. on Right - 2 Coys holding forward trenches - 1 Coy in defences near ARGOSY WOODS, 1 in reserve, attack on flank defence. 11th R.B. - 2 Coys in defence N. & E. of GERMAINE with supporting platoons covering flanks of the VAUX - GERMAINE spur. - 2 Coys in reserve immediately E of LANCHY. M.G. Corps in unimportant previously selected. In front of fact that dispositions would appear to have been only quite transient, 11 R.A.M.C. shuttles were dispatched to Bde to locate them but throughout the day, though sent back again & again to try to get in touch, it hampered subsequently, the account, also by the fact that practically no wounded from other Bde Groups passed through our A.D.S.'s during the day.	ARGOSY
		12 noon	Visited Bde. H.Q. but could get no definite information of location of units. Returned later and found Bde H.Q. had moved to position then unknown but later reported to be TOVILLE. No direct orders or instructions, with exception	
		3 p.m.	of money, having mentioned were received from Bde at any time during these operations though. The Ambulance was finishing up its billets at Bde. They acted greatly to the uncertainty of matters at different times, and to the responsibility of the C.O. in forming decisions.	
		4 p.m.	Visited A.D.S. at FORRESTE and found large number of wounded included sitting. Two cars arriving for evacuating them. Returned to UGNY and sent MAJOR BOYD afterwards and 2 large cars (2nd & 1st F.C.) And (all that were available) to A.D.S. FORRESTE to render with instructions to where so many wounded a fresh and then next point to MATIGNY, which place I had already selected as the next point to establish an A.D.S. as it was necessary from UGNY, becoming necessary.	See MAJOR BOYD attached narrative.

Army Form C. 2118.

WAR DIARY
or
INTELLIGENCE SUMMARY

(Erase heading not required.)

Instructions regarding War Diaries and Intelligence Summaries are contained in F.S. Regs., Part II. and the Staff Manual respectively. Title Pages will be prepared in manuscript.

Place	Date	Hour	Summary of Events and Information	Remarks and references to Appendices
UGNY	22/3/18	4.30 p.m. 5 p.m.	Message received from ADMS 20th Div. to withdraw to MATIGNY. At this time UGNY was heavily shelled and we were also fired upon with machine guns by enemy aeroplanes. No casualties. The detachment at LANCHY was withdrawn and sent on to FORRESTE with Major BOYD.	
MATIGNY	"	5.30 p.m.	Sent unit with transport back to LANGUEVOISIN under CAPT. BRODIE, a desert of infantry to get the main body of the rear arm thr (and at rise). With a small detachment and ADS at MATIGNY, I then proceeded to that place where I met ADMS 61st Div and ADMS 20th Div and ADS at MATIGNY from a 3.0 Aust. of 61st Div. was then a plan to take in ADS at MATIGNY from a 3.0 Aust. of 61st Div. was came in that the enemy was advancing rapidly. Major BOYD having arrived in return from FORRESTE I looked him after MATIGNY was ready (D 27 a 8.3" sheet 66 D) with party to join a collecting post for wounded who were now being in front the UGNY — MATIGNY road. All belonged to 61st Div. I looked some of these into the 2 lorries & 3rd just returned from C.C.S. and took them to VOYENNES (Off. Rest Sto) sending Major its cars back to Major BOYD who had no other cars that to use all types BOYD. of vehicle for the many wounded.	See attached narrative of Major BOYD.
LANGUEVOISIN	"		I then went on to LANGUEVOISIN to organize the next, & sent CAPT. BRODIE back to meet Major BOYD. These 2 officers carried on and cleared all wounded successfully withdrawing finally on Line being brought back to the SOMME and the bridges destroyed.	

2449 Wt. W14957/M90 750,000 1/16 J.B.C. & A. Forms/C.2118/12

WAR DIARY
or
INTELLIGENCE SUMMARY

Army Form C. 2118.

Place	Date	Hour	Summary of Events and Information	Remarks and references to Appendices
LANGUEVOISIN	23/3/18		H.Q. and Recy A.D.S. established at LANGUEVOISIN. (I 27 C central) Visited Bde H.Q. at ROUY-le-PETIT and learned that the Bde were holding the line of SOMME canal from BETHENCOURT to just S. of VOYENNES. On return sent 2 squads R.A.M.C. S.B.'s to each Bn. & later 3 squads under Sgt BARKER R.A.M.C. to be attached to Bde H.Q. These latter were never used and were returned to me in the following day. Sent Major BOYD with party & equipment to form A.D.S. at MESNIL St. NICAISE for left sector of Bde front and CAPT. BRODIE with similar pannier in A.D.S. at winmill. I22 d.1.3r. known as the QUIQUERY A.D.S. for Right Sector. It was found possible to send ambulance cars right up to the R.A.P's in VOYENNES. to bring cases to LANGUEVOISIN, where they were evacuated by M.A.C. to ROYE. H.A. wagons were also used in bringing wounded in this Sector. H.A.C. Reported to A.D.M.S. at NESLE in person.	
	24/3/18		Evacuation from VOYENNES sector continued as in previous day but after 4 pm cars could no longer go further than A.D.S. at QUIQUERY owing to withdrawal of our line from VOYENNES due to enemy having crossed canal at BETHENCOURT and S. of VOYENNES.	
		10am	Motor cyclist attached to Major BOYD reported with daily slates. Some afterwards came from P.A.D.M.S. that Major BOYD had been compelled to vacate A.D.S. at MESNIL-St-NICAISE owing to enemy shell fire. His whereabouts from now unknown to me. I received in following day several rumours that he had moved to ROUY-le-PETIT. No news of him there. The motor cyclist was then sent to A.D.M.S. with stats. and to ascertain M. JBVa NESLE to H.Q. 31 M.A.C. in case I'm Major BOYD & did not return till evening.	See accompanying A.D.S. of appendix from now onwards for information of Major BOYD

WAR DIARY or INTELLIGENCE SUMMARY

Army Form C. 2118.

Place	Date	Hour	Summary of Events and Information	Remarks and references to Appendices
LANGUEVOISIN	3/24/18	3 p.m.	Received word from A.D.M.S, who worked A.D.S established at NESLE. In the whole neighbourhood, I sent a detachment to work this A.D.S but could not then send an officer, being alone in charge of unit & A.D.S at LANGUEVOISIN. Later 4 p.m. Capt. BRODIE was sent with LIEUT. MONTGOMERY who had left the Bn the 11. K.R.R. and was in orders of A.D.M.S though attached to 60 to 90 Bde.	
		5 p.m.	Very heavy shelling of LANGUEVOISIN. Also machine gun fire on A.D.S by enemy airplanes. Wounded practically ceased to come in. Sgt. BARKER and squad returned from Bde H.Q. reported Bde H.Q. removed to MORLEMONT. Just N. of NESLE. As it seemed probable that the line of retreat of Bde would subsequently be through NESLE, taking the NESLE-ROYE road, and as there was already an A.D.S at NESLE in touch with Bde and my wounded were now coming to LANGUEVOISIN, I decided to withdraw unit to RETHONVILLERS. This play being also in direct line of evacuation of wounded from NESLE to ROYE.	
		6 p.m.	Accordingly withdrew unit. Army Wagon fired at by enemy airplanes whilst starting. My horse wounded & subsequently destroyed (at ABBEVILLE). Left small party with our trucking to evacuate any wounded coming in to MAC cars with our return to RETHONVILLERS whither also arrived at RETHUNVILLERS 8 p.m. having picked up Major BOYD and party at BILLANCOURT. He had two (S. Bt's) wounded & evacuated. Immediately established A.D.S. and notified CAPT. BRODIE, instructing him also to inform Bde H.Q. what I had did.	
RETHON- VILLERS		8 p.m.		

WAR DIARY
or
INTELLIGENCE SUMMARY.
(Erase heading not required.)

Army Form C. 2118.

Place	Date	Hour	Summary of Events and Information	Remarks and references to Appendices
RETHON-VILLERS	24/3/18	9 pm	CAPT BRODIE reported, accompanied by CAPT TOWNSEND & Lt MONTGOMERY having been ordered by Bde HQ to clear ADS at NESLE. Journey dutifully noted Bde HQ which were now just S of NESLE & reported my dispositions & that I proposed to withdraw next to CHAMPIEN, rest party in ADS at RETHONVILLERS.	
		11 pm	Sent next with Transport to CHAMPIEN. Transport to CHAMPIEN under Major BOYD, with CAPT BRODIE and Lt MONTGOMERY, all of whom were tired out. 9 remained in charge of ADS with Capt TOWNSEND & party at RETHONVILLERS. I now had 3 lorries, two cars of 6.0. M.T. Amb. 3 MAC cars + 4 lorries. All these I took steps to retain with me at all costs. During the night and throughout the French wounded came in steadily. The majority were French, these troops having come in during the night, but their Amb parts were not set up till midday. Supplied them with stretchers and blankets & evacuated them wounded with ours.	
	25/3/18		Afternoon very quiet, hardly any wounded. Bde HQ withdrawn to BILLANCOURT on morning. Enemy had advanced to within 1500 yds of ADS when it was evacuated.	
		3 pm	Reported to A.D.M.S. at CARREPUIS in person.	

WAR DIARY
or
INTELLIGENCE SUMMARY.

Army Form C. 2118.

Place	Date	Hour	Summary of Events and Information	Remarks and references to Appendices
CHAMPIEN	25/3/18	6 p.m.	Rejoined unit and sent Capt. BRODIE to A.D.S. at RETHONVILLERS with instructions to withdraw to crossroads at N.13.b.27. & bus B.H.Q. when necessary. Had on truck with Bde H.Q. Then he subsequently did. Bde H.Q. retiring to BALATRE.	
		8 p.m.	Received message from 3-9th Bde Staff Captain that enemy were advancing on two flanks, that it was proposed to withdraw unit to straighten line and that the Bde was probably to be relieved by the French & to come out about midnight. Immediately reported this to A.D.M.S. personally at ROYE. Arranged to withdraw unit to LAUCOURT on MONTDIDIER ROAD at once. Advised by G.S.O.2. to march through ROYE. Returned to CHAMPIEN and notified CAPT. BRODIE. Unit marched from CHAMPIEN at midnight, arrived at LAUCOURT at 3.30 a.m. 26/3/18. Billetted there. S.P.	
ROYE			returned to ROYE and sought A.D.M.S. but found he had left. Location unknown. Met Capt Brodie in ROYE 4.30 a.m. He had been sent back to report to unit by Bde H.Q. No information of Bde's whereabouts except that they were out of the line. Returned to unit in Capt.	B. BRODIE 1/A.C.y

Army Form C. 2118.

WAR DIARY
or
INTELLIGENCE SUMMARY.
(Erase heading not required.)

Instructions regarding War Diaries and Intelligence Summaries are contained in F. S. Regs., Part II. and the Staff Manual respectively. Title pages will be prepared in manuscript.

Place	Date	Hour	Summary of Events and Information	Remarks and references to Appendices
LAUCOURT BY ROYE	26/3/18	8 am	Received a visit from O.C. a French Inf. Bn. who told me the enemy were then entering ROYE from the north, that he went with other French troops was to form a line of defence between LAUCOURT & ROYE & during and to move at once. Passed this warning on to O.C. 53 C.C.S. who had no information or orders & prepared to move. Not knowing where 20th Div. were, they informed by a 20th Div. artillery officer that 20th Div. H.Q. was to be at FAVEROLLES. I decided to move towards MONTDIDIER.	
ROYE — MONTDIDIER ROAD			Received a report from O.C. 53 C.C.S. to help him remove his wounded. I turned over to him for this the 3 M.A.C. cars still with me, kept him all available 60 & 70 Amb. cars & also 4 lorries. Then whilst worked between 3-3 C.C.S. and LABOISSIERE Relay Camp had to 53 C.C.S. at HARGICOURT. Also arranged for him 3 ammunition lorries from ROYE. Many wounded were packed up also on road. Those had come from the line beyond ROYE & were walking or on limber wagons & lorries. Collected these & sent them all & up to LABOISSIERE & HARGICOURT. These must have been some 40 V. there.	

Army Form C. 2118.

WAR DIARY
or
INTELLIGENCE SUMMARY.
(Erase heading not required.)

Instructions regarding War Diaries and Intelligence Summaries are contained in F. S. Regs., Part II. and the Staff Manual respectively. Title pages will be prepared in manuscript.

Place	Date	Hour	Summary of Events and Information	Remarks and references to Appendices
ROYE – MONTDIDIER ROAD	26/3/18		On arrival at FAVEROLLES drew rations and ascertained from O.C. 20th Div. M.T. Column that 20th Div H.Q. were at QUESNEL on ROYE – AMIENS ROAD	
FAVEROLLES			Decided to push on through MONTDIDIER & get upon River AVRE and then work up left bank of that river to report Division	
FONTAINE SOUS MONTDIDIER			Proceeded to FONTAINE-SOUS-MONTDIDIER and billeted there. Reported location to A.D.M.S. at QUESNEL received orders to march to BRACHES to await instructions	
AUBVILLERS	27/3/18		Marched to AUBVILLERS & billeted there. BRACHES being fully occupied by French troops (cavalry) Met D.A.D.M.S. at BRACHES and received instructions to await orders in AUBVILLERS. Capt Brodie attached to 61st Fd. Amb. Received orders to march to BERTEAUCOURT through MOREUIL.	
BERTEAUCOURT	28/3/18		Marched to BERTEAUCOURT. There received orders to proceed to ABBEVILLE under orders of O.C. 62nd Fd. Amb. Marched to BOVES	
BOVES SAINS en AMIENOIS			then to SAINS en AMIENOIS billeted there. Very crowded	
SEUX	29/3/18		Marched to SEUX Billeted there	
WARLUS	30/3/18		Marched to WARLUS. Billeted there	
	31/3/18		Marched to ABBEVILLE & began to refit & refuel	

Appendix to
WAR DIARY
MARCH 1st 1918
60th FIELD AMBULANCE
Being Manuscript of Major C.A. BOYD RAMC

O.C. 60th Field Ambulance

The following is a copy of notes taken in connection with the operations of 60th F.A. detachments with which I was concerned during 22nd, 23rd & 24th March 1918.

22.3.18 I was ordered by O.C. 60th F.A. to proceed from UGNY to LANCHY to look for a suitable site and establish an A.D.S. at that place. I took with me Sgt. Cheal and a small holding party. I found that an ambulance of the 61st Divn was in occupation of practically all houses which had not been destroyed, but the O.C. of this Amb. placed a cellar and remains of a large house at my disposal. I established an A.D.S. in the cellar. Four bearer squads which had previously been sent forward from UGNY to find and report to the M.Os. 11th R.B. and 2nd S.R. who were reported to be in the vicinity of BEAUVOIS returned through LANCHY and reported that they had been unable to get into touch with these Batt'ns and that troops of the 61st Divn in BEAUVOIS could give no information as to their whereabouts. I then went forward myself to BEAUVOIS but I could get no news of the 59th Brigade units. At this time BEAUVOIS was being heavily shelled and transport & other details of the 61st Divn were preparing to evacuate and fall back on LANCHY so I withdrew these squads to UGNY in hope of getting some information there. (I found out later that early in the day the whole Brigade had been moved to a position further south. No information of this move had been received from Brigade HQ.) at about 6 p.m. during the O.C's absence an order arrived at UGNY from the Brigade to withdraw the F.A. to MATTIGNY. I then withdrew my party from LANCHY to UGNY to await the C.Os return. He had attended to no cases at LANCHY as the 61st Divn F.A. team was able to deal with all cases of their division. On the C.O's return to UGNY he sent me to FORRESTE with three cars (all that were available) and a loading party to assist the 61st Divn in the evacuation of wounded from that place whilst en route on the road (Village DOUILLY and FORRESTE we met a number of troops retiring, who told me that the enemy was in the outskirts of FORRESTE and that our troops were retiring in that area. I pushed on, loaded six stretcher cases and some sitting cases unable to walk. The enemy by this time was in the southern end of the village so I ordered my loading party under Sgt. Cheal to retire immediately and find their way to MATTIGNY. After the cars had been loaded I could not see six stretcher cases only left behind. These must have fallen into enemy hands as there was no means by which they could have been removed. I proceeded with the last car to MATTIGNY and established a dressing station at the Cross Roads there. Many wounded were collected there and sent on after being dressed. The evacuation at this time was extremely difficult and at one time I had nearly one hundred cases collected there with very little hope of getting them away as there was no MAC service available and a dressing station at VOYENNES to which earlier casualties had been sent on Rifflers and limbers etc. was sent up word that no more cases could be moved there + that all further cases must be evacuated to ROYE, a distance of 20 kilometres. As practically all cases coming through MATTIGNY belonged to units of the 61st Bde. I applied to HQrs of that Bde. (which at that time was at MATTIGNY) for help in evacuation. But was unable to get any assistance however an officer of an ambulance chain to whom I applied proceed to send in some lorries. An hour later these arrived and these together with another lorry which I immediately "requisitioned" partly relieved the congestion. Many wounded unable to walk but able to a certain extent to look after themselves went foot in wagons and limbers proceeding in the direction of VOYENNES. Two large cars and one Ford of the 60th FA travelled continuously to VOYENNES and back and later to ROYE with the most serious cases about 1 am 23.3.18 as practically all traffic through MATTIGNY which could be utilised for wounded had ceased, I walked to VOYENNES in the hope of being able to get some lorries there. In this there succeeded as no belonging to the Canadian Ry Troops were sent forward immediately. Capt Brodie arrived at about 2.30 pm to relieve me and I regret the DR of LANGUEVOISIN to which the ambulance had retired. Capt Brodie carried on until about 5.30 am when the line was withdrawn W. of BOUY when he returned to LANGUEVOISIN with the ADS party under Cpl Downs. As all collecting, dressing and evacuation of wounded at MATTIGNY had to be done in semi-darkness and in the midst of a constant stream of traffic no record could be kept nor particulars taken of casualties which passed through our hands. Two hundred and twenty three cases were sent back by lorries, motor ambulances and horse transport but nearly as many more must have been dressed and directed back as walking cases to VOYENNES where they would have even chance of being picked up by lorries.

On the morning of 23.3.18 I accompanied the D.C. to ROUY LE PETIT (HQrs 59th Bde.) The new position occupied by the Brigade was a line along the SOMME Canal from BETHENCOURT to S. of VOYENNES. It did not seem possible to evacuate cases from the N. Bd. of the line through ROUY LE PETIT to J... and to NESLE. The road from NESLE through MESNIL ST NICAISE to BETHENCOURT accompanied by Sgt Buckerton and a small party in four motor ambulances I went to MESNIL ST NICAISE and from a house at T.2 a 9.1. (sheet 66.D) provisionally. Then went forward along the NESLE BREGNY Road and found a dug outer road at C.17.a. where I established a temporary ADS. As many casualties were coming in from the 3rd Bde which as far as I could ascertain had been rushed up in our left and which had as yet no medical arrangements. I then went forward with

Sgt Rickerton along the BETHENCOURT road to endeavour to get into touch with the 11th R.B. at BETHENCOURT. The shelling all over this area was extremely heavy especially near the top of the hill at C.2.a.9.7. He met a Brigadier of the 8th Div who told him it was useless trying to get through as he had not yet been able to get a message through to one of his Batt's he returned to the A.D.S. at the sunken road. At about 5 p.m. a M.O. of the R. Berks (8th Div) which was in support here, established his R.A.P. in the sunken road. I then moved the A.D.S. back to I2.a.9.1. leaving the M.O. two of my stretcher squads and a wheel stretcher, having already cleared all cases from here. I then went to LANGUEVOISIN for bearers, stretchers dressings &c and on return to I2.a.9.1. went forward with six squads and with a stretcher. Having located the R.A.P. of the E.LANCS and W.YORKS of the 8th Div. we reached BETHINCOURT. Having cleared the 11th R.B. I returned to the A.D.S. leaving two squads with Capt Henry (M.O. 11th R.B.) and as many stretchers as he required. At about 6.30 a.m. (21.10) heavy enemy shelling was resumed and wounded coming in reported the enemy across the canal. At 11 a.m. reports by wounded showed the enemy advance to be fairly rapid in this sector. I decided to withdraw the majority of my party and most of my equipment to MESNIL LE PETIT. At this time there were seven stretcher cases at the A.D.S. and no cars had returned to me since 6.30 a.m. These cases were carried to I.1.c.5.3 across country. We were subjected to heavy shell fire on this trip (about a mile) and forgot to say that four bearers were wounded in addition to one patient again wounded. The wounded bearers continued to carry their cases till the new A.D.S. was reached. Fortunately, a lorry passing near this point was signalled and stopped and it took away all patients at that time at the A.D.S. I then returned to the A.D.S. at I2.a.9.1. and found Capt Henry there. He reported that he had lost touch with his Batt'. Shortly I withdrew the remainder of my party to MESNIL LE PETIT and carried on their till on infantry began to fall back to the right of my former A.D.S. when I retired to H.12.a.14., then to the Railway Crossing in H.11.a. At each of these points several walking wounded were dressed and sent to NESLE and those who could not walk were sent on any available vehicle to the rear area but these stretcher cases had to be carried to the cross roads in H.29.c. as no ambulance could be obtained. Further cases were dressed at H.10.d.2.5. and would have been directed to NESLE but for the fact that accounts about the position of the enemy were so conflicting. An officer in a motor car coming from NESLE was stopped at MANICOURT. He informed

4.

but that it was inadequate to either send cases on or take my party to NESLE as by the time stretchers of the enemy would be in the town. He also said that the dressing station there had closed and retired (the wounded) I now decided that I must in addition to take the stretcher cases, send Jnde R. walking wounded to the cross roads in H.29.c and to get into touch with HQre 60 Bde. Shortly after arrival at the cross roads I found that the J.A. was retiring to RETHONVILLERS when I reported.

The number of cases attended to of which particulars were taken, between noon the 23rd and the evening of the 26th was Officers 8. O.R. 96 but these figures did not represent a tenth of the total which passed through our hands. Accommodation at the A.D.S. was limited; there was no regular means of evacuation and as the building and vicinity were under heavy shell fire from 5.30 a.m. on the 26th all walking cases which did not need dressing were sent straight on to NESLE for transport. A list of names which contained over 200 names was lost but as these names were probably attended to in NESLE their names will have been taken there.

I cannot praise too highly the devotion to duty of Sgt. Cheal and Baxter Sr. and of all stores men of the J.A. who were with me during the 23rd to 26th. Pte Brooks on a bicycle which we found in the road acted as messenger and rendered invaluable service. We carried messages to and from the forward area, and it was mainly through his efforts we were able to commandeer returning ambulance lorries to evacuate cases on the 26th. Pte Kelly and Gibbs also worked hard and well without any relief from noon on the 23rd till the evening of the 26th. Their work is worthy of special mention though it is difficult to draw any distinction when all were so good.

With regard to the means of evacuation we were very much handicapped. Up to midnight on the 23rd we had a good service of cars and one lorry, in being all the ambulance cars lorries &c. all wounded had been cleared by midnight and all was quiet in the forward area. I sent a request to the O.C. M.T. by the but on learning to send me three cars at 5.30 a.m. (26th). At 6.30 a.m. no cars arrived & I sent an urgent message by the driver to form. One car and two lorries but unfortunately a motor cyclist at the A.D.S. in any future operations of a kind like these above described as absolutely essentially, situations must change which necessitate quick delivery of messages for cars etc and to notify necessary changes. In the position of the A.D.S. Instant means of communication it is very difficult to deal with casualties in a satisfactory manner. Notes by car wounded cannot be relied on as the route of these cars may not be always in the direction which you want to communicate.

C.A. Boyd. R.T.M.C.
O.C. J.A.
6.6.18.

Army Form C. 2118.

WAR DIARY
or
INTELLIGENCE SUMMARY
(Erase heading not required.)

WAR DIARY
of
60th FIELD AMBULANCE
FOR APRIL 1918

46/2902

COMMITTEE FOR THE
MEDICAL HISTORY OF THE WAR
Date 6 JUN 1918

Army Form C. 2118.

WAR DIARY
or
INTELLIGENCE SUMMARY

(Erase heading not required.)

Instructions regarding War Diaries and Intelligence Summaries are contained in F. S. Regs., Part II. and the Staff Manual respectively. Title Pages will be prepared in manuscript.

Place	Date	Hour	Summary of Events and Information	Remarks and references to Appendices
ABBEVILLE	1/4/18		Present with Unit — Major ASH (O.C.) Major BOYD, Lieut. MONTGOMERY (temporarily attached) Lieut & 2m JOHNSTONE. RAMC Personnel accommodated at Rest Camp. Transport in HT Details Camp. Unit engaged in preparing and refitting. Men 2 animals in good need of rest. Capt BRODIE attached for duty with 63rd and 2 BIRTON army M.O of VIII Corps. Reinforcement Camp.	
SOREL	4/4/18		The unit marched to SOREL and billeted there.	
"	5/4/18		Awaiting orders	
"	6/4/18		Lt & 2m Johnstone evacuated sick. Capt BRODIE appointed unit 3/4 MTBde	
HALLIVILLERS			The unit marched to HALLIVILLERS and opened 3/4 MTBde. Established small hospital and engaged in collecting & evacuating sick of Bde Group. Accommodation very limited.	
RAMBURELLES	10/4/18		The unit marched to RAMBURELLES with B/g 4 & 73 de Group. Great difficulty with transport owing to bad & hilly roads. Bgt major waters & s/s m Carr injured sick from Exam & U.K. heavy tram detained at BOULOGNE. also 13 O.R.	
INCHEVILLE	11/4/18		The unit marched to INCHEVILLE, Capt BRODIE & 15 O.R proceeded to ABBEVILLE (ROUVROY) to establish Corps Skin Centre there.	

WAR DIARY or INTELLIGENCE SUMMARY

Army Form C. 2118.

Place	Date	Hour	Summary of Events and Information	Remarks and references to Appendices
INCHEVILLE	13/4/18		Lieuts. R.H. RICHARDS, L. DONAHUE & E.F. McCARTHY, all MORC, USA, joined the unit for duty & taken on strength.	
"	14/4/18		Sgt HARDY and 14 O.R. proceeded to ROUVROY for duty at Corps Skin Centre. Unit enquiry (instructing) training arrk of B.S. & enough. Unit general training of about 70 Reinforcement & B.S. commenced.	
"	15/4/18		Lt. Col. BRODIE + party reported and having landed on steamer Reno. F.A. in rea of D.D.M.S. XVIII Corps. 2/2nd East Lancs	
"	17/4/18		H. Transport left at 8.50 p.m. 'to proceed by road to new area (TINQUES) to ERAGNE arriving 5 a.m. 17 instant. Very wet, dark night. March very trying to men & animals.	
BETHONSART	18/4/18		The unit marched to EU and entrained for TINQUES, where it detrained and marched to BETHONSART, whilst their motor Transport moved by road. H. Transport marched to BERNATRE for night.	
"	19/4/18		Unit engaged in collecting & erecting tents, reading out of B. de Group. Transport marched from BERNATRE to HERLIN-le-SEC for night.	
"	20/4/18		H. Transport reported unit, having marched from HERLIN-le-SEC to BETHONSART.	

Army Form C. 2118.

WAR DIARY
or
INTELLIGENCE SUMMARY
(Erase heading not required.)

Place	Date	Hour	Summary of Events and Information	Remarks and references to Appendices
BETHONSART	20/4/18		Sgt Davis and 3 O.R.s evacuated sick on 17th inst.	
"	21/4/18		Sgt Gunter wounded sick. L/Cpl TAPP RAMC promoted Cpl. from 16.2.18 inclusive. Training of Regtl S.B's continued, about 70 attending daily.	
"	26/4/18		Military Medal awarded to Sgt A.W. CHEAL, RAMC, Sgt J. BICKERTON, RAMC & Pte. T. KELLY, RAMC. Pte A.W. BROOKS RAMC & Pte C.R. GIBBS RAMC took on material issued from this A.D.C.	
"	27/4/18		Capt BRODIE proceeded to 11th D.L.I. and returned. Change of that unit. strength of unit from this day.	
"	30/4/18		O.C. 20 Div Train returned. Transferring unit. Capt J. KIRTON rejoined unit. 4 Reinforcement joined unit in duty. 1. HAWKIN MARKI received & returned. Strength of Unit. Officers 6. G.R. 168 RAMC + ASC 48 Officers 14 RAMC + ASC 1 10 Attd 2 RAMC on duty XVIII Corps Reinforcemt Camp. Or Special leave 1 ASC. Patients in hospital 10.	R.V.C. Ash Major RAMC a/o.c.

WAR DIARY
or
INTELLIGENCE SUMMARY.

Army Form C. 2118.

Vol 34 14/2983.

WAR DIARY
MAY 1918
60 FIELD AMB.

Confidential
May 1918

COMMITTEE FOR THE
MEDICAL HISTORY OF THE WAR
Date 9 JUL 1918

Army Form C. 2118.

WAR DIARY
or
INTELLIGENCE SUMMARY

(Erase heading not required.)

Compiled from Records of Daily Order Book.
by Lt Col A.C. HAMMOND SPARK

Instructions regarding War Diaries and Intelligence Summaries are contained in F. S. Regs., Part II. and the Staff Manual respectively. Title Pages will be prepared in manuscript.

Place	Date	Hour	Summary of Events and Information	Remarks and references to Appendices
BETHONSART	1/5/18		Capt J. KIRTON M.C. R.A.M.C. rejoined unit on completion of duty as M.O./c XVIIIth Corps Reinforcement Camp. No M7/104762 Sgt PATTERSON ASC/MT evacuated Sick.	
	2/5/18		MAJOR C.A. BOYD & 23 O.R. proceeded to Bois de la HAIE to take over DRS from a field ambulance of 4th Can. Div. Capt J. KIRTON proceeded to 51st FA for temporary duty. Pte. G.C. HIGH R.A.M.C. transferred from 62 nd to 160 field ambulance. Capt R.M. HUNTER R.A.M.C. reported for duty.	
	3/5/18		Unit moved by road from BETHONSART to Div Rest Station at Bois de la HAIE	
	4/5/18			

Signed 31-5-18 by A.C. Hammond Spark
Lt Col
O.C. 60th Field Ambulance

A.C. Hammond Spark
Lt Col
O.C. 60th Field Ambulance

Army Form C. 2118.

WAR DIARY
or
INTELLIGENCE SUMMARY
(Erase heading not required.)

Instructions regarding War Diaries and Intelligence Summaries are contained in F.S. Regs, Part II. and the Staff Manual respectively. Title Pages will be prepared in manuscript.

60th Field Ambulance   Summary of Events and Information by Lt. Col. A.C. HAMMOND SEARLE RAMC

Place	Date	Hour	Summary of Events and Information	Remarks and references to Appendices
CHATEAU de la HAIE near VILLERS-AU-BOIS	5.5.18		Took over command of this Unit from Major R.V.C. ASH (Acting O.C.). Capt J. MIRTON rejoined unit from detached duty with 61st G.R. Cpl. YOUNG T.J. & 6 (O.R.) Reinforcements reported for duty.	
	6.5.18		Divisional Rest Station in process of preparation and organisation	
	7.5.18		Lieut. DONAHUE J.H. (M.O.C. U.S.A.) & 11 O.R. proceeded for temporary duty with No. 8 C.C.S. Capt. MARWOOD M.J. Reinforcement reported for duty.	
	8.5.18		Accommodation of D.R.S. increased to 190. Number of patients in hospital at D.R.S. 163.	
	9.5.18		A/DDMS Mod. Board held on Pte. KEATES 14572 9/D.C.L.I. - before Mental Conclusion - President Self - Members Major ASH & Boyd. Conference at ADMS. Orders received to evacuate the bulk of patients in DRS & prepare to receive lightly wounded & sick in the event of active operations on the part of the Enemy. This was accordingly done. 96 patients were evacuated to CCS - 12 returned to duty - 8 retained in Hosp. Preparations made for reception of cases. Orders received 8.45 pm to detail	
		6.0 pm	1 M.O. & 7 O.R. to Establish a Detraining Centre at AHRUNS - Lt. McCARTHY (U.S.A) detailed.	
		8.45	Orders received for 1 M.O. Lt. RICHARDS (USA) detailed to report to O.C. 62nd F.A. at JENKS SIDING for temporary duty. 9/Cpl. TAPP RAMC reverted to Pte 9/2cps without pay - owing to being surplus to establishment. Preparations made for the reception of mildly gassed cases in the event of hostile action. Lt. McCARTHY (USA) returned to unit (3.8) RDM5 informed.	
	11.5.18	10.35 pm	Detraining Centre to RUITZ R20.a cent (368) RDMS informed. Visited Gas Centre SOUCHEZ - Bath & Gas Centre CARENCY - Sgt. ARMITAGE rejoined unit.	

2449 Wt. W14957/M90 750,000 1/16 J.B.C. & A. Forms/C.2118/12.

WAR DIARY or INTELLIGENCE SUMMARY

Army Form C. 2118.

60th Field Ambulance by Lt Col A C HAMMOND SEARLE

Place	Date	Hour	Summary of Events and Information	Remarks and references to Appendices
CHATEAU de la HAIE SUMMIT (near B.6.a. Sh. 36B.)	12.5.18	9 A.M.	MAJOR BOYD ordered to report for temporary duty to No 2 LOWLAND F.A. (52nd Div) to give instruction in Bearer work and methods of Evacuation as used in this Division and return after 2 days. Lieut RICHARDS M.T.C. returned from duty with 62nd F.A.	
	13.5.18		Capt L.W. WARD Dental Surgeon from No 8 C.C.S. arrived – attached for duty at this Div! Rest Station	
	14.5.18		Dental arrangements allotted. Capt WARD returned to F.C.S. by Orders D.D.M.S.	
	15.5.18		Lt RICHARDS proceeded to A.D.M.S. for temporary duty with 61st F.A. – to learn front and work. 2 N.Co's & 8 O.R. sent to 61st, 62nd FA's – (equally) to relieve bearers of these Ambulances. Number of Patients in Hospital 124.	
	16.5.18		Pte H.L. WSTREET A.S.C. M/T received transferred from 62nd F.A. Inspected Detraining Centre RUITZ SIDING. area forwarded report for transmission to D.D.M.S. XVIII Corps containing suggestions as to further equipment of same.	
	17.5.18		13 Reinforcements received. 180 patients in Div! Rest Station. Lt McCARTHY M.R.C. (U.S.A.) rejoined M.C. proceeded on Special Leave to U.K. Major R.V.C. ASH-FARTHY M.R.C. (USA) rejoined from detached duty at Detraining Centre RUITZ SIDING.	
	18.5.18		All Ordnance indents checked with D.A.D.O.S. Capt KIRTON detailed to inspect Detraining Centre daily. T/Capt a/Major C.A. BOYD R.A.M.C. awarded Military Cross	
	19.5.18		Evacuation to this D.R.S. commenced by Light Railway, arriving daily at 2.50 p.m. Also available for taking discharges back to CARENCY, SOUCHEZ etc.	
	20.5.18		1/Lt CO FCPL FARRH attached to 62nd FA to learn duties of train – in case of active operations. Number of patients in D.R.S. ordered to be reduced to 700	

WAR DIARY
or
INTELLIGENCE SUMMARY
(Erase heading not required.)

Army Form C. 2118.

Place	Date	Hour	Summary of Events and Information	Remarks and references to Appendices
CHATEAU de la HAIE SUMMIT	21.5.18		60th Field Ambulance by Lt Col A.C. HAMMOND-SEARLE. Lt RICHARDS MRC (OSn) returned from temporary duty with 61st FA. Total number of patients in Hosp: 141. A bombing raid on neighbouring village of MAISNIL BOUCHE resulted in casualties. The bodies of 2/Lt BAKER & 2/Lt MINTY R of 2/Lt PRIDEAUX-BRUNE, Lt MARSHALL, 3rd R.B. were brought in to this hosp.	
	22.5.18		Bodies removed to Mortuary of local cemetery by arrangement with the Div. The following wounded officers were attended to & evacuated 2/Lt KENNEDY, 2/Lt LITCHMARSH, B BEER 6, 2/Lt RAYNOR, 2/Lt WILLIAMSON, 3rd R.B. Also 2/Lt B REZNEO, 2/Lt PAYNE H Y/R.F. A very hot spell of weather is being experienced at present.	
	23.5.18		1 N.C.O. & 23 men returned from duty with 62nd FA. Major BOYD appointed to San-inten. Commenced work of digging in and revetting all the tents.	
	24.5.18		Special leave granted to Corporal HARTER.	
	25.5.18		6 Reinforcements reported for duty. Pte BRIDGEMAN of 45th FA exchanged for Pte HIGGINS of this FA.	
	26.6.18			
	27.5.18		Inspected entire route of evacuation of wounded by light Railway from LENS TUNNEL via ABLAIN-ST-NAZAIRE, BOUVIGNY-BOYEFFLES to RUITZ SIDING near BARLIN.	
	28.5.18		Permission obtained for the vacant beds (roughly 100) to be used for convalescent such as batches of gassed patients etc. All possible construction work - revetting & repairing put in hand. 105 cases Gased received 27/28. I.W.Co. & 2 OR. OR detailed for duty in forward area under O.C. 62nd FA - proceeded to HQ 62nd FA & now at Gas Centre CARENCY.	

Army Form C. 2118.

WAR DIARY
or
INTELLIGENCE SUMMARY

(Erase heading not required.)

Summary of Events and Information Lt. Col. A.C. HAMMOND-SEARLE

Place	Date	Hour	Summary of Events and Information	Remarks and references to Appendices
CHATEAU de la HAIE (SUNNIT)	29-5-18		60th Field Ambulance	
			Nothing special to report. 117 cases in hospital. Captain Major. C.A.M.C. arrived for special duty.	
	30-5-18		Court of Enquiry held on illegal absence of No 74/0.86444 Dr McMULLAN A.S.C. attached. Evidence elicited to the fact that this man was admitted to hospt. in BELFAST on 16/5/18 - (8 days after leave finished).	
	31-5-18		Remember in Hosp! 134. No returned to duty during the month (incomplete) 150. Lt. McCARTHY proceeded for duty with 61st FA in forward area for instructional purposes & O.R. transferred to O.C. 62nd FA	

A.C.Hammond Searle
Lt. Col.
O.C. 60th FA

31-5-18.

Army Form C. 2118.

WAR DIARY
or
INTELLIGENCE SUMMARY.
(Erase heading not required.)

Vol 33
140/3076

60TH FIELD AMB
WAR DIARY
JUNE 1918.

SECRET June 1918.

Army Form C. 2118.

WAR DIARY
or
INTELLIGENCE SUMMARY
(Erase heading not required.)

Summary of Events and Information Lt.Col. A.C. HAMMOND SEARLE

Place	Date	Hour	
CHATEAU de la HAIE SUMMIT	1-6-18		60th Field Ambulance. Nothing of importance to report. Patients 150 including 25 gassed.
	2.6.18		Capt KIRTON J. proceeded to Colonels Post A.D.S. for temporary duty under Lt 62nd FA and 6 O.R. 10 O.R. proceeded to forward area for work under CRE in connection with construction of a Relay Post. Major R.V.C. ASH returned from leave to UK. Inspection by Divisional Commander - 6 P.M. 2.6.18. Very satisfactory.
	3.6.18		Sgt A.H. HAMMETT RAMC reported sick. Members detached for duties with other units becoming excessive. ADMS asked to relieve a certain number returned. Request complied with.
	4.6.18		Major C.A. BOYD M.C. proceeded to Div. HQ as Acting D.D.M.S. during absence on leave to UK of Capt G.de W. GIBB. 2 O.R. (Ptes COLLINS & PAINE) of this Unit admitted to Hosp: suffering from Gas Shell results. Orders issued re issue of pyjamas to all P.U.O. cases. Also Scabies cases. Disinfector & hot air incinerator erected in this Hosp: 1800 Wounds were made in improvised hot air incinerator and a number of kits disinfected in about 14 days.
	5.6.18		Lt McCARTHY MRC (U.S.A) returned from temporary duty with 61st FA. 1 Rft O.R. RSC reported arrival for duty. Number in Hosp: 136. Gassed 21.
	6.6.18		
	7.6.18		Lt Mc CARTHY for medical charge of 20th Div. Reception Camp (late Div. Rest Wing.) Visited Detaining Centre RUITZ SIDING with Capt R.M. HUNTER M.O.I.C. who visits daily. Arrangements made with YMCA for supplies of chairs, tables, and comforts in case of necessity. Visited D.D.M.S. XVIII Corps in connection with above.
	8.6.18		Capt J. KIRTON M.C. returned from temporary duty with 62nd FA. 162 patients in Hosp: Inspection by DDMS XVIII Corps - Satisfactory.
	9.6.18		Col HUME Consultant Physician First Army - visited the hospital.

Army Form C. 2118.

WAR DIARY
or
INTELLIGENCE SUMMARY

(Erase heading not required.)

Instructions regarding War Diaries and Intelligence Summaries are contained in F. S. Regs., Part II. and the Staff Manual respectively. Title Pages will be prepared in manuscript.

Place	Date	Hour	Summary of Events and Information	Remarks and references to Appendices
CHATEAUVILLAINE			60th Field Ambulance OC Lt Col A.C. HAMMOND SEARLE	
SUR AIR	10.6.18		Received a certain number of Convalescent patients back from C.C.S. Adjusted this new move by exchanging to C.C.S. - Reserve beds occupied 52.	
SORMET	11.6.18		Visited by A.D.M.S - who read a Secret letter to all Officers.	
	12.6.18		Nothing Special to report. Numbers in Hospl. about 160.	
	13.6.18			
	14.6.18		Arrangements made for Sick of 20th Bde Reception Camp to attend at this hosp. 61st Bde horse show.	
	15.6.18		A/c A.D.M.S 24 O.R. rejoined from 61st FA and 25 O.R. from 62nd FA. Arrangements made for Sick of 59th Bde Details at MAISNIL BOUCHE to be seen by M.O. of 24th Bn resident there	
	16.6.18		Nothing to report.	
	17.6.18		Capt J. KIRTON proceeded for temporary duty with 61st FA at PAULINKS A.D.S. forward area. Visited right of Southern Sector of Line with A.D.M.S. Patients in hospl 153 including 62 P.U.O cases. Rain. Much needed - from spell of fine weather.	
	18.6.18			
	19.6.18		2 O.R. were Transferred to 61st FA to A.D.M.S yesterday.	
	20.6.18		(Warning) Order received from American Authorities for Lt Granville H. RICHARDS to join American forces. Verbal order received to withdraw Q. Swaggon & all personnel except holding party (NCO & 2 men) from Detraining Centre (RUITZ SIDING). RUITZ party withdrawn. Major C.N. BOYD returned for duty on return of Major C de W. GIBB D.A.D.M.S.	
	21.6.18		1 Officer Lt McCARTHY (M.R.C.) U.S.A. - 2 Cooks & 10 orderlies proceeded to No 1 C.C.S. for temporary duty. Number of patients in Hosp! 180 - including 60 Pyrexia cases. This compares very favorably with neighbouring divisions	

Army Form C. 2118.

WAR DIARY
or
INTELLIGENCE SUMMARY

(Erase heading not required.)

Instructions regarding War Diaries and Intelligence Summaries are contained in F. S. Regs., Part II. and the Staff Manual respectively. Title Pages will be prepared in manuscript.

Place	Date	Hour	Summary of Events and Information	Remarks and references to Appendices
CHATEAU de la HAIE (Somme)			60th Field Ambulance	Lt. Col. A.C. HAMMOND SPARKE
	22.6.18		Capt J. KIRTON returned from duty with 61st F.A. L'ABBÉ. (80 beds) Auxiliary Hosp established at CAMBLAIN L'ABBÉ (80 beds) Staffed from Field Ambulances to cope with present epidemic of mild pyrexial cases. Owing to sickness in 61st F.A. Capt J. KIRTON returned there for duty, arrived after arrival here. Members in hosp 176. P.U.O cases 65.	
	23.6.18		Assumed duties of A/ADMS owing absence on leave to U.K. of Col. B.T. WIMBATTS D.S.O. Visits to DDM.S in reference to Epidemic of Three day fever cases and overflow Hosp arranged at CAMBLAIN L'ABBÉ. Admitted 63 P.U.O. cases during the day. Members in hosp 196. Orders received to evacuate all P.U.O. beyond a certain number (50) to ordinary C.C.S. - 10 Aux Hosp. - 0 Gen! Hosp! in ESTAIRES having been received for same. Capt HUNTER RM. RAMC despatched on temporary duty to help at 61st F.A. whose officers are nearly all down with fever. 3. O.R. transferred to 82 w. F/A	
	24.6.18		Half of nursing orderly sent to 61st F.A. - relieved	
	25.6.18		D.D.M.S & B.D.M.S Capts inspected the Hosp. Three day fever epidemic in full swing - Only RAME & R.E (Signals) admitted to this hosp.	
	26.6.18		85 Cases of P.U.O left in hosp. 50 O.R. admitted from this unit in 24 hours. Period in hosp very short. 26 men discharged to duty today. MAJOR C.A. BOYD R.M.C. went on Special leave to U.K. - R.S.M. GOLTON R.S.C. reported for duty vice R.S.M. CROSS R.S.C.	
	27.6.18		Capt J. KIRTON reported for duty from attached duty with 61st F.A. Capt R.M. HUNTER R.A.M.C. relieved from attached duty as M.O./c of 80m. h./ auxiliary Sickness of Capt PROCTOR	
	28.6.18		10ff & 107 O.R. of this unit affected to date by prevailing Epidemic. (10M. & 6 O.R. recovered - 35 convalescent) - None Serious	

Army Form C. 2118.

WAR DIARY
or
INTELLIGENCE SUMMARY

(Erase heading not required.)

Summary of Events and Information Lt. Col. A.C. Hammond Searle

Place	Date	Hour		Remarks and references to Appendices
CHATEAU a la HAIE (SUMMIT)	29.6.18		60th Field Ambulance. 169 in Hosp! 1st Lt Granville H Richards M.R.C. (U.S.A) struck off strength of unit from 25/6/18 - Ordered to join A2nd Div. A.E.F.	
	30.6.18		Interviewed Capt Swift re care/ept of D.A.C. - Supply of drugs - etc. Visited 62nd SA. Instructions from D.D.M.S to take in P.U.O cases again - inspection of Battalion, up to limit of capacity. Visited Detraining Centre at RUITZ SIDING. Loose Communicated with reception of sandbagging. 5 OR. Survey to 61st SA additional - 20 working party.	

A.C.Hammond Searle
Lt. Col.
O.C. 60th FA.

Army Form C. 2118.

WAR DIARY
or
INTELLIGENCE SUMMARY.
(Erase heading not required.)

Vol 36
26/313

60TH FIELD AMB
WAR DIARY
JULY 1918

SECRET

COMMITTEE FOR THE
MEDICAL HISTORY OF THE WAR
Date -6 SEP

Army Form C. 2118.

WAR DIARY
or
INTELLIGENCE SUMMARY
(Erase heading not required.)

Instructions regarding War Diaries and Intelligence Summaries are contained in F. S. Regs., Part II. and the Staff Manual respectively. Title Pages will be prepared in manuscript.

Place	Date	Hour	Summary of Events and Information	Remarks and references to Appendices
			60th Field Ambulance Lt. Col. A.C. HAMMOND SEARLE	
CHATEAU de la HAIE (SUNNIT)	1-7-18		3. O.R. Transferred to 82nd F.A. Working party of 5 O.R. sent to BARLIN Detraining Centre. Complete meeting of Truts. Visited 61st F.R., M.T. Coy SAVY inspected and evacuation arranged	
	2.7.18		59th Bon Race Meeting. Visited Canadian Tramways Coy re P.U.O. Epidemic & loaning a N.C.O. R.A.M.C. to act as Orderly.	
	3.7.18		Examined & selected large number of men for reclassification by M.I.D. Assisted M.I.D. in examination etc. Very large numbers sent by surrounding Units & neighbouring Divisions entailing a great deal of clerical work for M.I.D.	
	4.7.18		Attended Conference at Office of D.D.M.S. VIII Corps. One Cpl R.A.M.C. lent to 1st Cau Tramways Coy to assist in the care of a large number of P.U.O. cases sick in Quarters	
	5.7.18		Inspected all R.A.P's in Southern Sector with D.A.D.M.S.	
	6.7.18		Inspected entire Northern Sector with D.A.D.M.S.	
	7.7.18		Orders received for Lt Col Stack 62nd to exchange with O.C. 35th F.A. issued by special messenger 11:30 p.m. 20th M.A.C. inspected. Major ASH visited Detraining Centre BARLIN. By exertion of all available billets & putting personnel into tents. Accommodation for hosp' increased to 238	
	8.7.18		Number of cases in Hosp' 207. P.U.O. 122. Epidemic slackening – hardly a case being evacuated. Receipt to Drerton C.S. M.T. Board held by order of military Secretary to C.u.C. on 200846 M/Cpl READ A.J. 2211 Duplunquur Coy.	
	9.7.18		Handed over duties of A/A.D.M.S. 20" to Col. R.S. WINGATE D.S.O. returned from leave to U.K. The BUCKLE trial on minor charge – aggravated his officer and then desired it to go further. Facts put before A.D.M.S. – who decided that there was no case requiring further investigation.	
	10.7.18		4 O.R. returned from Detraining Centre RUITZ SIDING	

WAR DIARY or INTELLIGENCE SUMMARY

Army Form C. 2118.

Summary of Events and Information: 60th Field Ambulance — Lt Col A.C. HAMMOND ◯ SPARR

Place	Date	Hour	Summary of Events and Information
10.7.18 (Cont) CHATEAU de la HAIE (SUNNY)	10.7.18 (Cont)	10.30	L/Cpl ACHESON G. 12 Kings (L'v'l) Regt found to have died in his sleep. Arrangements made for inquisition obtained for a post-mortem examination. Awaiting P.W.O. Major GIBB DADMS given assistance for slight accidental wound of knee.
	11.7.18		P.M. performed at No 42 C.C.S. Feeding — Tracheitis, & Acute Bronchitis. (Influenzal in Nature). P.M. attended by myself. Over 200 patients have been kept continuously in Hosp! for last 4 days. Discharges to duty for last month 381.
	12.7.18		16 O.R. sent to Detraining Centre RUITZ owing to lack of accommodation here — men & their beds not being weatherproof. Major C.D. BOYD M.C. R.A.M.C. returned from 14 days leave to U.K. Blankets loaned to M.O. R6 returned him to look after sick cases of P.U.O. in quarters. 211 in Hosp! P.U.O.'s 150.
	13.7.18		Capt. R.N. HUNTER R.A.M.C. proceeded on 14 days leave to U.K. (14th-28th). Weather Showery & cold. Gradual drop in P.U.O. cases.
	14.7.18		Inability to obtain coke retarding Disinfection & disinfestation of kits, clothing and blankets. Appeal made to Div H.Q. to obtain some how. Cuthority obtained from ADMS. to use D.O.C. Train for immediate issue.
	15.7.18		Q.M.S. — LUKE W.G. arrived for duty yesterday evening from 73 Gen! Hosp! Medical Board held on Pte PRICE as to fitness of service overseas. Duties XVIIIth Corps School PRESSIN — Exhibition Camp — from Sanitary point of view.
	16.7.18		Very Severe Storms in the night. Considerable flooding out of lines of camp — work of improving drainage hurried on. 241 cases in Hosp! B. O. R. fetched from RUITZ SIDING & proceeded for temporary duty with 61st F.A. [signed]
	17.7.18		
	18.7.18		Nothing to report. Still over 200 in J.P. — P.U.O. 140. Gradual fall in Account of Scabies in Division. Wordsthropor rearranged. Leaving only Scabies beds. Sku Centre at ESTRUX CAUCHES to take overflow.

Army Form C. 2118.

WAR DIARY or INTELLIGENCE SUMMARY
(Erase heading not required.)

Instructions regarding War Diaries and Intelligence Summaries are contained in F.S. Regs., Part II. and the Staff Manual respectively. Title Pages will be prepared in manuscript.

Place	Date	Hour	Summary of Events and Information	Remarks and references to Appendices
CHATEAU de la MAIE	18.7.18 (cont)		60th FA — Lt Col A.C. Hannoms Somme — Visited O.C. 159 Coy A.S.C. reference Fresh & Cold Storage Meat work and reviewed visits of Staff Sgt Janvier to Whether to prevent unnecessary deterioration of Transport fruit etc of experienced advice and to improve the Standard of Shoeing in the Unit. Inspected by A.D.M.S. — Satisfaction	
	19.7.18		Orders issued for the Disinfection - Disinfestation of Clothes & Kit of all patients admitted to this hosp! Still some difficulty in obtaining Cresol. Report of Camp being too visible from the air. Verified this by a flight over the Camp. Official report arose for — to enable me to obtain the necessary materials to reduce the visibility of huts & Camp generally.	
	20.7.18		Horse & Transport Show got up for the benefit of M.T. Must of whom were in hosp! to enable the expects in 59th Div Show. Judged by a.a. and a. 9 announced to be of the highest Standard.	
	21.7.18		3rd Anniversary of Arrival of Division in France. Celebrated by original members. Gradual fall in P.W.O.'s. Change of Type. A number of definite French Fever cases being now admitted. A.D.M.S. visited hosp! All whitewashed parts of camp being darkened by means of mudwash. Number of Patients sent 200.	
	23.7.18		Cold wet & stormy. Number of Patients only 180. General decrease noticeable in Sick admission rate.	
	24.7.18		Rotheig Special Report. A Good class of work in progress to reduce the visibility of the Camp from the Air. Improve Sanitary Appliances etc. Med'l Surgical Equipment of the Ambulance checked. Officers appointed	

Army Form C. 2118.

WAR DIARY
or
INTELLIGENCE SUMMARY
(Erase heading not required.)

Summary of Events and Information   Lt.Col. A.C. Hammond Starke

Place	Date	Hour	Summary of Events and Information	Remarks and references to Appendices
CHATEAU de la HAIE	25.6.18		60th Field Ambulance	
	26.6.18 (Cont)		to Relieve as follows Major MSH A.Sect, Major Boyd B.Sect, Capt Kirton C.Sect.	
	26.6.18		Admission rate still falling. Very determined bombing raid. 30.40 bombs being dropped over a period of several hours on surrounding district. One bomb fell close to the hospt. (300 yards) in details camp beside Div HQ. resulting in total demolition of several huts. Casualties received in this hospt from this alone 2 killed & 40 wounded. Another bomb fell at Corps Servmn - as a result of which 2 killed 15 wounded were received in this hospt. French Case hut were other casualties (dead) not brought to this hospt at all. Report received from R.O/16 Squadron R.N.S. that the camp now stands very well with surrounding Company as is quite numerous	
	27.7.18		Rainy + stormy weather. Gradual fall in typical cases still maintained as also fall in the number of admissions. Gunn being visited - very heavy satisfactory work finished. Physical training of men discharged from S.O. to Reception Camp ordered by Corps to be supervised by M.O. Major MSH detailed today a "rest to duty" on successive days	
	28.7.18		Nothing to report. P.U.O cases in Hospt now down to 75. Transport Inspection by O.C. Div Train - very good turn out.	
	29.7.18		Capt R.N. Hunter rejoined unit on expiration of 14 days leave to UK. c/o A.D.M.S. Capt R.N. Hunter detailed for temporary duty as M.O. 26th DAC. Arrangements made for a car party near to be ready nightly to start at a moments notice for scene of any neighbouring bombing. Dental Surgeon Capt. Proud R.A.M.C. - will be relieved by another after today's attendance.	
	30.7.18			
	31.7.18		P.U.O. have now reached a figure of 75 cases in hospt. from 130.140 at the height of the epidemic.	

Army Form C. 2118.

WAR DIARY
or
INTELLIGENCE SUMMARY

(Erase heading not required.)

Instructions regarding War Diaries and Intelligence Summaries are contained in F. S. Regs., Part II. and the Staff Manual respectively. Title Pages will be prepared in manuscript.

Summary of Events and Information Lt Col A.C. HAMMOND SEARLE

Place	Date	Hour		Remarks and references to Appendices
CHATEAU du HAIE	31/7/18	(cont)	At the same time a larger proportion of recurrent attacks probably definite Trench Fever is again seen. There is a definite fall in the Divisional Admission rate & the numbers have sunk to about 180 in hospt daily, instead of having to be kept (by evacuations) to a figure like 220 – 230 numbers returned to duty this month	

A.C.Hammond Searle
Lt.Col.
O.C. 60th F.A.

Army Form C. 2118.

WAR DIARY
or
INTELLIGENCE SUMMARY.
(Erase heading not required.)

War Diary
August 1918
60th Field Ambulance

Army Form C. 2118.

WAR DIARY
or
INTELLIGENCE SUMMARY
(Erase heading not required.)

Instructions regarding War Diaries and Intelligence Summaries are contained in F. S. Regs., Part II. and the Staff Manual respectively. Title Pages will be prepared in manuscript.

Place	Date	Hour	Summary of Events and Information	Remarks and references to Appendices
CHATEAU de la HAIE			60th Field Ambulance Lt Col A.C. HAMMOND S. EARLE	
	1.8.18		Change in weather. Very hot and oppressive. ADMS visited Im Sgt ARMITAGE Street before ADMS with a view to evacuation change of category.	
	2.8.18		Sgt ARMITAGE & Pte MENDER evacuated sick.	
	3.8.18		Lt McCARTHY, Lt DONAHUE M.O.R.C. rejoined for duty from No 1 C.C.S Lt DONAHUE told off to supervise physical training at 20th Div. Reception Camp Number in Hosp. 197. Major Boyd demonstrated wire Thomas extension at No1 C.C.S	
	4.8.18		Visited 20th Div Reception Camp re physical training & 20th D.R.C. Letters written to TRE & O.C. of 9th Riot D/Cpl ACHESON late of 10 Kings (disc 10.7.18) (past influenzal bronchitis recurring pneumonia). War Anniversary Communication Service.	
	5.8.18		Guard for Pte ANDREWS received at last. Lt struck at 1/8/18. Pte ANDREWS under charge of desertion and under observation as ? mental. (? sound) A patient Pte BEVERIDGE 7 Sc Rifles (Enteritis & Scarlet fever contact) broke out of hospital but was apprehended & brought back under arrest.	
	6.8.18		Cold & Stormy. 214 patients in hosp!	
	7.8.18		Visited by ADMS. Improvement in weather. Visited Mr FA. ref Disinfector transport etc. A.DONAHUE detailed in relief of Lt. RLEY 11th K.R.R. on leave to Paris. American Officers instructed in ricking.	
	8.8.18		A Demonstration awarag of Thomas Splint application for all Officers & Nursing Orderlies N.C.O's. His Majesty the King visited the Area during Post Itie hosp! at 2:45pm.	
	9.8.18		Lt DONAHUE (NRC) USA proceeded in Temporary relief of Lt RLEY USA - for duty with 11th K.R.R. (in the Line). During the absence of Lt DONAHUE - Capt J. KIRTON detailed to supervise physical instruction at 20th Div. Reception Camp	

WAR DIARY
or
INTELLIGENCE SUMMARY

Army Form C. 2118.

Place	Date	Hour	Summary of Events and Information	Remarks and references to Appendices
CHATEAU de la HAIE	9.8.18 (cont)		60th Field Ambulance Lt. Col. A.C. HAMMOND SEARLE	
			Capt R.M. HUNTER detailed to commence a weekly roster of Medical Officers who will take all Sick at M.I. Room for at least a week on end as tending to keep down numbers & improve treatment.	
	10.8.18		Inspected Physical Training at 20th Div. Reception Camp. At Moc Reb's visited owing to recrudescence of Dysentery M.O. S/Sections - arrangements made for rectal swabs to be taken of all diarrhoea cases.	
	11.8.18		Number of patients in Hosp.l 236. RAMC interfield Ambulance show of Ambulance wagons & water carts.	
	12.8.18		Major BOYD reconnoitred LA CHAUDIERE A.D.S. on receipt of orders to take over. An additional our battalion front. A.D.M.S. inspected the S.B. & was well satisfied	
	13.8.18		Major BOYD M.C. & 11 O.R. proceeded to LA CHAUDIERE A.D.S. to work in conjunction with 1 M.O. of 8th Div. Reception daily remaining there	
	14.8.18		Inspected Medical Posts of new Sector. Took up H.O.R. & made necessary arrangements for provision of Colour Equipment in anticipation of Early with-drawal of 8th Div. M.C.	
	15.8.18		Visited A.D.S. LACHAUDIERE. c/o R.D.M.S - Part of work inspect sent to 31st Div. three months ago returned true. Application made to D.D.M.S for return of 14 O.R. at 30 C.C.S. WARRANS (over 2 mths)	
	16.8.18		Patients in Hosp.l 168. Diarrhoea dysentery very mild & not many cases. Inspected A.D.S. & reconnoitred alternative routes of evacuation, over plank road across VIMY Ridge from GIVENCHY - SOUCHEZ and along LACHAUDIERE ANGRES Road to PAULINES. Suggestions sent to A.D.M.S entriguers to obtain permission of G. Staff	
	17.8.18			
	18.8.18			

WAR DIARY or INTELLIGENCE SUMMARY

Army Form C. 2118.

60th Field Ambulance A/Col A.C. HAMMOND SEARLE

Place	Date	Hour	Summary of Events and Information	Remarks and references to Appendices
19-8-18 CHATEAU A la HAIE	19.8.18		Remainder of working party returned from 61st FA. Route forward for change to via LICHAUDIÈRE ROAD – ANDRES – Car Relay Post at PAULINES. R.T.S. Water Officer Corps visited reference water supply of this hospital.	
	20.8.18		Visited A.D.S. LICHAUDIÈRE. New route of evacuation via PAULINES now in use. 1H C.R. returned from WAVRANS (No 30. C.C.S.). 1 Sgt transferred from 61st F.A. reported for duty.	
	21.8.18		Visited D.M.Y. Cap. (GOUY SERVINS) ref water supply to this hosp! which is still cut off daily. 2 Squad of Bearers sent to A.D.S. PAULINES – to be used at CRUMPCORNER (S.11.c.1.9) RELAY POST & R.A.P. CYRILTRENCH.	
	22.8.18		The hottest day of the year. O. Donahue Sent up to A.D.S. to relieve A McCarthy who returned to this unit for duty. Request for storage tank of 1600 gallons made to "Q".	
	23.8.18		Battery of importance reports. A.D.S. heavily shelled ant damage to kitchen gear. (but not personnel) Capt Wo'se Shoe.	
	24.8.18		Major Boyd returned from A.D.S. on relief by Capt Kidston & O.R. proceeded for duty at Hard RELAY POST (BALSAM). Major C.A. BOYD R.A.M.C. proceeded to 2nd Div H.Q. as A/DADMS vice Major CHANDLER	
	25.8.18			
	26.8.18		A.D.M.S. inspected men for reclassification. 204 in hosp! P.U.O. is continuing to decline – numbers in hosp! now only 63. Mild epidemic of diarrhea – in which occasional dysentery cases are discovered by rectal swab examination. Number in Hosp! 27.	222
	27.8.18		Lt. McCARTHY MRC(USA) took over Med! charge of 20th DAC & Capt R.N. HUNTER this Hosp! was today visited by the Corps Commander who inspected in detachment & expressed himself very satisfied. Numbers in hosp! 222.	

Army Form C. 2118.

WAR DIARY
or
INTELLIGENCE SUMMARY

(Erase heading not required.)

Summary of Events and Information: **60th Field Ambulance.** Lt. Col. A.C. HAMMOND-SEARLE

Place	Date	Hour	Summary of Events and Information	Remarks and references to Appendices
CHATEAU de la HAIE SUMMIT	28.8.18		Relief of 1 Sgt. 10 O.R. Sent to A.D.S/4 CHAUDIERE). 1/Lt. McCARTHY Officer i/c Strength of Mess Kit from 26th inst.	
	29.8.18		Evacuation of Left Battalion ACHEVILLE Sector arranged with O.C. 62nd Fd Ambulance place through A.D.S. L/CHAUDIERE. Conference of O.C.'s Field Ambulances at Div HQ reference further on inspections by Corps Commander.	
	30.8.18		Visited L/CHAUDIERE A.D.S. and forward Area. Intermittent heavy shelling. Inspected Cellar behind A.D.S. to be prepared as Gas-Clothes Changing Room. Pte. DONAHUE U.S.A returned(Sick) from A.D.S. 29/30. Capt R.M. HUNTER proceeded for duty to A.D.S. H. O.R. Sent to detraining Centre BARLIN in relief. 26. Men inspected for Reinforcation - proving to Chevrin A.T.D. H. O.R. proceeded to A.D.S. L/CHAUDIERE in relief of Bearers in forward Area. Number of patients in hosp! 171. 22 diarrhoea cases still in hosp! PUO down to 41. Weather Cold – Somewhat Stormy.	
	31.8.18			

A.C. Hammond-Searle
Lt Col.
O.C. 60th F.A.

Army Form C. 2118

WAR DIARY
or
INTELLIGENCE SUMMARY
(Erase heading not required.)

War Diary
September 1918
60th Field Ambulance

140/3259

JL 38

17

Army Form C. 2118.

WAR DIARY
or
INTELLIGENCE SUMMARY

(Erase heading not required.)

Instructions regarding War Diaries and Intelligence Summaries are contained in F.S. Regs., Part II. and the Staff Manual respectively. Title Pages will be prepared in manuscript.

Place	Date	Hour	Summary of Events and Information	Remarks and references to Appendices
CHATEAU de la Haie SOMMET	1/9/18		60th Field Ambulance. Lt Col A C HAMMOND Serg[?]. A.O.R. proceeded in relief to LACHAUDIERE. Lt QM LUKE proceeded on leave to U.K. 14 days.	
	2.9.18.		Inspected MAISNIL BOUCHE Y.M.C.A. etc. Report to Div Q "re bad sanitation" replacement of orderlies by men of our own Div.	
	3.9.18 4.9.18		Nothing special to report. Conference of O.C's Field Ambulances at D.H.Q. with a view to requirements and possibilities of dumping equipment in case of a move forward. Major R.V.C. ASH visited LA CHAUDIERE. Considerable shelling around A.D.S. – No direct result of too much movement in tin open.	
	5.9.18		Medical Board. Consisting of A.D.M.S., D.A.D.M.S. & Self of Gr TATE 2nd Bde R.B. – Postponed. Large numbers of gassed cases through A.D.S. roughly 250. Chiefly 12th R.B. & 51st	
	6.9.18		Visited LA CHAUDIERE. Fixed new path via LAFOUR FARM. – Suitable for low of recovery. About 40 cases gassed – awaiting evacuation. Nearly all very mild cases which have cleared up in the new time.	
	7.9.18		List suggested permanent reduction in YA Equipment submitted to DHQ as requested. Patients in hosp'. 201. Diarrhoea 16. diminishing. Gassed cases 22 eyes mostly rather severe. Sgt Major WILSON returned to leave.	
	8.9.18		Capt J. KIRTON M.C. relieved by Major R.V.C. ASH at LACHAUDIERE. Gassed patients mostly suffering from severe Eye symptoms – necessitating a number of evacu- ations. Number in Hosp'. 208. A.D.M.S. visited Hosp'.	
	9.9.18		Visited Detaining Centre – RUITZ SIDING – Satisfactory. 1 N.C.O & CRUMP carried to OPEN TRENCH line of evacuation.	
	10.9.18		Med Inspector of Troops [?] about 60 men of various divisions for Reclassification. Visited ADS LACHAUDIERE	

WAR DIARY
or
INTELLIGENCE SUMMARY

Army Form C. 2118.

Summary of Events and Information: 50th Field Ambulance   Lt. Col. A.C. Hammond Searle

Place	Date	Hour	Summary of Events and Information	Remarks and references to Appendices
CHATEAU de la HAIE	11.9.18		Accompanied ADMS to H.Q. Corps in connection with certain projected matters. 1 Squad proceeded to reinf. to MDS – S.D.R. returned from ADS.	
	12.9.18		Weather very wet and stormy. Number in hosp. 208. Receiving high no. of sick of foot disease numbers. Conference at Div HQ.	
	13.9.18		Visited AIX NOULETTE H.A. HQ. & reconnoitred the place and surroundings. Reduction of numbers of patients ordered 2 hours down to 750. Conferred at Div HQ. further reduction.	
	14.9.16		D.R.S. Lt. Donahue MRC (USA) sent to 20th Div. Recep. Camp (MAISNIL BOUCHÉ) in relief of Capt. Tennant 62nd FA.	
	15.9.16		Reconnoitred road from Calonlefort to AIX-NOULETTE ref. suitability for walking wounded. Sojourned & contemplated change of a new Recon. cross road between AIX-NOULETTE & CARENCY. ADS auto suitability for transference of stores required from here to there. Patients in the DRS have during the past 8 days been reduced from about 800 to 80 by orders of A.D.M.S.	
	17.9.18		Conference of O.C.'s FAs at A.D.M.S office. Lt. Qu. Lowe returned from leave U.K.	
	18.9.18		Visited Forward Area. The is at shelling in the neighbourhood of LYCHAUDIER R.II.G.	
	19.9.18		Nothing special to report. Weather wet and stormy. D.R.S still being kept down to about 80 patients.	
	20.9.18		Visited Detraining Centre RUITZ. Arrange for encampment of tents and save Area Crown and out se up air of road.	
	21.9.18 22.9.18		3 Reinforcements arrived. Visited CRS to arrange for help in connection with report of your road. Nature of water supply – which is being continually cut off.	

Army Form C. 2118

WAR DIARY or INTELLIGENCE SUMMARY

(Erase heading not required.)

60th Field Ambulance   Lt. Col. A.C. HAMMOND Served

Place	Date	Hour	Summary of Events and Information	Remarks and references to Appendices
CHATEAU de la HAIE (Bruay)	23.9.18		Permission received from D.D.M.S. to increase Nuremberg cases in DPS (+VD) As 100. There has been a decline in sickness since the diarrhoea epidemic has been controlled. Second report on water supply sent to C.R.E. Corps. Major R.W. ASH M.C. relieved at the A.D.S. LA CHAUDIÈRE by Major C.H. BOYD M.C. R.A.M.C.	
	24.9.18		Orders received to post marquees at Detraining Centre BARLIN as Rcpt N3 – followed by orders to withdraw equipment and personnel. Visited Detraining Centre and Superintended demolition. 8 O.R. required on completion of outwork at BARLIN.	
	25.9.18		Conference of F.A. Commanders at A.D.M.S. Office. 4 O.R. proceeded to A.D.S. in relief.	
	26.9.18		Visited A.D.S., forward area. Capt R.N. HUNTER proceeded to A.D.S. in relief of Capt J. KIRTON. 12 O.R. proceeded to reinforce forward posts of CYRIL Sector in anticipation of requirements. 60th Inf. Bde participating in a small operation in conjunction with 2nd and 4th of 8th Division	
	27.9.18		Capt J. KIRTON proceeded on leave to U.K. 8 O.R. returned from duty in the forward area – reinforce posts. Night operation by 61st Bde in conjunction with 8th Div on our right. Completely successful. All objectives gained. 29 prisoners. Casualties light. L/c CHAUDIÈRE Rear to 60th Inf Bde – next involved. Weather cold and unpleasant.	
	28.9.18		Rotary Special Report. No patients in Hosp.l	
	29.9.18		Lt. DONOHUE M.R.C. (U.S.A) returned on completion of duty with 3rd Cav Regt Cav.	
	30.9.18		Men in Hosp.l Diarrhoea now well under control. Only about 6 cases under treatment on the average. A.D.S. Fraser Shelled yesterday with the "Blue Cross". No casualties.	

A.C.Hammond
Lt Col
O.C. 60th F.A

"Original"

War Diary
of
O.C. 60th Field Ambulance

1st October 1915 - 31st October 1915

WAR DIARY or INTELLIGENCE SUMMARY

Army Form C. 2118

Place	Date	Hour	Summary of Events and Information	Remarks and references to Appendices
CHATEAU de la HAIE (SUCHET)	1/10/18		60th Field Ambulance. Lt. Col. A.C. HANNON SMYTH In anticipation of moving onwards - Visited 60th Bde HQ - and went forward to recce in the Company HQ at QUARRIES (T16c9.8) East of VIMY as a future ADS - at present used as an R.A.P. Reconnoitred route of evacuation back to LOCHNADIARR. Discussed arrangements at ADS - Two runners sent to Bde HQ. O.C. 32 LR Coy interviewed as to train arrangements for evacuation of wounded	
	2/10/18		Visited Bde HQ and A.D.S, LOCHNADIARR. Called at LENS JUNCT, Injury Officer, 9 P.D.I.P. BERLIN Forward Squad reinforced. All squads forward of ADS being doubled. Called on ADMS and conferred. Working out of WW & R8 at SUMMIT. Holding party set up at QUARRIES at T16c9.8 with a view to preparation as an ADS	
	3/10/18		Visited Bde HQ & ADS - Went forward along NEW BRUNSWICK ROAD to QUARRIES at T16c9.3 accompanied by M.T. Sgt PSC reference places of roads for cars. Car board BERLIN received - time 17.30. Motor-cyclist attached to M.D.S. Evacuation of CYRIL Sector taken out of our hands by ADMS owing to shifting of Intrebrigade boundary. Personnel Manning Medical Posts accordingly returned to MDS LOCHNADIARR. 1 Officer 1 NCO & 32 OR Div. S. Coy reported for duty.	
	4/10/18	6.30pm	Revisited Forward Area & A.D.S. Extra rations & medical comforts taken up to posts. Stretcher bottles. hundred Nahsels Sent forward for coats today. Purpose: Preparation of equipment just up and take over LOCHNADIARR tomorrow. A.D.S. visited forward area. visited OC 12th R.B. & Advance Relay Post at T13a and without authority. Orders received forward as to be stationed at LH CHAUDIER which tomorrow. MDS MAJOR RVC Ash proceeds to LOCHNADIERE last night	
	5/10/18		Orders for relief of SH in the line received during the night Capt. RV HUNTER returned from forward Area. Returned. CAPSOOM, SR Lt. Col. RH HUNTER proceeded with 20 OR. to MOUVELIN as holding party for 61st FA. Major RVC ASH, MC & Major BOYD MC returned from A.D.S. on handing over here to 36th FA. 12 & Dr. 65 OR reported bush on completion of duties in forward area	

1875. Wt. W593/826. 1,000,000. 4/15. J.B.C. & A. A.D.S.S./Forms/C. 2118.

WAR DIARY or INTELLIGENCE SUMMARY

Army Form C. 2118

Place	Date	Hour	Summary of Events and Information	Remarks and references to Appendices
(SUMMIT) CHATEAU de la HAIE	6.10.18	18.00	66th Field Ambulance. Lt Col R.C. HAMMOND SEARLE. Personnel Transport moved to CAMBLIGNEUL. Unit evacuated by 10.00 C.C. Sawing place all cases remaining in D.R.S. - 25 Sent to No.7 C.C.S. hours. 16 of cases remaining in D.R.S. - 25 Sent to No.7 CCS	
	7.10.18		LIGNY-ST FLOCHEL – A/Div Temporarily as Corps Rest Station – M patients taken on to CAMBLIGNEUL	
		4.m.m.	Capt R.M. HUNTER & 20 O.R. rejoined unit from HOULLINS. C/o DDMS for Sent for duty (Detraining) at TINQUES. Instructions received from	
	8.10.16		Proc'd to Oct for him. During his short special leave. Visited 59th Bde HQ, & 2S/R at BERLES. Training of unit commenced. D.A.D.M.S. Sent to See ADHS reference a Corps Relief ordered. Relief cancelled	
	9.10.18		Visited B9 C 59th Bde reference training of R.S.B.'s. Examined 6 O.R. of 2 S/R & charge of category. Lt DONAHUE M.R.C (USA) proceeded to TXRKR in temporary relief of ABLEY granted leave to UK. R.S.B.'s now y'sent by B9. C 59th Bde letter sent	
	10.10.18		HQ for Relief. Examined 2 OR DLI re change of category. Visited DHQ	
	11.10.18		By desire of B9.C 59th Bde arranged for major Boyd to meet R.S.B.'s at SAVY daily and instruct them there. Major Boyd today visited all R.M.O's & inspected programmes as to Completeness etc.	
	12.10.18		Visited DHQ. Training of R.S.B.'s arranged and commenced at SAVY. Daily training of Unit carried out daily. Sick arrival. Average number of patients in hospl. 8. Visited Bde HQ & all Batt HQ to arrange for additional training of R.S.B's by R.M.O's.	
	13.10.18		Evacuation Cas. Capt J KIRTON M.C. returned from leave to UK.	
	14.10.18		Visited 12 KRR 9 Y/Som L.I. Lecture (propaganda) to whole unit on "Franchise". "D America	
	15.10.18		Lectures delivered on 'Care of Disabled Soldiers' and 'Lt Lichnowski Memoirs'. ADMS inspected	
	16.10.18		HQ. Training proceeding normally Medical Board on A/Capt Hick RC 11th R.B. 16 Potember hosp. ADMS interviews. & addressed medical officers	

1875 Wt. W593/826 1,000,000 4/15 J.B.C. & A. A.D.S.S./Forms/C. 2118.

Army Form C. 2118

WAR DIARY
or
INTELLIGENCE SUMMARY
(Erase heading not required.)

Instructions regarding War Diaries and Intelligence Summaries are contained in F. S. Regs., Part II. and the Staff Manual respectively. Title Pages will be prepared in manuscript.

Place	Date	Hour	Summary of Events and Information	Remarks and references to Appendices
60th Field Ambulance			Lt Col. A.C. Hammond-Searle	
	17.10.18		Visited 189 Coy A.S.C. Coy replacement Supply wagon horse. Ordered rearing out disinfection of billet No 3 Coy A.S.C. Not Safar called out by Sanitation	
	18.10.18		treated M.O. 2/S Rifles in connection with O.C.S.M. case. Called at No 12 Stationary Hosp! Re ref to this case - now diagnosed P.U.O ? post epileptiform convulsion M.O. 2/S Rifles instructed accordingly. Called at Div. H.Q.	
	19.10.18		Nothing special to report	
	20.10.18		Granted leave to UK handed over to Major R.V.C. ASH. MC	
2			A.C. Hammond-Searle Lt. Col. R.A.M.C.	

WAR DIARY or INTELLIGENCE SUMMARY

Army Form C. 2118

Place	Date	Hour	Summary of Events and Information	Remarks and references to Appendices
CAMB-LINGNEUL	27.10.18		Assumed command of Unit during absence on leave of Lt. Col. A.C. HAMMOND-SEARLE	Major R.V.C. Ash in lieu of Lt. Col.
	27.10.18		CAPT. KIRTON. J. M.C RAMC rejoined unit on completion of duty as M.O. to 11/KRRC. Training of unit continued normally. Average number of Patients in hospital daily during past week = 150. Influenza on 11th Bn. 1/KRRC. Villetta et BETHONSART continue without abatement.	
	28.10.18		1st Lieut. J. L. DONAHUE MORC USA returned from leave to Paris today. Country tryeing held at TINQUES Auto fatal accident to French civilian (woman) on evening of 24th inst caused by Ambulance Car driven by Driver J. Cook A.S.C. M.T. attached 60 O Field Ambulance. Capt R.N. HUNTER proceeded on temporary duty with 61st Field Ambulance at DOUAI. 1st Lieut J. L. DONAHUE MORC USA evacuated sick to No.12. Stationary Hospital.	
	29.10.18		CAPT. R.N. HUNTER. RAMC rejoined unit on completion of duty with 61st Field Ambulance at DOUAI	
	30.10.18		The Unit marched to SAVY and entrained for VELU. 20th Division having been transferred from VIII Corps 1st Army to XVIII Corps 3rd Army. From VELU which was reached at 7 p.m. the personnel proceeded to CAMBRAI by bus transport - by noon.	
CAMBRAI	31.10.18		Unit arrived in CAMBRAI at 3 a.m. went into billets; H.Q. at No 5. RUE DE PERONNE. Strength of unit - officers 5 -; O.R. 231. Lt. Col. HAMMOND SEARLE. on leave to U.K.	

R.V.C Ash. Major 'Ram'
A/O.C. 60 Field Amb A.

R.V.C Ash. Major 'Ram'
A/O.C. 60 Field Amb A.

114/3401.

60 F.A.

COMMITTEE OF
MEDICAL HISTORY OF THE WAR
Date 16 JAN 1919

Army Form C. 2118

60 7th Field Amb

WAR DIARY
or
INTELLIGENCE SUMMARY
(Erase heading not required.)

Instructions regarding War Diaries and Intelligence Summaries are contained in F. S. Regs., Part II. and the Staff Manual respectively. Title Pages will be prepared in manuscript.

Place	Date	Hour	Summary of Events and Information	Remarks and references to Appendices
CAMBRAI	1.11.18		Strength of Unit – Officers. J.O.R. 2.31 Officers present with unit MAJOR. R.V.C. ASH. MAJOR A.C. BOYD, CAPT. J. KIRTON, CAPT. R.N. HUNTER. LIEUT + Q.M. W.G. LUKE. Lt. J.L. DONAHUE. M.O.R.C. Lt Col A.C. HAMMOND SEARLE. on leave to U.K. U.S.A. evacuated sick on 29.10.18. Established hospital for light cases. 15 patients in hospital.	
	3.11.18		The unit moved by road, under 57th Bde order, to CAUROIR	
AVESNES lez AUBERT	4.11.18		The unit moved by road, under 57th Bde order, to AVESNES-LEZ-AUBERT. and took over buildings at the MAIRIE: from detachment of 61st Fd. Amb. Prepared sub-(parted) hospital for Fever cases from XVII Corps troops (2) Stagnil Post for other ranks to be evacuated by train to Corps Sick collecting Station – NOTRE DAME de GRACE – CAMBRAI. Whole site very dirty & insanitary – a great deal of work to be done. Continued preparations	
	6.XI.18		Returned from leave to U.K. and took over command of unit from Major ASH. Much work of clearing up & repairs necessary also in round to render the place weatherproof.	
	7.XI.18		Beds for 72 serious cases put up & wards arranged. 53 patients in hosp. Accommodation for about 250 patients allotted.	

R V C Ash.
Major R.A.M.C.

R V C Ash
Major R.A.M.C.

WAR DIARY or INTELLIGENCE SUMMARY

Army Form C. 2118

Summary of Events and Information Lt Col A.C. Hammond. Score

Place	Date	Hour	Summary of Events and Information	Remarks and references to Appendices
NESNES les AUBERT	8.xi.18		Divn HQ at VENDEGIES - Corps HQ also moved there. Work of repairs and salvage continues. Large quantities of salvage being collected. Visited DDMS XXIII Corps at VENDEGIES.	
	9.xi.18		Arrangements made with AC of S Q midland in CAMBRAI to help and provide clean clothing & to disinfect the dirty : OC 7/3 F.A. will send 30 beds tents to be erected at St AUBERT STATION in preparation of reception of some 250 cases of Sick from Divisions - acting as a Staging post on their way to XXII Corps Sick Collecting STATION CAMBRAI (3/3 F.M.) - whither they are to be moved by train. Extra rations, medical comforts and coal arranged for from AD XXII Corps M.T. Coy. ST AUBERT. DDMS inspected this hosp.	
	10.xi.18		Camp of 30 bell tents erected at ST AUBERT STATION. Six bell tents arrived in the evening. Great irregularity of train service yesterday. 200 blankets received from OC 7/3 F.A. to increase accommodation of this Influenza hosp.	
	11.xi.18		News of cessation of hostilities at 11AM received. DDMS visited here.	
	12.xi.18		During the night about 120 Sick were passed through staging camp at ST AUBERT. In accordance with instructions of DDMS only local sick were admitted here from today and gradual evacuation of Influenza hosp is being carried out with a view to possibly rejoining the Division. 80 cases evacuated today.	
	13.xi.18		Visited Corps Staging Camp. 21 cases received during the night. Orders received from Corps for collection of Corps Triage forthwith - Corps Staging Camp accordingly struck, lent the reception of a small number (10) beds - for emergencies. Remaining 10 cases on stop. Accept no wounded or disabled as to walk home of DDM.S	
	14.xi.18		Visited Corps HQ at BAVAY. Constructed DDMS wishes as to closing down of this hosp. and arranged for return of village Haunch to our Surplus stores ST AUBERT	

WAR DIARY or INTELLIGENCE SUMMARY

Army Form C. 2118

Place	Date	Hour	Summary of Events and Information	Remarks and references to Appendices
AVESNES le AUBERT			60th Field Ambulance	Lt Col A.C. Hammond. S&MRA
	16.XI.18 16.XI.18		Staging Post shut down & routine resumed in to Corps O.O. J. Hospital supplies of British patients - 2 French Soldiers in Hospital & many civilians under treatment. Weather very cold	
	17.XI.18		Rotary Special Report - A large number of French civilians under treatment and two French soldiers in Hosp.	
	18.XI.18		Lt. A. Power took over duties of A.D.M.S. today. Orders received for Capt Hatton + Hunter to proceed to XIII Corps Staging Post + Capt Donahue to Scottish Rifles. 2 Motor Cars + 1 Ford car to proceed this morning. Major R.V.C. O.S.M. proceeded on leave to U.K. leaving only Major Boyd and myself	
	19.XI.18		Considerable number of French civilians under treatment for Influenza.	
	20.XI.18		6 civilians consulted with Cards hip Japonais Rotary Special Report. Large amount of furniture collected by French Officer with aid of fatigue party. Stated + Crown Inn room. Box of valuables dug up.	
	21.XI.18 22.XI.18 23.XI.18		Rotary Special Report. Employed all day sorting French Stores. Ditto. Evacuating order received from A.D.M.S relative to move of Division. O.C. on HQ visited this am. Whence taking over. Accident to Sgt Lynes. Shed at finger blown off by detonator in salvage. Evacuated to CCS. 1 NCO + 3 O.R.s + 1 medical equipment sent to Warranties & Petit to open an Room. There were under Capt Hatton + Hunter. Verbal Message received from A.D.M.S to send Major Boyd M.C. but only remaining officer to HQ Reply sent to that effect that account of work precluded possibility of compliance	
	24.XI.18 25.XI.18		Capt Donahue returned for duty. Away two nights at B.O.S.P.A. by A.D.M.S. Capt R.N. Muntz + J. Hatton report 4 for duty. Civilian Rear Guard slightly less Several severe cases evacuated to CCS. Official report made by the Deputy of the District for this. 2nd day. Official report made by French Government on occurring its number of cases under treatment	

Army Form C. 2118

WAR DIARY
or
INTELLIGENCE SUMMARY
(Erase heading not required.)

60th Field Ambulance Lt Col A.C. HAMMOND-SMITH

Place	Date	Hour	Summary of Events and Information	Remarks and references to Appendices
GOEULZIN to AUBERT	26.xi.18		3 further serious cases amongst French Civilians evacuated to CCS at CAUDRY. 51st Brigade arrived in the area	
	27.xi.18		Unit move complete by road to CAMBRAI - % B.G.C. with 59th Bde group. Capt J. KIRTON M.C. proceeded to 11th D.C.s as 2/i/c in relief of Capt BRODIE transferred to UK. Major C.A. BOYD MC RAMC proceeded to DHQ as A/ADMS in relief of Major Coe W.9IBA granted leave to UK.	
CAMBRAI	28.xi.18 30.xi.18		Nothing Special to report. Unit in billets repairing much cleaning up. Unit reimbursed at CAMBRAI and moved to MARIEUX AREA. Billetted at LEALVILLERS	

A.C.Hammond-Smith
Lt Col
O.C. 60th FA

ORIGINAL

98/41
146/3481

COMMITTEE FOR THE WAR
MEDICAL HISTORY OF THE WAR 1919
Date

WAR DIARY

of

60th FIELD AMBULANCE

1st December 1918 – 31st December 1918

CONFIDENTIAL

Dec. 1918

Army Form C. 2118

WAR DIARY
or
INTELLIGENCE SUMMARY
(Erase heading not required.)

Instructions regarding War Diaries and Intelligence Summaries are contained in F.S. Regs., Part II. and the Staff Manual respectively. Title Pages will be prepared in manuscript.

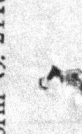

Place	Date	Hour	Summary of Events and Information	Remarks and references to Appendices
LEAUVILLERS			60th Field Ambulance Lt Col R C HAMMOND STORIE	
	1.xii.18		Transport having moved from CAMBRAI by road 29/xi - 1/xii, rejoining unit.	
	2.xii.18		Grading of unit from Educational point of view proceeded with.	
	3.xii.18		G.S.O.1 visited F.A. Site - corroborating the poor quality of the site both for Latrines and personnel of unit. Capt CO J HENRY 2nd O/c 11th R.F.A having been relieved by Capt LODGE PATCH - reported here for duty.	
	4.xii.18		A.D.M.S and C.R.E visited this F.A. Accompanied them to TOUTENCOURT with object of selecting another site. A dilapidated Camp - excellently situated at TOUTENCOURT - HERISSART Chosen - Sectors to Potassine R.E repairs.	
	5.xii.18		Double guard & large working party dispatched to TOUTENCOURT C.R.E had already commenced work with materials at hand. Owing to the decrepit state of motor Ambulance Cars - A.D.M.S requested to apply for the attachment of our M.A.C Car.	
	6.xii.18		Capt DONAHUE MRC (USA) evacuated to C.C.S Sick. Took a view to further evacuation to the Base. Owing to breakdown of Ambulance Cars. Evacuation very difficult & entailing considerable hardships on the newcomer.	
	7.xii.18		Major R.V.G. MSH returned from leave to U.K.. New Camp near TOUTENCOURT progressing - 1 Sect of 3d Coy RE lately of Forceu.	
	8.xii.18		Camp Site at TOUTENCOURT progressing. 30 men of the unit assisting	
	10.xii.18		A.D.M.S visited Field Ambulance, Evacuating order to base so fatiguing received.	
	12.xii.18		New Camp progressing slowly owing to shortage of material & labour. All available men from this unit assisting. Request to D.D.Q to expedite work.	
	13.xii.18		C.R.E visited New Camp at urgent request and agreed as to the need for further and more rapid work on the huts. D.M.S advised accordingly. Men hospital not to be transferred for another 3 days or so.	

WAR DIARY or INTELLIGENCE SUMMARY

Army Form C. 2118

Place	Date	Hour	Summary of Events and Information	Remarks and references to Appendices
			66th Field Ambulance Lt Col A C Hammond SMO	
14.XII.18 LEALVILLERS	14.XII.18		ADMS visited FA. Investigated complaint re shortage of light. 9 quarts of paraffin recently received	
	15.XII.18		Major R.N.C. ASH - M.C. + Capt R.N. HUNTER proceeded to New Camp TOUTENCOURT. Considerable increase in numbers weekly. Troops Douse GPI's inspection. A good deal of parties set to be sent to Newer huts weatherproof.	
	16.XII.18		ADMS visited FA. Capt R.N. Hunter detailed as OB (? A) Officer to 2/3 Rifles and for emergency beds in the village of TOUTENCOURT.	
	17.XII.18		Hosp.' opened for (60 cases) at New Camp TOUTENCOURT.	
TOUTENCOURT	18/19.XII.18		Remainder of Unit (with exception of HTPSC) moved to TOUTENCOURT by road. Weather very cold & boisterous. Very few sick being received. Orders received re care over medical charge of 239 P.W. Camp CLAIRFAYE & 26 Labour Group ACHEUX. Reutilization of miners — Sick. — Causing considerable deficiency among M.T. personnel. ADMS visited the Camp.	
	20.XII.18		DDMS Tropical Camp and X-rays, & horses of Cholsford work in progress.	
	21.XII.18		ADMS visited camp and gave instructions reference period of his leave. Assumed duties of A/ADMS vice Col B.J. Wingate on leave to U.K.	
	22.XII.18			
	23.XII.18		Visited D.M.Q. Divisli at 61st FA.	
	24.XII.18		Div. & returned of Major Rogerson 63rd FA. -- ref departure of Major Quinn appointing DADMS 33rd Div. Visited D.M.Q. and 61st FA. Leaving Capt STALLARD K.U.R.	
	26.XII.18		Visited D.M.Q. & 63rd FA. Capt R.N. HUNTER granted 14 days leave to U.K. departed on 24th. Very few sick being received at present. — Average number in Hosp. 12.	
	27.XII.18			
	28.XII.18		Visited D.M.Q. Heavy rain & much rain and cause considerable delay in work on the Camp.	
	31.XII.18		Confidential reports on all Officers Submitted. Weather very bad — delay in completion of camp. Visited D.M.Q. corner Camp Proceeding normally. Number of patients admitted small.	

O. C. Hammond Lt Col

Army Form C. 2118.

WAR DIARY
or
INTELLIGENCE SUMMARY.
(Erase heading not required.)

20 DIV
Box 1835 Vol 4
140/290

16

Instructions regarding War Diaries and Intelligence Summaries are contained in F. S. Regs., Part II. and the Staff Manual respectively. Title pages will be prepared in manuscript.

WAR DIARY
60TH FIELD AMB
JANUARY 1919

Place	Date	Hour	Summary of Events and Information	Remarks and references to Appendices
Jan. 1919				

WAR DIARY or INTELLIGENCE SUMMARY

Army Form C. 2118

Place: 60th Field Ambulance
Summary of Events and Information: Lt. Col. A.C. Hammond Smith

Date	Hour	Summary of Events and Information
1.1.19 Tourneour		Gen'l holiday. Recommendations for Roumanian & Italian Decorations sent in
2.1.19		Report on Suggested Alterations in RAMC Organisation for Field Ambulances forwarded
3.1.19		Report on reduction of personnel to a working minimum sent in to D.D.S. Lecture to Units on Demobilisation. Evidence work greatly increased by Demobilisation work and the numbers of reports called for. Slight improvement in weather. Admissions still low
6.1.19		Visited D.H.Q. Demobilisation continues in the Corps yesterday a fresh batch of privates Group 43 - Slip men Sect. Work of Construction proceeding normally. Horse Lines still v. bad - Regretted impression by D.A.D.V.S. T.O.C. Train - who were unable to remedy it - evidence of infection by O.C. 159 Coy A.S.C. at my request. Number sick being received - Slaveing Gwell - an average of 8.9 men only - and Civilian cases for treatment in a C.R.A.
7.1.19 8.1.19		Capt. J. Kirton M.C. having been relieved by Capt. Houston R.A.M.C. Gwdh as M.O. 1/6 11th Rd A.I.T. advised evact. Court of Enquiry held on illegal absence of Pt. McKenna (absent 21 days) Capt. W.J. Henry proceeds to 91st Bde R.F.A. for duty in relief of Capt. Wake proceeding leave to U.K. O.C. B.J. Wingate D.S.O. having returned from leave to U.K. re-assumes duties of A.D.M.S. as from 7th. B.Q.C. 69th Bde inspected Horse Lines by my request and morning hosp - an regards improvement
9.1.19		Visited D.H.Q. in connection with Confidential Reports on all Medical Officers
11.1.19		A.D.M.S. visited the Camp Leave of Capt. R.N. Hunter extended to 15th inst.
12.1.19		Court of Enquiry on 17 Pats - illegal absence without leave - to number proceeding of 21 R.M.R. Sgd. A. Member - Member Major R.V.C. T.S.M.M.C.
13.1.19		A.D.M.S. inspected Camps - Wards - Accounts &c
15.1.19		Horses classified by Remount Officer. Capt. Hunter's leave extended to 15.1.19
17.1.19		10 men demobilised. RAMC Strength now only 146. Difficulties of M.T. still acute owing to deficient.
19.1.19		New D.D.E. for I.A.S. received. Constructional work in Camp nearing completion. Number of patients still very small - averaging 8-9 in hospital
20.1.19		Visited D.H.Q. reference Collection of Sick from ROSEL already being carried out by car attached to M.O. 1/c 217th F.G. Coy. Visited DDMS for ADMS. Received telephone orders to cancel order to collect from there

Army Form C. 2118

WAR DIARY
or
INTELLIGENCE SUMMARY
(Erase heading not required.)

Instructions regarding War Diaries and Intelligence Summaries are contained in F.S. Regs., Part II. and the Staff Manual respectively. Title Pages will be prepared in manuscript.

Place	Date	Hour	Summary of Events and Information	Remarks and references to Appendices
			60th Field Ambulance Lt. Col. A.C. HAMMOND-SEARLE	
Berthen Rouge	21.1.19		G.O.C. 20th Div. & A.D.M.S. visited and inspected the Camp.	
	22.1.19		Capt R.N. HUNTER whilst on leave to U.K. - transferred to Home Establishment and struck off the strength of the Unit accordingly.	
	23.1.19		Transport inspected by O.C. Div. Train - who expressed himself very satisfied.	
			Lt-Qr-Mr LUKE R.A.M.C. proceeded on 14 days special leave to U.K.	
	25.1.19		Sgt. Clerical Sergeant Staff Sgt. Orders received from A.D.M.S. to recp. Gunner R.G.A. for treatment in hospital - copies enclosed. Capt. W.T. HENRY rejoined unit. No.2 Gr R. BEER, R.A. having returned from leave.	
	26.1.19		Capt. J.W. HENRY ordered to proceed to 62nd F.A. for P.M. examination of R.G.W. from BERNEVILLES who died.	
	27.1.19		9 Prisoners of War in Hospl. (Guard obtained). Sick from Brigade & still very small in numbers. Heavy snow fall.	
	29.1.19		Q.M.S. DIGBY - P.O.R. having been ordered to report to A.D.M.S., ABBEVILLE, Capt. W.T. HENRY R.A.M.C. assumed the duties of Q.M. of the Unit pending relief of Q.M. LUKE from U.K. Statement of Strength of Ambulance forwarded - with a view to stopping further dispersal allotments - owing to inability to arrive M.D. 20 O.R. proceeded demobilised	
	31.1.19		Capt. J. KIRTON proceeded on temporary duty to 84th Labour Group at LONGPRÉ. but the move was postponed at the last moment owing to doubt as to the location of the place in question	

A.C. Hammond-Searle
Lt. Col.
O.C. 60th F.A.

A.C. Hammond-Searle
O.C. 60th F.A.

WAR DIARY
or
INTELLIGENCE SUMMARY

Army Form C. 2118

60 Ya Amb

J8 4 B 14·0/5524

SECRET

WAR DIARY.

February 1919.

No. 60 Field Ambulance

60th F.A.

Feb 19/19

WAR DIARY or INTELLIGENCE SUMMARY

Army Form C. 2118

Place	Date	Hour	Summary of Events and Information	Remarks and references to Appendices
			60th Field Ambulance Lt.Col A.C.Hammond-Searle	
TOUTENCOURT	1.2.19		Capt J. Kirton. M.C. proceeded for temporary duty to 84th Labour Group LONGPRÉ. Pte FLOOD RAMC Tried by F.G.C.M. here today. A.D.M.S inspected Camp. Lieut Staugth reduced to 135 minus at least 25 O.R. not likely to return from leave. Severity been unofficially heard to have been remonstrated. No satisfaction can be got in the matter of Enquiry official intimation enabling them to shorten the stay.	
	4.2.19		Weather very cold & windy. Deep snow. Pte Luke still very sick. Sentence of finding by G.C.M. promulgated on parade. Awarded 28 Days F.P. No.1 - Taken to F.P. Camp at P.H.S.	
	6.2.19		Very heavy fall of snow - Yesterday - affecting even a tram to tour portent. Thaw today restored passability of tracks.	
	7.2.19		Intense cold - very severe frost. One case clinical Diphtheria admitted fr. 239 P.Lab.Coy.	
	9.2.19		1 P.G.W. at CLAIRFAYE died suddenly. A second case " "	
	10.2.19		Post-mortem examination of him P.G.W. shewed membraneous ulceration of Tonsils putrefy aphthonitis. This man made no complaint of his throat when he came sick - as far as could be ascertained from the Interpreter. Similarly case of Diphtheria admitted on 7th inst: made no complaint as to his throat & was only discovered in course of examination to have any thing wrong with the throat. A.D.M.S visited the camp. Pte LUKE returned from leave to U.K. last evening	
	12.2.19		3rd day of sunshine. Centre of anticyclone. P.G.W. in Hosp: Now 16 - British 6. News of impending move to TERRAMESNIL. Brigade closing up.	
	13.2.19		Request by B.de Major S.Fr Bde to convey body of a man 118th R.E. to Doullens for burial complied with. Camera Bac Major War junction to bring would be necessary.	
	14.2.19		Proceeded to TERRAMESNIL with Staff Captain 69th Bde & chose new Camp site. Pte R.A.M.S sent.	
	15.2.19		Heavy Thaw. Major ASH & Self completed arrangements at TERRAMESNIL. Advance party sent.	
	17.2.19		Pte HOOD returned fr. F.P. Camp on closing of same. G.H.Q list No 226 - Capt J.KIRTON M.C. to be a/major from 24th Dec 1918. 9 horses demobilised today.	

1875 Wt. W 593/826 1,000,000 4/15 J.B.C. & A. A.D.S.S./Forms/C. 2118.

Army Form C. 2118

WAR DIARY
or
INTELLIGENCE SUMMARY
(Erase heading not required.)

Place	Date	Hour	Summary of Events and Information	Remarks and references to Appendices
			60th Field Ambulance Lt. Col. A.C. HAMMOND-SEARLE	
TOUTENCOURT 18.2.19			Divisional Commander inspected the Camp. Complaint made by Pte Hood as to Conduct of F.G.C.M. Div! Commander declined to see him - directing that any complaint should be put in writing and passed through usual Channels	
	19.2.19		Complaint by Pte Hood submitted to D.H.Q. Cadre Establishment definitely Selected and Sent in to Corps H.Q. Major A.S.H. proceeded in advance to take over new Site of F.A. at TERRAMESNIL - Forge advance party and most of Stores already there.	
	20.2.19		Unit moved by road to TERRAMESNIL	
	25.2.19		A.D.M.S. visited F.A. Capt HOOSTON 62nd A Fd Amb. Transferred to 11th R.B. (HERRISSART).	
	26.2.19		A.D.M.S. visited F.A. and read out to the J.J.H.ZOOD the Divisional Commanders Ruling with reference to his complaint - in the presence of myself & Capt W.J. Henry. The prisoner expressed himself as Satisfied	
	26.2.19		Visited D.H.Q. re Unicycle Condition resulting from demobilisation of horses and return askew for. Divisional Commander inspected the F.A.	
	27.2.19		Instructions received for No 1 11th R.B. to proceed to VAUCHELLES. Car provided. Instructions received for 289 P.O.W. Coy & 20 Div MT. to be handed over to 61st Div. as regards medical care Practically no sick received. Any cases have been invariably to be sent on direct to C.C.S. owing to nature of cases. Letter written pointing out that no hospital Strength is F.A. owing to the numbers attached and who are not retaining here in effect only 14 men above cadre Strength.	
	28.2.19		Capt W.J. HENRY proceeded for temporary duty to 57th Labour Group, GREVILLERS. 13 O.R. demobilised	

A.C.Hammond Searle
Lt.Col.
O.C. 60th F.A.

A.C.Hammond Searle
Lt.Col.
O.C. 60th F.A.

Army Form C. 2118.

WAR DIARY
or
INTELLIGENCE SUMMARY.
(Erase heading not required.)

Vol 44
wo/3554

60th Field Ambulance

WAR DIARY

MARCH 1919

Army Form C. 2118

WAR DIARY or INTELLIGENCE SUMMARY
(Erase heading not required.)

Place	Date	Hour	Summary of Events and Information	Remarks and references to Appendices
			60th Field Ambulance Lt. Col. A.C. HAMMOND. SEARLE	
TERRAMESNIL	1.3.19 5.3.19		A.D.M.S. visited the Ambulance. No of sick capable of being detained in the FA almost negligible. Another 600 Arrived almost completely demobilised. Owing to the number relieved 2 officers & 79 O.R. – numbers in Camp at almost down to Cadre strength.	
	7.3.19		F.O.R. demobilised. A.D.M.S. visited Ambulance & noted details of number of men detached at 1 O.R. detailed for No 6 Stationary Hosp.	
	8.3.19		A.D.M.S. visited the unit. 1 O.R. recalled before leaving BOULOGNE as a detainable man should have been sent. Examined Rifleman MAX WEBB 11th R.B. for the information of Divisional Commander (innovative, neurotic, release on compassionate grounds not justified). 1 Detainable O.R. sent to No 6 Staty. Hosp.	
	9.3.19 10.3.19		Orders received to hand in "C" Sect equipment and to pack — Park as much as possible of remainder of unit equipment. 2 further detainable O.R. sent to No 6 Stationary Hosp. Surplus equipment sent to Ordnance under GRO 6286	
	11.3.19		D.D.M.S. & A.D.M.S. Corps visited unit. Visited MONDICOURT to arrange for reception of personnel & transport	
	12.3.19		B Sect equipment & remainder of "C" Sect + 1 Ambulance wagon proceeded to MONDICOURT and parked (under guard) at Div. Transport Park. Conference of F.A. Commanders at 61st F.A. Lt METZGER U.S. M.R.C. joined the unit for duty. A.D.M.S. visits the unit. Cpt. W.T. HENRY – who is Officer of the Strength of the unit	
	13.3.19 14.3.19		A Sect Equipment & remainder of C Sect + 1 Ambulance wagon proceeded to Div. Transport Park MONDICOURT. Dr SNOW revisited dispensed for 2 weeks leave. 2 O.R. demobilised.	

Army Form C. 2118

WAR DIARY or INTELLIGENCE SUMMARY

(Erase heading not required.)

Summary of Events and Information — Lt. Col A C Hammond-Searle

Place	Date	Hour	Summary of Events and Information	Remarks and references to Appendices
TERRAMESNIL	15.3.19		60th Field Ambulance closed for the Division of Patients - other than local Sick. Attending. A.D.M.S. visited F.A.	
	17.3.19		Attended conference at Div. HQ re Divisional Code Book.	
	18.3.19		Visited 62nd & 61st F.A.'s ref. above. Lt. METZGER M.R.C. (U.S.A.) proceeded to 27th Bde R.G.A. Divisional services in relief of Lt. FLETCHER. A.D.M.S. visited F.A.— French civilian to hosp. DOULLENS. 20th Div. I.H.Q. ceased to function. Administration of Division handed over to Staff of 61st Bde. A.D.M.S. not included in Cadre — Duties of S.M.O. 61st Bde or 20th Div:!	
	19.3.19		Cadri handed over to true.	
	21.3.19		Reconnoitered D.D.M.S. to MONDICOURT. Arranged for transfer of ex-A.D.M.S. office to 62nd F.A. — & took over the duties — incidentally — Col wing at heavily increased to XVII Corps as D.D.M.S.	
	22.3.19		A.O.R. detailed for duty with 18 C.C.S. Office of S.M.O. 61st Bde (20th Div. Cadre) transferred to H.Q. of 62nd F.A. MONDICOURT. Visited & shall continue to visit daily.	
	25.3.19		Q.R. transferred to No 6 Stationary Hosp. Weather very cold. Heavy snow fall. In accordance with W.O.'s wire. Major R.V.E. ASH M.C. & Major J. KIRTON M.C. R.A.M.C. are struck off the strength of the F.A. from this date and revert to the Joux of Captain on ceasing to Command Stations of this F.A.	
	29.3.19		Accompanied D.D.M.S. to DOULLENS & interviewed & Parie re certain Sanitary defects. Orders received to send 2 cars to M.T. Coy with drivers — Sillingen with drawal. No 70/146. Dr. ROOSE C.E. & escort returned BREMT.	

A. Hammond Searle
Lt Col
O.C. 60th FA

A. Hammond Searle
Lt Col
O.C. 60th FA

Army Form C. 2118

WAR DIARY
or
INTELLIGENCE SUMMARY
(Erase heading not required.)

60th Anti

98 46
140/3550

60th T.A.

WAR DIARY
APRIL 1919

O.C. Hammond Scale

Army Form C. 2118

WAR DIARY
or
INTELLIGENCE SUMMARY
(Erase heading not required.)

Summary of Events and Information: **60th Field Ambulance** Lt. Col. A.C. HAMMOND-SEARLE

Place	Date	Hour	Summary of Events and Information	Remarks and references to Appendices
TERRAMESNIL	1/4/19.		Visited Capt PROCTOR RTO 2nd Bde R.T.O. Gave orders from him to hand over to W.O.E. Collier DDMS office he instructions as to Capt R.T.O. to report here. Gen Snell to fetch Capt BLEY – stopped from release.	
	2.4.19.		R.T.O's inspection Transport at MONDICOURT. Pte NASON dew on sick called on S.M.T.O. XVII Corps Ref enquiry of replacement of drivers Major R.V.E. ASH proceed of our temporary duty to ZONGRÉ. Pte NASON Group in relief of Capt J. KIRTON (on leave to U.K., transferred to Ste Labour Group).	
	3.4.19		Papers to re DRome returned from D.M.Q. with permission to dispose of Cars previously	
	4.4.19.		To HQ R.N.S.C dispatched to hd.' Air' Train.	
	5.4.19.		6 OR attached #6 C.C.S to be struck off strength	
	6.4.19.		#6 C.C.S, Cav.4, 3rd Army. M.T Replacement obtained by direct intimation to S.M.T.O. Visited 61st JA. re return of 20 mules ordered from the 3 Bn's, Paris Leave for	
	7.4.19.		men. Medical attendance of R.T.O Camp Lourcamps also 61st JA & wabs m.o. 6 X mules proceed for dispersal. letter to Q. ref impossibility of moving the remainder of the vehicles	
	10.4.19		Visited D.D.M.S.	
	13.4.19		Truans as to shortage of regretable rations forwarded	
	16.4.19		All M.O's accept the JA. Counter quites have been placed with S.M.O Doullens. Area the at half C.C.S. Orders received for Capt BLEY MRC (U.S.A) to proceed for duty to St GERMAIN's near PARIS – Car to be given over by the S.M.O allocated for such division received for R.A.M.C during the week in order to. Inquire 4's D.D.' with 2.0.	
	20.4.19		Visited S.M.O XVII Corps Group Pt. Capt BLEY proceeded to St GERMAINS. Visited S.M.O Doullens Area - reference Capt Townsend	
	23.4.19		Capt R.V.E. ASH M.C. returned from leave from St Labour Group LONGPRE on relief by Capt J. KIRTON returned from leave to U.K. Pte CAVE retained details until love from Br DOELEN re demobilization of Dr HURLEY on compassionate grounds. No division today.	

Army Form C. 2118

WAR DIARY
or
INTELLIGENCE SUMMARY
(Erase heading not required.)

Instructions regarding War Diaries and Intelligence Summaries are contained in F.S. Regs., Part II. and the Staff Manual respectively. Title Pages will be prepared in manuscript.

Lt. Col A.C. Hammond Searle   60th Field Ambulance

Place	Date	Hour	Summary of Events and Information	Remarks and references to Appendices
TERRAMESNIL	26.4.19		Pte MORLEY demobilised on compassionate grounds. D.D.M.S called reference claims. Division Roster and any special cases regarding Special demobilisation.	
	28.4.19		Capt R.V.C. Ash reported for duty to D.M.O. Doullens Area. Dr Critten demobilised. Orders received to send in 2 large cars for disposal. Visited Corps 9 Coy. Received verbal authority to retain 2 cars & Send Army Services over this number. Authority from 20th M.T. Coy received for transfer Landin M.T. to this M.A.	
	29.4.19		Claims Officer 20th Div. Rouen visited F.A. in connection with damage to No. 38 billet Terramesnil, repudiated by this F.A.	
	30.4.19			
	1.5.19		1 car transferred to No. 15 M.A.C. (Doullens) Car returned as "not acceptable" owing to cracked chassis	

A.C. Hammond Searle
Lt Col
O.C. 60th F.A.